Toward a
True Alliance

MIKE M. MOCHIZUKI
Editor

Toward a True Alliance

*Restructuring U.S.-Japan
Security Relations*

BROOKINGS INSTITUTION PRESS
Washington, D.C.

About Brookings

The Brookings Institution is a private nonprofit organization devoted to research, education, and publication on important issues of domestic and foreign policy. Its principal purpose is to bring knowledge to bear on current and emerging policy problems. The Institution was founded on December 8, 1927, to merge the activities of the Institute for Government Research, founded in 1916, the Institute of Economics, founded in 1922, and the Robert Brookings Graduate School of Economics and Government, founded in 1924.

The Institution maintains a position of neutrality on issues of public policy. Interpretations or conclusions in Brookings publications should be understood to be solely those of the authors.

Library of Congress Cataloging-in-Publication data
Toward a true alliance : restructuring U.S.-Japan security relations /
   Mike Mochizuki (editor) ... [et al.].
      p. cm.
   Includes bibliographical references and index.
   ISBN 0-8157-5800-6 (cloth : alk. paper). — ISBN 0-8157-5801-4
(pbk. : alk. paper)
      1. National security—Japan. 2. National security—United States.
   3. Japan—Military relations—United States. 4. United States—Military
   relations–Japan. I. Mochizuki, Mike.
   UA845.T647 1997
   355'.033052–dc21   97-21062
                                                                 CIP

9 8 7 6 5 4 3 2 1

The paper used in this publication meets the minimum requirements of the American National Standard for Information Sciences— Permanence of Paper for Printed Library Materials, ANSI Z39.48-1984

Typeset in Times Roman

Composition by Linda C. Humphrey
Arlington, Virginia

Printed by R.R. Donnelley and Sons, Co.
Harrisonburg, Virginia

Foreword

EVEN in the post–cold war environment, the security relationship between the United States and Japan continues to benefit both countries and contribute to East Asian security. The alliance remains an effective means of deterring threats to the sea lanes in the Pacific, averting the proliferation of weapons of mass destruction, and contributing to regional stability that is essential for trade to flourish. The alliance is also a source of reassurance. Americans have a reliable friend in East Asia to help maintain a stable equilibrium, while Japanese feel secure that the United States will help them if their country should face threats from its neighbors. The relationship also reassures Japan's neighbors that it can achieve security without dramatic increases in its military forces, possession of nuclear weapons, or a radically altered regional security role. Finally, the alliance provides a framework for promoting preventive diplomacy. Washington and Tokyo can better harmonize their diplomatic efforts to reduce the risks of conflict and to consolidate, in concert with others, a generally benign and favorable political and territorial status quo in the area.

Unfortunately, after the disintegration of the Soviet Union, public support for the alliance in both the United States and Japan, while broad, is somewhat shallow. Both Tokyo and Washington currently emphasize its usefulness as a "hedge against uncertainty," but this rationale, although plausible, can scarcely stir much public enthusiasm. The alliance will certainly have to adapt to changing circumstances if it is to be politically sustainable at home and effective abroad in meeting security challenges. The danger of a regional crisis or even military conflict, such as on the Korean peninsula, makes this task especially urgent.

In December 1995, Koichi Minaguchi, then chairman of the advisory board of the Nomura Research Institute (NRI), proposed that his organization and Brookings conduct a joint study on how the U.S.-Japan security relationship might be restructured to deal better with the post–cold war world. The binational project began in June 1996 with the participation of Mike Mochizuki and Michael O'Hanlon from Brookings and Satoshi Morimoto and Takuma Takahashi from NRI. This book is the product of their collective effort. It analyzes the process now under way between the United States and Japan to redefine the alliance, dissects the debates on security policy in both nations, assesses the changing strategic environment in the East Asia–Pacific region, and examines ways to improve bilateral defense cooperation as well as change the U.S. force structure in Japan. At the end of the book, the four contributors jointly propose recommendations, some of them controversial, for strengthening the alliance and dealing with regional security issues.

Research and writing for this volume by the two Brookings scholars grew out of projects funded in part by the Carnegie Corporation of New York and the John D. and Catherine T. MacArthur Foundation. The Tokyo Club Foundation for Global Studies assisted with the funding for this project. The Brookings Institution extends its gratitude to all these institutions.

The views expressed here are those of the authors and should not be ascribed to the Nomura Research Institute, or to the trustees, officers, or other staff members of the Brookings Institution.

Michael H. Armacost
President

July 1997
Washington, D.C.

Acknowledgments

THE AUTHORS are grateful to Michael Armacost, Richard Armitage, James Auer, and Edward Lincoln for reading the manuscript and providing trenchant comments and criticisms. Even when we disagreed with them, their comments helped sharpen the argument.

We also appreciate the efforts of the many who generously shared their knowledge and opinions during the course of this project. They include Masaaki Aguni, Christopher Ames, Carl Bradshaw, Robert Crumplar, Robert Dobson, Michael Green, Akikazu Hashimoto, Hideo Higa, Morihiro Hosokawa, Hajime Izumi, Matake Kamiya, Tomoyuki Kojima, Toru Kusukawa, C. H. Kwan, Seiichi Masuyama, Matashiro Nakagawa, Nobuyuki Nakahara, Masashi Nishihara, Eric Nyberg, Hisahiko Okazaki, Masaomi Omae, Masahide Ota, Seizaburo Sato, Gary Shiffmann, Junji Shimada, Motoo Shiina, Stephen Solarz, Masayoshi Suzuki, Yoshindo Takahashi, Kurayoshi Takara, Choko Takayama, Yoshifumi Tamada, Hitoshi Tanaka, Kazuyoshi Umemoto, Akio Watanabe, Noboru Yamaguchi, and Yoshihide Yoshida.

Mike Mochizuki and Michael O'Hanlon give special thanks to Hirokazu Nakaima and the Okinawa Keizai Doyukai for making it possible to visit Okinawa, talk with many Okinawan officials and citizens about the U.S.-Japan security relationship, and be briefed at Kadena Air Base. Kinichi Yoshihara and the Asian Forum Japan graciously hosted a regional conference in Tokyo on the subject of this book in September

1996. During our trips to Japan we learned much from discussions with U.S. officials in Japan and with Japanese experts from the Defense Agency, Japan Democratic Party, Japan Association of Corporate Executives (Keizai Doyukai), Japan Forum on International Relations, Japan Institute of International Affairs, Kazankai, Liberal Democratic Party, Ministry of Foreign Affairs, Institute for International Policy Studies, National Institute of Defense Studies, New Frontier Party, New Party Harbinger, Policy Studies Group, and Social Democratic Party.

Satoshi Morimoto and Takuma Takahashi acknowledge the assistance of the following NRI staff members: Donna Vandenbrink, Shui-Yung Li, and Kanako Nishiwaki.

As project coordinator and editor of this volume Mike Mochizuki wishes to thank the Brookings staff who ably helped in this endeavor. Research assistance was provided by Kaori Nakajima Lindeman with the help of interns Isamu Azechi, Satoko Kato, and Michael Wong. The administrative assistants were Trisha Brandon and Megan DeLong. James Schneider edited the manuscript, Yoshiko Tanaka verified its factual content, Caroline Polk proofread the pages, and Sherry Smith prepared the index.

Editor's Note

IT IS the custom in Japan to place the family name before the given name. We follow this practice when referring to Japanese authors who have published in Japanese. We therefore cite the author of "Ajia no ashita to Nichi-Bei dōmei" as Okazaki Hisahiko. Japanese authors, however, often employ English-language conventions when they publish in English by placing their given names before their family names, that is, Hisahiko Okazaki. Therefore, when citing English-language publications by Japanese authors, we do likewise. We also refer to Japanese persons in the body of the text according to the same convention, placing their given names first.

Contents

xi

Part Three: Policy Recommendations

Toward a
True Alliance

Introduction

As Japanese and American officials were preparing for the April 1996 bilateral summit that would release a security declaration reaffirming the U.S.-Japan alliance, the Nomura Research Institute proposed to the Brookings Institution a joint project to examine how the alliance might be redefined and even restructured to respond more effectively to the security challenges and opportunities presented by the East Asia–Pacific region. The continuing uncertainties regarding North Korea's intentions toward South Korea and the tensions generated by the confrontation of Taiwan and China demonstrated the precarious nature of security even as the region as a whole was enjoying unprecedented prosperity and stability. In addition, reaction to the rape of a schoolgirl by U.S. servicemen in Okinawa in the fall of 1995 exposed the fragility of public support in Japan for the U.S.-Japan alliance. These developments gave the proposed inquiry by NRI and Brookings a greater sense of urgency and purpose.

Instead of convening a conference with scores of participants, as is often done in U.S.-Japanese projects, the two institutions decided to organize a small group of researchers (two from each) to engage in a series of intensive discussions over a period of time. The framework would provide the researchers an opportunity not only to exchange views in a more candid manner, but also to have their views evolve as a result of the interactions. The project team (Satoshi Morimoto and Takuma

1

Takahashi of the Nomura Research Institute and Mike Mochizuki and Michael O'Hanlon of the Brookings Institution) held their first meeting in Tokyo in June 1996. This occasion involved a discussion of the April 1996 summit between President Bill Clinton and Prime Minister Ryutaro Hashimoto and the policy implications of the U.S.-Japan Joint Declaration on Security. In addition to mapping out the project and the division of labor, the researchers had an opportunity to hear the views of other Japanese experts and policymakers about various aspects of East Asia–Pacific security.

A second meeting was held in September 1996 to present and critique the papers written by each of the researchers. In addition, members of the group participated in a conference sponsored by the Asian Forum Japan, which made it possible to discuss the regional implications of the April 1996 joint declaration with policy analysts from China and the Republic of Korea as well as other specialists from Japan and the United States. Mochizuki and O'Hanlon also visited Okinawa to get a firsthand look at the situation there.

The final face-to-face interaction took place in November 1996 to discuss further revisions of the papers and finalize the joint policy recommendations. Throughout the project, the participants also communicated frequently by e-mail and fax regarding specific issues as the papers were being expanded and revised.

This edited volume, which is the final written product of this endeavor, is divided into four sections. The first (chapter 1) analyzes the motivations, process, and results of the U.S. and Japanese official reviews of the security relationship and critiques the incremental approach to redefining the alliance that is being pursued by the two governments. Mochizuki argues for a new strategic bargain between the United States and Japan and a more comprehensive and integrated approach to alliance restructuring.

The second section (chapters 2–4) describes the strategic context for the alliance. Chapter 2 by Mochizuki dissects the strategic debates in both the United States and Japan and recommends a new synthesis that would draw on the strengths of the various schools of thought. He explores what such a synthesis might look like in concrete policy terms with respect to Korea and China. Chapter 3 by Morimoto analyzes the evolving security environment in East Asia by examining the changing roles of the major powers (Russia, China, the United States, and Japan), the situation in Korea, and the nascent efforts to develop a new regional security framework. He suggests the need to follow a dual-track strategy of traditional balance-of-power approaches and multilateral initiatives to promote security cooperation. Chapter 4 by Takahashi analyzes the security implications of economic growth in the East Asia–Pacific region and argues that the dynamics of regional development and interdependence tend to ameliorate rather than exacerbate traditional geopolitical rivalries. He recommends adopting a policy of assurance as the best way to integrate China into the regional order as a force for stability.

The third section discusses how bilateral defense cooperation might be improved and the U.S. force structure in Japan altered to strengthen the domestic political support for the alliance in both Japan and the United States. Chapter 5 by Morimoto discusses both the political problem of U.S. bases in Okinawa and the challenges confronting the review of the bilateral guidelines on defense cooperation mandated by the U.S.-Japan Joint Declaration on Security. He argues that Japan must be willing to exercise its right to collective self-defense if it is to become a true ally of the United States. Chapter 6 by O'Hanlon evaluates the current U.S. military presence in Japan in terms of its costs and its role in possible regional contingencies. He then analyzes options for restructuring U.S. forces and bases in Japan to reduce the political backlash that the American military presence has engendered in Okinawa while maintaining and even strengthening the ability of the United States and Japan to respond militarily to security threats in the region. Morimoto and O'Hanlon agree that the U.S. marine combat forces can be removed from Okinawa without jeopardizing the defense missions of the alliance and should be removed.

Chapter 7 by O'Hanlon assesses the implications of theater missile defense (TMD) programs for U.S.-Japan security interests and bilateral cooperation. He argues that although technical questions and uncertainties in the Northeast Asian security environment make the promise of TMD technology unclear, he acknowledges that its potential utility is considerable. He therefore favors Japan's cooperating with the United States both technically and financially in the development, procurement, and operation of TMD, especially the U.S. Navy's upper-tier system.

The final section presents the policy recommendations that emerged from this project. As a comparison of the preceding chapters would show, the four members of the project have somewhat different perspectives on regional security and defense policy and disagree on some specific issues. The policy recommendations presented in chapter 8, however, represent the consensus of the group. To achieve this consensus, some of the policy prescriptions mentioned in the individual chapters are not included. Despite the differences among them, the participants agreed that the U.S.-Japan security relationship needs to undergo a much greater restructuring than is now being contemplated by the U.S. and Japanese governments if it is to evolve into a true alliance.

CHAPTER ONE

A New Bargain for a Stronger Alliance

Mike M. Mochizuki

WHY SHOULD the U.S.-Japanese security relationship continue as before, even after the Soviet threat, which had originally inspired this arrangement, has collapsed? One response to this question might be to point to other existing or potential threats in East Asia, such as from North Korea or China. Although straightforward and easily understood, such a rationale for the transpacific alliance presents dilemmas for both Washington and Tokyo. Although military vigilance against North Korea is still necessary, an improvement in relations between Pyongyang and Seoul and even Korean reunification are not far-fetched developments as we enter the twenty-first century. Japan and the United States indeed share the ultimate objective of peaceful Korean reunification. Justifying the U.S.-Japan alliance primarily on the basis of the North Korean threat could therefore sow the seeds of the alliance's eventual demise if and when Korean unity is finally realized.

The rise of China as a regional superpower may provide a more enduring justification. Tensions across the Taiwan Straits in March 1996 created a context for revitalizing the alliance during the April summit in Tokyo between President Bill Clinton and Prime Minister Ryutaro Hashimoto. But if the United States and Japan want to avoid containing China and prefer to engage it and integrate it into the regional order, officials in Washington and Tokyo cannot openly invoke the so-called China threat to reinvigorate the security relationship.

5

If common threats are inadequate rationales, other arguments for the alliance have survived in unofficial and informal discussions. In the United States many analysts still view the security link as a way to contain Japan strategically. A Japan loosened from the tie with the United States might remilitarize or decide to develop nuclear weapons. Fears from Japan's neighbors about such a prospect could then trigger a destabilizing regional arms race. For the Japanese the bilateral security relationship allows their country to avoid hard choices. By relying on America's security guarantee, Japan can concentrate on its commercial interests, especially in Asia, without contributing much to the security order that makes its relentless foreign economic expansion possible. Without the political-military cover provided by the United States, Japan would have to spend much more on defense to counter hostile neighbors or deal more forthrightly with its militarist past and absorb more Asian products so as to nurture friendly relations with the rest of the region.

Although these arguments may still be compelling within their respective publics, they foster distrust as they traverse the Pacific. The American logic of containing Japan offends Japan's national honor and perpetuates Japanese insecurity about their democratic institutions and their ability to control the military. The Japanese logic of cheap-riding under America's security umbrella feeds American resentment about Japan's economic success and undermines U.S. domestic support for the alliance.

A more benign rationale for the alliance advocated by some is that of reassurance. The U.S. military presence in and defense commitment to Japan reassures Japanese psychologically that their country will be secure in an uncertain environment, obviating the need to develop military capabilities to defend itself on its own. This effect in turn reassures the rest of East Asia against the danger of Japanese remilitarization. But the problem with the concept of reassurance is that it is far from clear how many U.S. forces in Japan and East Asia and what kind are necessary or sufficient to reassure the Japanese and other East Asians. This rationale also does not provide a good way of determining the appropriate Japanese contribution to regional security. In the end, sound defense planning requires thinking about potential threats and the military capabilities necessary to deter them. Furthermore, a strategy of reassurance does little to delineate how Japan and the United States can work together and separately to shape a more positive security environment.

To provide a more compelling and durable foundation for U.S.-Japan security, officials in Washington and Tokyo initiated a process to redefine the alliance. The relationship must now evolve beyond its original bargain: a U.S. commitment to defend Japan in exchange for Japan's willingness to provide the United States with access to military bases on Japanese territory. It must become a more reciprocal partnership to preserve regional peace and stability. Although President Clinton and Prime Minister Hashimoto implicitly blessed this approach to revamping the alliance during their April 1996 summit, the means to achieve redefinition are still either narrowly cast or too vague. The centerpiece of the process has so far been a review of the 1978 guidelines on bilateral defense cooperation. Defense officials on both sides have chosen an incremental approach. Bilateral military cooperation is to be strengthened by working *within* the existing policy parameters. The Japanese constitution is not to be amended or to be reinterpreted; the bilateral security pact is not to be revised; and the current U.S. force structure in Japan is not to be altered. Moreover, alliance redefinition is to be primarily a bureaucratic process with public discussions kept to a minimum.

Although this book endorses the effort to reinvigorate the alliance, it argues that there is both a need and an opportunity for a more thorough restructuring than the one under way. As the explosion of discontent in Okinawa after the rape of a schoolgirl by American servicemen in September 1995 indicated, more must be done to lighten the burden on Okinawa for maintaining the security arrangements. Given the strong domestic opposition to the transfer of Okinawan bases to Japan's main islands, the reduction of troops and bases on Okinawa will inevitably require a binational, not just a Japanese, solution. The burgeoning Japanese budget deficit suggests that there are limits to how much Tokyo can continue to increase its host-nation support for U.S. forces in Japan. And with the end of the cold war, more Japanese financial contributions may not be enough to convince Americans that Japan is not free-riding on U.S. security policy. But how far should Japan go in cooperating militarily with the United States?

For most U.S. policymakers the geopolitical interest in preventing the rise of a hostile regional hegemon or coalition might be sufficient to justify the security engagement in East Asia. But the same cannot be said for much of the American public. After the collapse of the Soviet Union, other objectives such as improving commercial access to East Asia and promoting democratic values have become just as, if not more, important in the calculations of U.S. citizens. Although the Pentagon has articulated these goals as part of its overall East Asian strategy, the results have been mixed at best as America's trade deficit with the region as a whole continues to grow and as most East Asian states resist Washington's human rights and democratization agenda. Getting Japan to do more militarily may be inadequate for buttressing domestic American support for the alliance. The alliance must also serve U.S. economic interests and advance its basic political values.

To transform the security relationship into a true alliance, the United States and Japan must strike a new strategic bargain. Currently, Japan is a passive partner for regional security whose primary role is limited to letting the United States use bases on its territory for contingencies beyond the defense of Japan. Under a new bargain, Japan would expand its security horizons beyond defending its homeland and assume more of the diplomatic and military risks for maintaining peace in the region. As Japan becomes a more active ally, the United States would streamline its military presence to alleviate Japanese domestic pressures. The alliance would move away from the pattern of American paternalism and Japanese dependency toward a more equal partnership in which Washington truly consults with Tokyo and Tokyo is willing to take more initiative on security matters.

Japanese and American Reviews of Defense Policy

Although the Japanese and American reviews of their defense policies began independently, they developed into an interactive process. In early 1994 Prime Minister Morihiro Hosokawa appointed a blue-ribbon advisory group chaired by Hirotaro Higuchi to examine the future of Japanese defense policy with an eye to revising the National Defense Program Outline (NDPO), the policy framework for defense planning. Hosokawa believed a thorough reassessment was needed because of the dramatic international political and economic changes that had transpired since the the NDPO was approved in 1976. In addition, the realignment of political forces after the split within the Liberal Democratic party provided a favorable domestic context for the review. In joining the non-LDP governing coalition led by Hosokawa, the Socialist party had abandoned its policy of unarmed neutrality and agreed to support the maintenance of the Treaty of Mutual Cooperation and Security between Japan and the United States. There was now an opportunity to broaden the political consensus in support of the nation's defense policy.

Although the Higuchi report in August 1994 did not recommend major departures from current policies, it did attempt to frame these policies in a new way.[1] At the outset, the report urged a "coherent and comprehensive security policy" that made use of an array of policy instruments, including diplomacy, economics, and defense capabilities. It suggested moving from a "cold war defense strategy" to a "multilateral security strategy."[2] Although Japan's own defense capabilities and cooperation with the United States would remain important pillars of Japanese security policy, these elements should now be viewed more from the vantage point of cooperative security. As a consequence, the Higuchi group emphasized greater participation of the self-defense force in UN peacekeeping operations, more active government support for international arms control processes, and government promotion of regional security dialogues.

To strengthen U.S.-Japanese security cooperation, the report advocated
— improvement of bilateral policy consultations and exchanges of information;
— promotion of "joint formation and studies of unit operation plans as well as joint training on the assumption of various circumstances";
— facilitation of mutual logistical support by concluding an acquisition and cross-servicing agreement similar to that between the United States and NATO member states;
— promotion of joint research, development, and production of weapons and other defense-related systems; and
— improvement of support arrangements for U.S. forces in Japan by streamlining joint use of facilities and by consolidating and realigning these facilities as necessary.

Regarding Japan's own defense capabilities, the Higuchi advisory panel recommended
— improving command, control, communications, and intelligence systems;
— strengthening joint operational abilities among the ground, sea, and air self-defense forces;
— promoting the maneuverability and combat readiness of the self-defense forces; and
— adjusting the size and structure of the self-defense forces.

This last recommendation encompassed a reduction in the ground forces, reductions in the number of ships and aircraft for antisubmarine and antimine warfare, improvement in surveillance and patrol functions as well as antisurface and antiaircraft battle capabilities, reductions in air fighter units and fighter planes, consideration of midair refueling and long-range air transport capabilities, and acquisition of antiballistic missile systems.

Given the interest in UN peacekeeping activities and concerns about Japan's response to a Korean crisis, the Higuchi group discussed constitutional issues concerning collective security and the right of collective self-defense, the right of a country to consider an attack on a country with which it has close, friendly relations as an attack on itself and to act jointly to counter that attack. But in the end, it shied away from recommending that Japan should exercise its right of collective self-defense. Indeed, it did not address this matter explicitly in the report. By the time the panel had drafted its recommendations, Japan had a new prime minister, the socialist Tomiichi Murayama, who would certainly have rejected the Higuchi report if it had advocated reinterpreting the constitution in favor of exercising the right of collective self-defense.[3]

The Pentagon's East Asian Strategic Review

While the Higuchi committee did its work, the U.S. Defense Department conducted its own review of East Asian strategy in the wake of the so-called bottom-up review of defense policy completed in September 1993. This regional assessment culminated in the February 1995 East Asian Strategic Review.[4] The EASR was the successor to the Bush administration's East Asian Strategic Initiative (EASI) reports.[5] The reports outlined a process for restructuring and reducing forces in the region "without jeopardizing [the Pentagon's] ability to meet its security commitments" in three intervals: phase 1, 1990–92; phase 2, 1993–95; and phase 3, 1995–2000. This procedure was to be flexible enough to enable modifications in response to regional developments, especially in nations where the United States kept forward-deployed forces.

The Clinton administration, however, ended the EASI reduction of military personnel. The February 1995 EASR declared instead America's "commitment to maintain a stable forward presence in the region, at the existing level of about 100,000 troops, for the forseeable future." Although the end of the cold war removed the need to deter the Soviet military, tensions over the North Korean nuclear program and continuing uncertainties about the North Korean regime motivated American defense planners to keep a robust military presence in the region.

In addition to deterring North Korean aggression and having the capacity to respond effectively during a Korean military crisis, policymakers stressed the general reassurance mission of U.S. forces. East Asians were voicing concerns about America's staying power in the region either because of its lack of will or because it was a declining power. If they began to believe that the United States was disengaging militarily, geopolitical tensions in the region would increase and the East Asian states would begin to engage in a destabilizing arms race. Some East Asians feared the remilitarization of Japan; others worried about not having a reliable power to balance the rise of China. The Clinton administration, therefore, maintained the number of troops in the region to reassure Asians psychologically. This meant the presence of about 45,000 military personnel in Japan for the forseeable future.

But Clinton officials did not stop there. Just as their predecessors did, they encouraged Japan to strengthen defense cooperation with the United States. During the height of the cold war, such a policy was easily understandable. But after the Soviet collapse, and in the wake of the U.S. intention not to further reduce its military deployments in East Asia, asking Tokyo to contribute more to defense matters was puzzling. Why did Japan need to take a more prominent military role in the alliance? Why not just maintain the status quo?

Three concerns operated here. One was how sustainable the alliance would be during an actual crisis. Japan's awkward response to the Persian Gulf crisis and war of 1990–91 impressed upon U.S. officials the danger that Tokyo might balk in another crisis. The alliance weathered Desert Shield and Desert Storm with primarily financial contributions from Japan because American casualties were so low. Another regional conflict might not have such a favorable outcome. Moreover, a crisis closer to Japan, like one on the Korean peninsula, would test the alliance more severely. If the crisis led to a military confrontation and the conflict did not go well, the American people would expect Japan to contribute more than just financial support and U.S. access to bases in Japan. Under the existing framework of U.S.-Japan defense cooperation, the possibility that the alliance would fail such a test was too high for comfort. Therefore, to counter arguments that Japan was a free or cheap rider on America's security guarantee, Pentagon officials initiated a bilateral process (the so-called Nye initiative, named after Joseph Nye, assistant secretary of defense for international security at the time) to spur defense cooperation.

A second concern was to respond to signs that Japan was beginning to hedge against a worsening of U.S.-Japan relations.[6] President Clinton's tough trade policy was eroding Japanese domestic support for the alliance and signaled to the Japanese that Washington did not value the security relationship as much as before. Japanese commentary that Japan should turn more to Asia after decades of being dependent on the United States began to appear with greater frequency and resonance. The Higuchi report further raised concerns in the Pentagon that Japan might be trying to gradually increase its autonomy. Although the report treated the security relationship with the United States as one of the pillars of Japanese defense policy, it gave comparable attention to UN peacekeeping operations, multilateral security dialogues and institution building, and the development of autonomous long-range transport, intelligence gathering through satellites, and defense technnology and industrial capabilities. The fact that the report discussed "multilateral security cooperation" *before* "the enhancement of Japan-U.S. security cooperation" worried some Japan watchers in the Defense Department. To check this hedging tendency, the Pentagon launched the Nye initiative.

Not surprisingly, many Japanese interpreted Nye's dictum that "security is like oxygen" to mean that the Clinton administration was abandoning its aggressive trade tactics and putting priority on security issues. The brinksmanship in the bilateral automobile talks that followed the 1995 release of the Pentagon's East Asian strategy report, however, demonstrated the inaccuracy of this interpretation. The idea was not to deemphasize U.S. economic interests in favor of security, but rather to promote simultaneously and with vigor *both* U.S. economic and security interests. In fact, tightening the security relationship would permit Washington to pursue an assertive trade policy without pushing Japan away from it politically.

The third calculation in encouraging Japan to do more on the defense front concerned the rise of China.[7] U.S. policymakers understood that China viewed international politics through the lens of realpolitik. Beijing emphasized the tensions in U.S.-Japan relations and the emergence of a multipolar dynamic in the Asia-Pacific region. Although the U.S.-Japan security relationship served China's interest by restraining Japanese rearmament, U.S.-Japan economic frictions would inevitably cause Japan to become more independent politically and less willing to toe the American line. This trend provided China with an opportunity to advance its own economic and strategic interests. Given this calculus, an effective American way to counter China's hope of playing a multipolar game and to restrain Chinese behavior was to strengthen U.S.-Japan security relations. A Japan that would be willing to stand with the United States in an East Asian crisis and even to fight shoulder to shoulder would certainly give pause to the Chinese. But insofar as the Clinton administration wanted to pursue a policy of engaging China, it did not want to give the impression that the United States was revitalizing the U.S.-Japan security relationship to contain China.

The Nye Initiative and Japan's New National Defense Program Outline

Just before the U.S. Defense Department released the East Asian Strategic Review, American and Japanese officials quietly began working-level discussions on security cooperation under the Nye initiative. This bilateral exchange using bureaucratic channels contributed to the Japan Defense Agency's own review that culminated in a new planning guide to replace the original National Defense Program Outline. Formally approved by the Japanese cabinet in November 1995, the new NDPO mandated a restructuring and streamlining of the self-defense forces along the lines recommended in the Higuchi report. The mandate included eliminating unnecessary forces and equipment and implementing a reorganization and modernization program to make the self-defense forces more compact and able to respond more quickly and flexibly. For example, the new program outline will make the self-defense ground forces lighter and more mobile to deal with a greater variety of missions, including disaster relief and international peacekeeping.

The Nye initiative shaped the new NDPO in two ways. First, it emphasized more strongly than either the 1976 NDPO or the Higuchi report the importance of Japan-U.S. security arrangements to Japanese defense policy. The 1995 NDPO mentions "Japan-U.S. security arrangements" eleven times in the text; the old NDPO did so only twice. Second, the new NDPO broadened the geographic scope of national defense.

Should a situation arise in the *areas surrounding Japan,* which will have an important influence on national peace and security, take

appropriate response in accordance with the Constitution and relevant laws and regulations, for example, by properly supporting the
United Nations activities when needed, and by ensuring the smooth
and effective implementation of the Japan-U.S. Security Arrangements. [italics added][8]

This sentence was included despite resistance from the Cabinet Legal
Affairs Bureau (Naikaku Hōsei Kyoku), which raised questions about
the constitutionality of going beyond a doctrine strictly oriented toward
self-defense.[9] The previous program outline had not referred to possible
Japanese responses to situations that did not involve direct or indirect
aggression against Japan. Drafters of the new NDPO wanted to reinvigorate the security relationship by allowing Japan to cooperate actively
with the United States to promote regional security. Only by redefining
the alliance in this way could Japan check the isolationist tendencies in
the United States. The new program outline was a breakthrough that permitted not only bilateral studies about how to respond to regional contingencies, but also eventual coordination of military operations. To
avoid an acrimonious debate, however, the Murayama cabinet down-
played the new NDPO's historical significance and emphatically reaffirmed the government's position that the constitution prohibited the
exercise of the right of collective self-defense.

The Clinton-Hashimoto Summit

Japanese and American defense officials initially intended to cap the
bureaucratic security discussions conducted under the Nye initiative and
the drafting of the new NDPO with a bilateral summit reaffirming the
U.S.-Japan security relationship. The summit was to be held immediately
after the Asia Pacific Economic Cooperation (APEC) meeting in Osaka
scheduled for November 15, 1995. Things, however, did not turn out as
planned. The rape of the Okinawan schoolgirl by American servicemen
in early September posed one of the most difficult political challenges to
the alliance in recent memory. Japanese popular support for the security
relationship dropped sharply, and demands for a reduction of U.S. forces
on Okinawa increased dramatically. Governor Masahide Ota, who was
elected on a platform to reduce the American military presence on
Okinawa, refused to sign the mandatory extension of land leases for U.S.
military use. A few antiwar landowners had refused to renew the leases.

The U.S. and Japanese governments tried to defuse the situation through conciliatory gestures and the creation of a Special Action Committee on Okinawa just two weeks before the summit. SACO's purpose was to find ways of "reducing the intrusion of U.S. forces' facilities and personnel on the Okinawan people."[10] But despite this initiative, there was a real possibility the president's visit would be marred by embarrassing questions related to the rape and the future viability of U.S. bases in Japan. What was to have been a triumphant summit seemed headed toward a public relations disaster.

Despite the misgivings it aroused in the East Asia–Pacific region, President Clinton's decision not to attend the APEC summit in Osaka because of the budget battle in Washington turned out to be a blessing in disguise. Policymakers gained more time to deal with the aftermath of the rape. The selection of Ryutaro Hashimoto as prime minister after Murayama's resignation in January 1996 brought forth a better counterpart to Clinton for reaffirming the security relationship. Believing resolution of the Okinawa issue was critical to the longevity of his government, Hashimoto quickly began searching for a way to get the Futenma Marine Air Base returned to Okinawa, a top priority for Okinawans. Known for his hawkish views on defense, Hashimoto was also more enthusiastic than Murayama about strengthening the alliance. Finally, China's attempt to intimidate Taiwan during the island's first democratic presidential election in March provided a good context for convincing Americans and Japanese alike about the strategic importance of the bilateral security partnership.

These developments cleared the way for initiatives that might not have been taken had the summit been held as originally scheduled. First, just before the rescheduled summit of April 1996, the two governments signed an Acquisition and Cross-Servicing Agreement (ACSA) that mandated Japanese logistical support for U.S. forces during peacetime in the context of training, joint exercises, peacekeeping operations, and humanitarian missions. This support could include supplying fuel, spare parts, and military components to the U.S. military as well as food, water, and clothing. To implement this agreement, the Japanese government announced first that it would not apply the three principles against arms exports. In the new domestic and international climate, this move stirred little controversy in Japan.

Second, Tokyo and Washington decided to insert into the Japan-U.S. Joint Declaration on Security an agreement to review the 1978 Guidelines for Japan-U.S. Defense Cooperation. The aim would be to improve bilateral coordination and cooperation to handle "situations that may emerge in the areas surrounding Japan and which will have an important influence on the peace and security of Japan." Third, SACO issued an interim report two days before the summit that contained bold measures to defuse the discontent on Okinawa. Washington agreed to return the Futenma Marine Air Station in five to seven years, and Tokyo agreed to pay for a new Marine Corps helicopter port. The United States also decided to reduce by about 20 percent the total acreage of American military facilities on Okinawa, terminate live artillery exercises over Highway 104, adopt more stringent noise reduction initiatives around U.S. air bases, and relinquish the Sobe Communications Site located on the land of one of Okinawa's most active and famous antimilitary landowners.

At the summit itself, President Clinton declared in the joint declaration on security (see the appendix) that "100,000 forward deployed military personnel in the region, including about the current level in Japan" were required "in the prevailing security environment." In welcoming this "U.S. determination to remain a stable and steadfast presence in the region," Prime Minister Hashimoto agreed to continue Japanese contributions, financial and otherwise, to maintain U.S. forces in Japan. The joint declaration on security also outlined in general terms the intention of the two countries to work "jointly and individually . . . to achieve a more peaceful and stable security environment in the Asia-Pacific region." The document noted the following objectives:

—cooperation with China with the aim of encouraging Beijing to "play a positive and constructive role" in the region;

—encouragement of and cooperation with Russia's ongoing reform, and reaffirmation of full normalization of Japan-Russia relations as important to regional peace and stability;

—continuation of efforts regarding stability on the Korean peninsula in cooperation with the Republic of Korea; and

—development of multilateral regional security dialogues and cooperation mechanisms such as the Association of Southeast Asian Nations (ASEAN) Regional Forum, and eventually, security dialogues regarding Northeast Asia.

In addition to regional issues, the two countries agreed to work together on other security matters, including UN peacekeeping and humanitarian relief operations, acceleration of the Comprehensive Test Ban Treaty negotiations, prevention of the proliferation of weapons of mass destruction and their means of delivery, facilitation of the Middle East peace process, and implementation of the peace process in the former Yugoslavia.

Notwithstanding the success of the summit, it marked only the beginning of the redefinition of the alliance. Complex issues remain in implementing the plans for the base realignment and reduction in Okinawa. The joint security declaration suggested but left unanswered critical questions about the alliance's future.

What should the United States and Japan do together and separately on behalf of the regional security goals articulated by Clinton and Hashimoto? Their statements were much too vague to guide policy. What is the desirable Japanese military role in regional security from the perspective of both deterrence and crisis management and response? What kind of expanded Japanese military contribution would give the alliance a new lease on life instead of letting it remain a source of tension? Should the United States seek Japanese participation in military patrols and even combat operations during crises, or is logistical support in the rear enough? Should Japan's participation in UN security activities be limited to peacekeeping operations, or should Tokyo be encouraged to become involved in more difficult peacemaking or peace enforcement operations? If the appropriate policy is to have Japan contribute more in military terms to regional security, how should this evolution be managed so as not to become a destabilizing factor in the region? To what extent and in what way can and should U.S. force deployments change in response to greater defense cooperation by Japan as well as changes in the regional environment and advances in military technology? Although maintaining the alliance and keeping a robust U.S. military presence in the East Asia–Pacific theater may be essential to regional stability, they are by no means sufficient. Therefore, how should the United States and Japan coordinate their diplomacy and economic policies to deal with security challenges and shape a better strategic environment? What should be the relationship between bilateral and multilateral approaches to security issues? What initiatives to reduce tension, measures to build confidence, and arms control processes should Japan and the United States promote?

The Inadequacy of Incrementalism

As fundamental as the questions about the nature of the alliance are, the U.S. and Japanese governments have adopted an incremental approach to redefining it. In fact, since the April 1996 summit, officials in Tokyo have backpedaled, contending that the joint declaration was a reaffirmation *(sai-kakunin)*, not a redefinition *(sai-teigi)*, of the bilateral security relationship.[11] Incrementalism has the following characteristics. First, the improvement of defense cooperation will proceed within the framework of the existing Japanese constitution and the U.S.-Japan security treaty. The constitution will not be reinterpreted or revised; the security pact and the Status of Forces Agreement, which governs the U.S. armed forces' use of facilities and bases in Japan, will not be formally altered, and Japan will continue to adhere to its "exclusive defense-oriented" *(senshu bō'ei)* policy. Second, despite a commitment to lessen the burden on Okinawa, the aggregate number of U.S. troops in Japan and their force structure will remain the same. Third, redefinition of the alliance will primarily be a bureaucratic process among security policy specialists in both countries, and open discussion will be minimized. When questions are raised in public forums such as the Diet, Japanese officials will deemphasize the significance of what is occurring to avoid political controversy.

Different calculations lie behind Tokyo and Washington's pursuit of incrementalism. In Japan, domestic political constraints have steered policymakers toward this approach. Political realignment and the end of single-party governments finally induced the Japan Socialist party (now the Social Democratic Party of Japan, or SDPJ) to change its longstanding platform of unarmed neutrality and accept both the U.S.-Japan Security Treaty and the constitutionality of the self-defense forces. For the first time since the end of the U.S. occupation, this change has presented Japanese defense officials with an opportunity to formulate policy on the basis of a broad multipartisan consensus. But at the same time, the participation of the Social Democrats in government has made an expansion of Japan's defense responsibilities more difficult. Given their interest in preserving the present coalition between the Liberal Democratic party (LDP), the SDPJ, and the New Party Harbinger (Shintō Sakigake), even LDP security hawks have acquiesced to incrementalism.[12] The Defense Agency and the Ministry of Foreign Affairs have also adopted this approach for fear of politicizing the issue. In their view, revising or even reinterpreting the constitution and the bilateral security treaty would impede the process of strengthening U.S.-Japan defense cooperation. A rancorous debate would eat up precious parliamentary time and could even trigger public demonstrations. It would therefore be more efficient to do things quietly in the context of bilateral discussions between Japanese and American bureaucrats responsible for defense policy.

Although Prime Minister Hashimoto favors a proactive security policy much more than his pacifist predecessor did, he has tempered his defense agenda to sustain parliamentary support for his government from the dovish Social Democratic party and the New Party Harbinger. Nevertheless, he has adopted two ways to move things forward. One is to expand the scope of individual self-defense. Heretofore the right of individual self-defense referred primarily to defending against attacks on Japanese territory. Now the government would like to broaden the meaning to include the rescue of Japanese citizens abroad who may be endangered by local conflicts. The overseas dispatch of self-defense forces for such missions should be constitutional. With the large number of Japanese business personnel and their families now living in foreign countries, business has welcomed this initiative. Alarm about the ineffective response to both the Hanshin earthquake and the Aum Shinrikyo sarin gas attack in 1995 has probably made the Japanese people more receptive to such an expansion of the concept. The hostage crisis in Lima reinforced this trend.

The second way of advancing incrementalism involves the review of the 1978 Guidelines for Japan-U.S. Defense Cooperation to promote coordination during regional contingencies. In contrast to the 1978 guidelines, which refer only to bilateral consultations and study, the aim of the new guidelines would be to facilitate actual coordination at the operational level. Rather than pushing for a conceptual breakthrough at the start, Hashimoto has asked defense officials to consider specific scenarios and determine which actions are permissible under the present interpretation of the constitution, which are impermissible, and which lie in the gray zone between. The promotion of bilateral defense coordination could begin with those tasks that are clearly permissible, and if politically possible, even approve tasks in the gray zone. Many of the so-called gray-zone activities relate to Japanese logistical support for American combat operations and will require clarification about what constitutes the use of force for Japan.[13]

In the United States, a delicate balancing act led policymakers to embrace incrementalism. The logic of maximizing deterrence and the ability to respond quickly to crises called for Japan to perform as a great power with the will and capacity to act outside its defense perimeter in concert with the United States. But the logic of restraining Japanese autonomy and of not increasing regional geopolitical tensions suggested that it would be imprudent to push Japan too far too quickly. Even within the Pentagon, sharp disagreement existed about whether to urge Japan to take on new defense missions even in cooperation with the United States. A Japan that can do more for regional defense, some defense analysts argue, would be a Japan less dependent on the United States and less willing to follow America's strategic lead. This ambivalence explains why Washington still wants Tokyo to work within the present constitution and opposes a revision of the security pact to strengthen its mutuality. In addition, moving beyond the existing policy might repoliticize the defense debate in Japan, jeopardizing the steady progress that has been made in the past two decades in broadening Japanese domestic support for the alliance.

As understandable as this cautious and tentative approach to change is, incrementalism has serious shortcomings. First, and especially in Japan, it may impede expanding Japan's contribution to the alliance. Even winning approval for gray-zone activities will require strong political leadership and commitment. The Cabinet Legal Affairs Bureau is likely to retain its restrictive reading of the constitution and argue that gray-zone functions lie outside the bounds of constitutional permissibility.[14] The bureau contends that Japan cannot exercise its right to collective self-defense. But in addition is the agency's doctrine concerning the "integration of the use of force" (buryoku kōshi no ittaika). Developed in the context of the 1990–91 Persian Gulf crisis, the doctrine tries to define what kind of support activities would entail the use of force. Such activities would be prohibited unless performed only as an exercise of the individual self-defense right. According to the bureau, even the transport of medical and food supplies to combat areas would fall under this prohibition.[15]

Interministerial rivalries can also obstruct defense cooperation. The Ministry of Post and Telecommunications, the Ministry of Transportation, and other domestic-oriented agencies are resisting Defense Agency efforts to develop a legal framework to deal with military emergencies and permit U.S. military and the self-defense forces access to civilian air facilities, ports, and communications networks during a crisis. Political forces such as the SDPJ will cooperate with these government agencies to impede redefining the security relationship. Contrary to the bureaucratic view that incrementalism will result in faster progress, without determined political leadership it may not only be painstakingly slow but could also establish new policy hurdles. For two decades defense policymaking in Japan has required compensating the pacifist opposition with new restrictions on the military to get its acquiescence for measures that strengthen defense. A strategically coherent restructuring of the bilateral alliance will require changing this pattern.

The second problem with incrementalism is that the ultimate objective of alliance redefinition remains vague. American and Japanese defense officials have stated that Japan should do more to cooperate with U.S. military forces, but how much and in what way is unclear. On the American side the lack of clarity stems not only from a desire to avoid controversy in Japan, but also from a concern about pushing Japan too hard. On the Japanese side the prodefense forces want to use American pressure to chip away at the domestic political constraints on the Japanese military. The greater the U.S. pressure, the better. But to Japanese pacifists and many Asians who fear remilitarization, Washington's effort to redefine security relations is unwittingly strengthening Japanese nationalistic groups that seek greater strategic autonomy. U.S. defense officials, however, want to do precisely the opposite: check Japan's quest for autonomy and strengthen its link with the United States. Vagueness about what kind of security alliance is ultimately desirable widens the gap between Japanese and American motives.

Vagueness is related to a third shortcoming of incrementalism: the lack of a frank and open discussion of security issues in Japan, particularly at the parliamentary level. The guardedness, the result of a laudable government effort begun during the cold war to depolarize the intense ideological conflict over security matters, may have outlived its usefulness. The time is now ripe in Japan to stop sidestepping the hard security questions and to debate candidly specific policy choices. For two decades Japanese officials have deemphasized the strategic significance of changes in security policy even while expanding the scope of Japan's defense to include defense of sea lanes out to 1,000 nautical miles, joint exercises with U.S. forces, dispatch of minesweepers to the Persian Gulf, and participation in UN peacekeeping operations. This deemphasis inhibits public interest in and knowledge about defense issues. There are no research centers independent of the government to evaluate official policy, and Japanese politicians with more than a cursory knowledge about the details of security policy are woefully few. A continuation of this situation is healthy neither for Japan nor for the alliance. The lack of openness also breeds distrust from Japan's neighbors, even though the Japanese government has conscientiously published its annual defense white papers and myriad publications explaining defense budgets and procurements.

Some might argue that it is better to delay addressing the hard issues until a crisis occurs that will compel Japanese leaders to act boldly in coordination with the United States. But as Japan's reaction to the Persian Gulf crisis suggests, the possibility of paralysis is just as great as the possibility of an effective and timely response. And paralysis is not the only danger. Unless Japan becomes better prepared to handle security crises, it might overreact as well as underreact. The public's meager knowledge of security issues could provoke mass hysteria during an emergency. Rather than the prime minister and his government taking the lead to fashion an appropriate and measured response, ultranationalistic forces could take advantage of political immobility to push the country in a militaristic direction. To overcome the impasse, some political and military leaders might even urge a response to crisis through extralegal means. Such a Japan would be destabilizing for both the East Asia–Pacific region and the world.

There is therefore a pedagogical purpose to making the process of redefining the alliance more open and frank. If Japan is to take a more prominent part in ensuring international security, the practice and institutions of civilian control over military policy must become more effective. A review of the constitution or the security treaty may temporarily aggravate the work of bureaucrats, but a public debate about these matters may be just what is necessary to raise the consciousness of Japanese citizens and politicians and to nurture attention to Japan's international interests beyond the pursuit of economic gain.

Another flaw in incrementalism is that it has the effect of limiting flexibility. In turning the number of troops (100,000 military personnel forward deployed in East Asia) into a symbol of U.S. commitment, the Clinton administration has made it more difficult to adjust forces in response to technological and political developments. Reassuring Asian friends and allies is an important political objective, but it need not be done by highlighting numbers. More critical than the number of troops is America's ability to perform crucial military missions with the cooperation and help of allies. Depending on the will and capacity of Japan to assist in military operations, America could alter its force deployments without jeopardizing deterrence and the ability to respond to crises. Explaining the adjustments fully in these terms and being more attentive to the region will more than adequately confer the necessary psychological reassurance to East Asian states. Of course, the United States will need to maintain a core military presence, given its unique ability to integrate intelligence and operations. The Hashimoto cabinet's intention to work within the concept of individual self-defense excessively restricts the ways U.S.-Japan defense cooperation can deal with regional contingencies. A conceptual breakthrough that involves recognizing Japan's right to collective self-defense would open up new options for tightening the alliance.

Finally, incrementalism suffers from an overly narrow agenda. Since the April 1996 summit, security policy officials on both sides of the Pacific have been preoccupied with developing new guidelines for bilateral defense cooperation and implementing the plans for consolidating, realigning, and reducing the U.S. military facilities on Okinawa. As vital as these matters are, maintaining peace and stability in the Asia-Pacific region requires more than military means. The American military presence and the U.S.-Japan security arrangements may be necessary to regional security, but they are by no means sufficient. In redefining the alliance, Washington and Tokyo have not adequately discussed the coordination of diplomacy and economic policy to nurture a more benign regional environment. The reference to "multilateral regional security dialogues and cooperation mechanisms" in the Clinton-Hashimoto joint declaration on security is almost an afterthought. The Asia-Pacific region is undergoing revolutionary economic and social changes that will inevitably have profound political consequences. The United States and Japan, two of the most powerful countries in the region, have an opportunity to establish an order that can accommodate these changes peacefully. But the joint policy agenda must be deepened and broadened beyond the range of defense incrementalism.

Domestic Politics and Transpacific Linkages

Ultimately, changes in the strategic environment will shape alliance restructuring. Renewed tensions with North Korea created by its nuclear program will revive U.S. expectations of Japanese cooperation on policy for economic sanctions and even military options. An outbreak of war on the Korean peninsula will probably lead to American requests for at least Japanese logistical support in addition to unhampered access to military facilities in Japan. Hesitation from Japan would severely strain the alliance; and if American casualties were high, the security relationship might become politically unsustainable after the war if Japan's support were considered inadequate. A U.S. military confrontation with China would pose similar challenges. Given its ever growing economic interests in China, Japan is likely to become deeply divided between siding with the United States and taking a neutral stance. If Japan chose neutrality, the alliance itself could be endangered.

A more benign regional security environment could also fundamentally alter America's outlook. Korean reunification or even the reduction of tensions between North and South Korea would cause the public and many political leaders to question the necessity of maintaining a large military presence in Northeast Asia. Of course, a deterioration in relations with China might offset the effect of positive Korean developments and ultimately reinforce America's forward deployment, with some adjustments. But if Sino-American relations were to improve as well, especially as a result of Chinese political liberalization, the geopolitical value of the security partnership with Japan would diminish. Washington would become much more serious about pursuing the cooperative security agenda embraced by American liberals and Japanese pacifists.

But in addition to these possible international developments, the interaction of American and Japanese politics will shape the alliance's future. Domestic pressures could compel leaders to move beyond incremental alliance redefinition and even consider revisionist ideas. Internal trends could also present an opportunity for both governments to be bolder about restructuring the security relationship. In the coming years, the security dialogue is likely to revolve around three domestic issues: Okinawa and the distribution of U.S. bases in Japan, budget constraints and trade imbalances, and the Japanese constitutional question regarding collective defense and security.

Okinawa and the Distribution of U.S. Bases

For the moment, American and Japanese policymakers appear to have successfully defused the Okinawans' complaints. The adjustments announced in April 1996, especially the return of the Futenma Marine Air Station, demonstrated that both Tokyo and Washington were giving serious attention to the aspirations of Okinawans. Although the prefectural referendum held in September 1996 showed strong support (nearly 90 percent) for a reduction of U.S. military facilities on the island, the turnout of less than 60 percent suggested that the intense anger that had exploded after the rape had subsided.[16] Just before this vote, the Japanese Supreme Court ruled against Okinawa and for the national government's right of eminent domain regarding the leasing of Okinawan land for U.S. military use. But instead of gloating over this decision and the relatively low turnout rate in the referendum, Hashimoto acknowledged that the central government had not been sensitive to Okinawan interests and offered the prefecture a variety of economic benefits. In response, Governor Ota announced his willingness to sign the order to renew the leases for U.S. military use on land owned by antiwar activists. The prime minister was thus able to call a general election without turning this contest into a plebiscite on U.S. military presence in Japan.

But the Okinawa problem is far from resolved. The return of Futenma is predicated on finding a site for a heliport that can assume some of the functions performed by the base. Strong local opposition to the construction of a new military facility, even a modest one, led Tokyo to resist the Pentagon's proposal for a heliport constructed in Marine Camp Schwab, located in central Okinawa. Japan's counterproposal of augmenting facilities within Kadena Air Force Base posed problems of air traffic safety and noise levels. U.S. and Japanese officials then turned to an offshore facility as an alternative, but feasibility questions prevented SACO from making a conclusive decision on this matter by the time it issued its final report in November 1996. Since then, Okinawan residents have expressed their preference for a landfill facility over an offshore one. Although it would be imprudent to rush a decision on the heliport at the risk of adopting an unworkable plan, an extended delay would be politically damaging. In 1974 the United States agreed to return the Naha Military Port pending the construction of a new port. Because of resistance from Urasoe City, the proposed site of the new facility, the transfer has yet to take place. A similar deferral on Futenma would dissipate the goodwill generated by SACO's work.

Another problem is the process for renewing land leases for U.S. military use. Most Okinawan landowners (about 29,000 out of 32,000) who rent their property for American military use do so voluntarily and welcome the financial compensation. The mainstream landowners' association has indeed opposed Governor Ota's campaign to dismantle U.S. military bases on the island. But some 3,000 antiwar activists own small plots totaling about 91 acres that are located in many critical U.S. military facilities such as Kadena Air Force Base.[17] They have refused to extend their leases voluntarily. The legal process for determining eminent domain in these cases involves a review by a prefectural land use committee appointed by the Okinawa governor.[18] Under Governor Ota this committee has become more receptive to the antiwar landowners by reducing the length of the mandatory renewals and by prolonging the review process. As a result, many leases were due to expire in mid-May 1997 before the Okinawa land committee ruled on the Defense Agency's request to renew them under eminent domain. Faced with the possibility that U.S. military use of this land would become illegal, the Hashimoto government hastily pushed through legislation in April 1997 to make this use legal even after the leases formally expired and while the prefectural land use board is continuing its deliberations. That an overwhelming parliamentary majority consisting of all the significant political parties except the Social Democrats and Communists backed this bill did indicate broad support for the alliance with the United States, at least at the national political level.

The April 1997 special legislation, however, provides only a temporary Band-Aid for the land-leasing issue. The power of the antiwar landowners derives not from their numbers but from their ability to mobilize the support of the Okinawan citizenry, most of whom are irritated by the intrusion of the U.S. military presence into their daily lives and angry about the burden they have to bear for the U.S.-Japan security relationship. If the national government does not follow through on its commitment to lessen this burden as well as to facilitate the prefecture's economic development independent of the U.S. bases, the prefectural land use committee may be emboldened to formally reject the Defense Agency's petitions for eminent domain. But the minister of construction has the power to reject such a decision and compel the prefectural board to rehear the case. Under the April 1997 legislation the U.S. military can still legally use the land as long as the deliberative review continues, but this is a fragile basis for giving legal legitimacy to American bases in Okinawa. To correct this flawed process, Ichiro Ozawa, leader of the New Frontier party, and some other politicians advocate removing the authority to decide eminent domain cases regarding military bases from the prefectural to the national level.

A more alarming danger is the possibility of another incident with a political impact comparable to the rape. The chances of this happening are great no matter how much effort is devoted to tightening discipline or ensuring citizen safety. More than 4,700 serious crimes have been committed by U.S. military personnel since the reversion of Okinawa in 1972. The number of sexual assaults has been high relative to other areas where the U.S. military is located.[19] After the return of Okinawa to Japan, there have been 121 aircraft accidents (of which 36 were aircraft crashes) and 133 brush fires, burning an area of about 1,340 hectares.[20] A serious accident or incident could again ignite Okinawan anger and perhaps trigger widespread violence comparable to the Koza riots of 1970. As a result, the antibase movement could spread to the main islands and jeopardize the entire U.S.-Japan security relationship. This possibility suggests that a piecemeal response to the Okinawan problem may prove inadequate.

For Okinawans the salient matter is fairness. About 60 percent of U.S. military personnel in Japan are stationed in Okinawa; 75 percent of the total acreage of the military facilities under exclusive use by U.S. forces in Japan is in Okinawa, although the prefecture comprises only 0.6 percent of Japanese territory. American bases occupy about 10 percent of the land in the entire prefecture (and 18 percent of the area of the main island of Okinawa), making it by far the prefecture with the highest percentage of land used by the U.S. military.[21] After Okinawa are Shizuoka prefecture with 1.2 percent and Yamanashi with 1.1 percent.[22] From the time of reversion in May 1972 to January 1996, the area of U.S. military facilities on Okinawa decreased only 15.5 percent. In fact, after reversion, the acreage of Marine Corps facilities increased as the corps took over some of the facilities made available by the departure of army units. Although the April 1996 agreement reached in SACO will reduce the total acreage of U.S. facilities by another 20 percent, Okinawa will still have a much greater percentage of its land controlled by the U.S. military than have other prefectures. The Pentagon is willing to return more land to get the percentage down further, but much of this property belongs to landowners who prefer to receive their rents or do not have other immediate prospects for profiting from it. The Okinawans desire most the return of land near urban areas that is presently obstructing development.[23] Moreover, local residents find the American practice of returning small parcels of land at a time especially irksome because it makes long-term economic planning impossible.

Most Japanese opinion polls confirm strong public support for reducing U.S. military bases in Okinawa, but there is formidable opposition to transferring these facilities to the main islands. According to a May 1997 survey conducted by the *Asahi Shimbun*, 72 percent of the respondents favored a gradual reduction of the U.S. bases and 15 percent wanted a total withdrawal. Only 8 percent supported the status quo. But 53 percent of those surveyed opposed moving the Okinawa facilities to the main islands, while 38 percent were in favor.[24] Business appears to share the public's view. In a poll of Japanese corporate executives conducted by the *Far Eastern Economic Review*, 82.1 percent believed that the United States should reduce its military presence on Okinawa.[25]

Japanese analysts who enthusiastically back the alliance with the United States frequently argue that the situation on Okinawa is a domestic matter, not a bilateral one. Insofar as the island bears an unfair burden for maintaining the U.S.-Japan security relationship, moving some of the military facilities and activities to Japan's main islands would be ideal. But strong opposition from other prefectures makes this option politically infeasible. Insisting on such a move is likely to ignite antibase movements on the main islands as well. As an alternative, the national government may increase its compensation to Okinawa by boosting subsidies and granting preferential economic regulations, tariffs, and visa requirements. One proposal attracting attention is to turn Okinawa into a free port, which would permit it to capitalize on its geographic location to become a commercial intersection for the region. These ideas resonate in Okinawa because of its economic overdependence on the military bases. Whether such economic measures would be sufficient to make Okinawans willing to accept a large U.S. military presence for the foreseeable future remains to be seen.

Japanese politicians have begun to raise fundamental questions about how U.S. military facilities in Japan serve Japanese interests and how they might be used in various regional contingencies. Some are searching for ways to reduce the American military presence in Okinawa (and elsewhere) without undermining the alliance or the U.S. ability to perform critical military missions. This undertaking suggests that an effective response to the problems of Okinawa will require adjustments in the security relationship as well as changes in domestic policy.

Trade Imbalances and Budget Constraints

Despite the occasional assertions that Japan is a free rider on U.S. security policy, most American politicians acknowledge the strategic benefits of having access to military bases in Japan and appreciate the financial support the country provides to help defray the cost of maintaining American forces there. Nevertheless, economic tensions between the two can still threaten the security relationship. Even after decades of intense trade negotiations, Americans believe that the Japanese market is much less open to foreign goods than their own market. Although few political leaders would like to use the U.S. security commitment as leverage to pry open Japanese markets, the hostility that trade negotiations generate inevitably weakens the goodwill between the two countries. Americans who suffer from the economic dislocations caused by imports from Japan and the rest of Asia will certainly question why the United States must provide security for Japan while Japan reaps the benefits of Asian economic growth at their expense. At the moment, however, the decline in the U.S. trade deficit, coupled with Japan's poor economic performance in recent years, has muted arguments about linking security and trade to pressure Japan to open up its market. In fact, the initiative to redefine the security relationship has buttressed the traditional fire wall between economic and security issues. Moreover, the burgeoning trade deficit with China and China's saber rattling over Taiwan have diverted attention from Japan. Up to a point, the difficulties of Sino-American relations will cause U.S. leaders to more greatly value the strategic link with Japan.

American public support for the security relationship with Japan remains strong. A February-March 1996 Gallup poll of both ordinary citizens and opinion leaders found that 66 percent of citizens believed that the U.S.-Japan Security Treaty was in America's security interests, and 75 percent favored maintaining it. Among opinion leaders, 83 percent believed that the treaty served U.S. security interests.[26] A May 1997 Louis Harris survey of American opinion yielded a similar result: 79 percent supported the security treaty, and 76 percent wanted the United States to sustain its military influence in the Asia-Pacific as before for regional stability purposes.[27] But there does exist some support for changing the terms of the alliance. For example, in the Harris survey, 48 percent of the American respondents favored maintaining the U.S. military bases as they are now, but 44 percent supported a gradual reduction and 5 percent a total withdrawal. The Gallup poll revealed a divergence between ordinary citizens and opinion leaders in that 42 percent of the ordinary citizens and 66 percent of the opinion leaders believed Japan should increase capabilities for its own defense.

Of course, dramatic political or economic changes will affect American views on these questions. For example, if tensions in East Asia were to increase, more Americans might feel that Japan should increase its military capabilities. Conversely, a resolution of the Korean conflict could raise the percentage of Americans who favor reducing the number of U.S. bases and forces in Japan as well as South Korea. If the trade imbalance with Japan again worsened, both leaders and ordinary citizens might insist on greater Japanese sharing of the defense burden. But at this point, there is little strong public advocacy in the United States for altering security arrangements with Japan. If this attitude continues, American initiatives to alter security relations are likely to result from an overall reassessment of defense programs because of budgetary pressures and the incorporation of new military technologies, not from a reevaluation of Japan policy per se (see chapter 6).

The initiative for change may now be Japan's because of strong public and elite support for reducing the U.S. military presence in Okinawa and to some extent the rest of Japan. And Japan's own budgetary constraints may lead it to seek to change the host-nation contributions (*omoiyari yosan*). During the Diet deliberations on the latest bilateral agreement increasing the contributions, dissent came not only from the Social Democrats but also from conservative politicians, including younger Diet members from the ruling Liberal Democratic party. As its budget deficits grow, Japan will increasingly resist further escalations in the contributions and may even try to reduce them. This is especially possible if it incurs large expenses in transferring U.S. military facilities on Okinawa. The Defense Agency also increasingly resents the *omoiyari yosan* for eating up more and more of the defense budget.[28] Given these trends, host-nation support will become less sustainable as a way of sharing the defense burden.

The Constitutional Question and Collective Self-Defense

After decades of stalemate between revisionists and preservationists, Japan is finally addressing the constitutional questions that affect its security policies. In 1955 when it was founded, the Liberal Democratic party made revising the postwar constitution one of its main political goals. The opposition, led by the Japan Socialist party, however, vigorously opposed revision and even mobilized like-minded conservatives in the LDP for the cause. Rather than achieving the two-thirds majority necessary to amend the constitution, the LDP's strength in the Diet dwindled steadily and the party eventually tabled its revisionist objective. In this context the government staked out the middle ground in interpreting Article 9 of the constitution. Japan, it said, can have military forces for the purpose of national defense in a strict sense because no nation-state can deny itself the right to self-defense. As confirmed in both the UN Charter and the 1960 U.S.-Japan Security Treaty, Japan also has the right of collective self-defense in terms of international law.[29] But in April 1960, during the contentious parliamentary deliberations over the revised treaty, Prime Minister Nobusuke Kishi stated that the constitution prohibits Japan from *exercising* this right.[30] In 1972 the government clarified this point by affirming that the constitution limits Japan's right to use force to the minimal extent necessary to defend the nation and therefore "prohibits exercising the so-called right of collective self-defense to prevent armed attacks against other nations." [31]

But if Japan cannot exercise its right of collective self-defense, how has it justified in constitutional terms providing military bases to the United States for the purposes of maintaining security in the Far East? The government has argued that this policy does not have any direct bearing on whether Japan can exercise the right of collective self-defense. Because the use of force is permitted under the constitution only for its own defense, the relevant constitutional test is whether these measures are integrated with the "use of force." According to the government's interpretation, merely providing the United States with bases in Japan does not constitute the use of force, but rather relates only to Japan's exercise of its territorial sovereignty.[32] The government, however, has skirted the issue of whether there are any Japanese *constitutional* constraints on how the United States can use its military bases in Japan for purposes other than the defense of Japan. Nevertheless, official notes exchanged when the 1960 Security Treaty was signed obligate the United States to consult with Japan beforehand if the bases are going to be used for military combat operations beyond the defense of Japan. Japan has interpreted this affirmation of prior consultation as giving it the right to veto American military operations from Japan. [33]

The Persian Gulf crisis and tensions in 1994 over North Korea's nuclear program raised the matter of Japanese participation in and support for operations that do not directly relate to its own defense as well as the question of dispatching self-defense forces overseas. Although the Cabinet Legal Affairs Bureau has usually invoked the criterion of whether an action is integrated with the use of force in judging what is constitutionally permissible and what is not, these questions are far from settled.[34]

As early as 1959 the bureau questioned whether Japan was able under the constitution to provide supplies to U.S. forces as part of an operation for "peace and security in the Far East." In October 1980 the bureau argued that Japan could not participate in a UN force if its mission involved the use of force.[35] During the Persian Gulf crisis the Japanese cabinet submitted the United Nations Peace Cooperation bill to mandate more visible Japanese support for the multinational coalition against Iraq. Although the Diet failed to pass the legislation, government officials struggled to define which support activities would constitute integration with the use of force and which would not. According to the Cabinet Legal Affairs Bureau, the crucial test involves the timing and physical distance of such activities in relation to actual combat. Logistical support or medical assistance intimately linked by temporal sequence to a combat operation or that takes place at or near a combat area would be integrated with the use of force and therefore proscribed. But even these criteria leave ambiguous the constitutionality of various support operations that are certainly within the realm of possibility. For example, would Japanese vessels be able to provide supplies to U.S. ships engaged in a naval blockade against North Korea? A clear answer has yet to be given.[36]

To escape this legalistic morass, many proponents of a stronger alliance with the United States or more active Japanese participation in UN security activities urge that the constitution be reinterpreted or revised so that Japan can exercise the right of collective self-defense. This advocacy received a big boost when the influential Japan Association of Corporate Executives (Keizai Dōyukai) issued a report in May 1996 urging reconsideration of the government's interpretation of the constitution.[37] The Japanese public also appears to breaking away from its longstanding silence about constitutional revision. According to a March 1997 poll conducted by the *Yomiuri Shimbun*, 44.9 percent of the respondents favored revising the constitution and 36.8 percent opposed revision.[38]

Although a mid-1996 survey of Diet members showed the strongest support for an incremental improvement in military cooperation with the United States, significant numbers of national politicians advocate more dramatic change. Of the 225 who responded to the questionnaire, 93 Diet members (41.3 percent) believed that the constitution precludes the right of collective self-defense but that bilateral military cooperation should be promoted case by case within the constraints of the constitution.[39] Twenty-four Diet members (10.7 percent) supported reinterpreting the constitution to permit the exercise of the right. But 51 (22.7 percent) backed an outright revision of the constitution to make it less restrictive regarding security policy. Only 37 (16.4 percent) believed that Japan, in sticking to its constitution, should emphasize peaceful forms of international cooperation rather than military cooperation with the United States. Although 41.3 percent backed the government's current incremental changes, what is striking is that 33.4 percent wanted, through constitutional reinterpretation or revision, to move more vigorously toward greater military cooperation with the United States. Most of those who backed a pacifistic approach came from either the Social Democratic or Japan Communist parties. With the demise of the Social Democrats in the October 1996 election, Diet support for a strict pacifistic position is likely to decrease.

These trends do not mean that Japan will revise its constitution anytime soon. The two-thirds parliamentary majority necessary to amend it still represents a formidable barrier. But changes in public opinion, the realignment of party politics, and the frequent commentary on constitutional issues in opinion journals and the daily press demonstrate that the Japanese are now engaged in a debate about their constitution with an eye toward increasing their country's participation in promoting international security. Whatever the outcome, this debate will at least increase popular awareness of security issues and stimulate the creation of nongovernmental institutions for analyzing and influencing state policies in military matters. Such developments can only help strengthen the mechanisms of civilian control over the defense establishment.

Rather than repolarizing Japanese politics, openly addressing the constitutional question creates an opportunity to develop a new domestic consensus. Instead of viewing revisionism as a reactionary movement or a rejection of Japanese pacifism, politicians can frame the problem increasingly in terms of harmonizing the three documentary pillars of security policy: the constitution, the UN Charter, and the U.S.-Japan Security Treaty. The government will initially focus on two tasks: expanding the concept of individual self-defense so that it encompasses more than what is minimally necessary to defend Japan and relaxing the restrictions on the integration of the use of force (*buryoku kōshi no ittaika*) so that Japan can provide greater rear support for U.S. forces as well as participate more actively in UN peacekeeping operations. These two steps would lay the political groundwork for the approval of both collective self-defense and collective security, either through constitutional reinterpretation or a formal amendment.

An Integrated Approach to Alliance Restructuring

Transforming the U.S.-Japan security relationship into a true alliance will first require forging a new domestic consensus in both Japan and the United States. Although an uneasy political stalemate in Japan has long steered policymakers toward defense minimalism, recent trends present an opportunity to mobilize political support for a more activist security policy. In the wake of the October 1996 election held under the new electoral system, the Social Democratic party has become only a minor political force and the new Democratic party (Minshutō) led by politicians born since World War II has emerged as a pivotal group. Unlike the pacifistic Social Democrats, the Democrats are more willing to include a healthy dose of realism in their dovish outlook. For example, in advocating a reduction of U.S. military facilities in Okinawa, the Democratic party, as compensation for the change, advocates that Japan take on new defense functions within the framework of the constitution. This new party thus has the potential to become a political bridge between the realism of mainstream conservatives and traditional pacifism. Because the Social Democrats have faded as an obstructionist force in defense policymaking, there is an opportunity to develop a new consensus around a synthesis of both realist and pacifist ideas (see chapter 2).

For the United States, the critical challenge will be to develop a strategic vision and a clearer sense of priorities. Its geopolitical isolation, coupled with high deficits, economic inequality, high crime rates, and other pressing domestic problems, will inevitably tug the United States toward a less ambitious, more inward-looking foreign policy. Yet America's stake in the global economy and its sense of historical mission will also restrain the isolationist impulse. What will be increasingly debated is not whether it should be involved internationally, but the terms of that involvement. Despite America's temptation to resort to unilateral action, the active support of allies will become more and more critical to sustain domestic support for foreign engagement. In East Asia, American foreign policy encompasses multiple objectives: preventing the emergence of a regional hegemon or hostile coalition, deterring attacks on allies and defending them if deterrence fails, checking the proliferation of weapons of mass destruction, improving access to the region's growing markets, and promoting democratization and protecting human rights. Welding these different goals into a coherent strategy is hard enough in the abstract. In practice, the task becomes virtually impossible without presidential leadership in defining priorities and mobilizing a domestic political consensus, especially in Congress. Without such leadership, policy will be ad hoc, inconsistent, and essentially reactive.

The time has come for Japan and the United States to strike a new strategic bargain. Under current arrangements the alliance may not weather a severe security crisis. When shared vital interests are at stake, Japanese financial contributions will be inadequate to convince Americans about the alliance's importance, especially after the collapse of the Soviet Union. Preventing a rupture therefore requires altering the terms of the security relationship *before* a crisis occurs. Although the Pentagon has temporarily defused tensions on Okinawa by agreeing to return the Futenma Marine Air Station in five to seven years, there is now widespread support in Japan for a gradual but significant reduction of the U.S. military presence in Okinawa and elsewhere in Japan. Rather than stubbornly sticking with 47,000 U.S. troops in Japan, the United States should determine what forward deployments are absolutely critical for deterrence and crisis response. Because America's most important military assets in Japan are its air and naval power, the Pentagon should make the adjustments necessary to sustain Japan's willingness to host these assets. In return, Japan should take the appropriate steps to support U.S. regional military operations and facilitate rapid deployments into and out of Japan during an emergency. If such a bargain can be struck, the marine combat forces in Okinawa could be removed without harming the integrity of U.S. military missions (see chapters 5 and 6 for a fuller development of this argument). This would go far in consolidating Japanese political support for the alliance well into the next century.

As the alliance becomes more reciprocal, the United States must genuinely consult Japan, not merely inform it of decisions already made. Although the two countries agreed to prior consultation when they signed the 1960 security pact, the mechanism has never been used. Because support for U.S. military operations beyond Japan would provoke such intense domestic controversy, Tokyo appeared to prefer not to be consulted. The Japanese government has applied such strict criteria for times when Washington would have to consult that the U.S. government has never had to get Japan's formal permission to use bases in Japan for military operations in Southeast Asia or the Middle East. Indeed, Japan has given the United States freer rein on the use of overseas bases than America's European allies have, even though Japan has projected a much stronger pacifist image.[40] Japan's abdication of its right to be consulted has fueled public distrust about bilateral defense cooperation. A healthier alliance demands that the concept of prior consultation be resuscitated. As Japan musters the courage to say yes to collective defense and security missions, it should also gain the right to say no to the United States when it disagrees with U.S. policy. The U.S.-Japan alliance would then evolve toward something akin to America's strategic relationships with the major west European allies.

Finally, the importance of the alliance for regional security makes improving it much more than a bilateral matter. Greater Japanese military support for U.S. forces may strengthen deterrence and the ability to respond to regional crises, but it may also aggravate Asian concerns about Japan's possible remilitarization. Some Asian states might interpret the new arrangements as a precursor to American military disengagement. Any attempt to restructure the alliance must therefore be sensitive to its effect on the region. Japanese leaders must also deal more forthrightly with Japan's militarist past to reassure Asians that militarism is not growing. And U.S. leaders must convince the region that changes in U.S. force structure do not weaken America's capacity to deter aggression or respond effectively when it occurs. Indeed, the adjustments are designed to make U.S. forward deployments in Japan politically more sustainable.

As critical as deterrence and crisis management are, they are by no means sufficient to promote regional security. As the two largest economies of the Asia-Pacific region with formidable diplomatic resources, the United States and Japan have an opportunity to work together to reduce tension and prevent crises. Thus far, alliance redefinition has done little to address the steps the two countries can take together and separately to lessen the possibility of military conflict in the region. The United States and Japan must develop an effective regional strategy to reduce tensions and prevent crises. Keeping 100,000 troops in the region is a poor surrogate for a comprehensive Asia policy. More realism is necessary in claims about what this military presence does. The "regional cooperation" section of the April 1996 Japan-U.S. Joint Declaration on Security did nothing more than list in general terms common security goals regarding Korea, China, Russia, and Southeast Asia. What is desperately needed is a concrete coordinated policy to achieve these objectives.

Notes

1. Advisory Group on Defense Issues, *The Modality of the Security and Defense Capability of Japan: The Outlook for the 21st Century*, August 12, 1994.

2. The original Japanese phrase for *multilateral security strategy* is *takakuteki anzen hoshō senryaku*. Although the Japanese government's translation of *takakuteki* into English is *multilateral*, the word can also be translated as *multidimensional*. If it is translated as *multidimensional*, the concept has less of a connotation that Japan should gradually move away from a policy focused on bilateral U.S.-Japan security to one focused on multilateral or multinational institutions. The idea would be to embed the bilateral security relationship in a more multidimensional or multifaceted framework. I wish to thank Akihiro Magara of the Asian Forum Japan for pointing out this distinction to me.

3. Interviews with members of the Higuchi advisory group.

4. Office of International Security Affairs, *United States Security Strategy for the East Asia–Pacific Region* (U.S. Department of Defense, February 1995).

5. The two EASI reports were *A Strategic Framework for the Asian Pacific Rim: Looking toward the 21st Century* (Department of Defense, April 1990) and *A Strategic Framework for the Asian Pacific Rim: Report to Congress 1992* (Department of Defense, April 1992).

6. Peter Ennis, "The 'Nye Initiative': Can it Save the U.S.-Japan Security Alliance?" *Tokyo Business Today*, vol. 63 (June 1995), pp. 38–41; and Patrick M. Cronin and Michael J. Green, *Redefining the U.S.-Japan Alliance: Tokyo's National Defense Program* (Washington: Institute for National Strategic Studies, National Defense University, 1994), pp. 7–10.

7. Yoichi Funabashi, "Nichi-Bei Ampō saiteigi no zen kaibō," *Sekai*, vol. 622 (May 1996), pp. 27–31.

8. Defense Agency, Japan, *Defense of Japan 1996: Response to a New Era* (Tokyo, 1996), p. 279.

9. "'Futenma' no shinso," *Mainichi Shimbun*, morning edition, August 9, 1996, p. 2.

10. "Public Affairs Plan: Special Action Committee on Okinawa (SACO)," briefing memorandum, U.S. Forces in Japan, December 18, 1995.

11. This was despite the emphasis on alliance redefinition found in press accounts of the summit. No doubt the officials wanted to deflect criticisms from pacifists that the substance of the security pact had been secretly altered. See for example the following assessment found in a journal closely tied to Japan's Ministry of Foreign Affairs: "21 seiki no anzen hoshō o kataru," *Gaikō Forum* (*Kinkyū zōkan*), vol. 9 (May 1996), pp. 24–39.

12. Yamazaki Taku, "Watashi no shūdan-teki ji'eiken kō," *This Is Yomiuri*, vol. 78 (August 1996), pp. 198–203.

13. According to a study conducted by an LDP Diet member specializing in defense matters, some operations are probably permissible under the current interpretation of the constitution and the existing legal framework if there were a military crisis on the Korean peninsula: disposing of abandoned mines, providing the United States with information acquired for the purpose of national defense, allowing U.S.

military personnel aboard aircraft engaged in rescuing overseas Japanese nationals, offering to U.S. forces on a temporary basis facilities and locales beyond those currently designated for American military use, facilitating procurements by the Defense Facilities Administration Agency, providing U.S. forces in Japan with extra personnel, supplying fuel for emergency landings, receiving wounded soldiers in domestic hospitals, guarding U.S. military bases in Japan, and cooperating in terms of funds and supplies.

The following roles would be clearly prohibited: participating in combat operations; supporting in an integrated fashion U.S. combat operations involving, for instance, searching for targets and minesweeping in combat waters; and providing logistical support (supplies, equipment, and transport) for U.S. forces in combat areas. The gray-zone modes of Japanese support that could be permissible but would require a top-level political decision include escorting U.S. warships and military aircraft as well as civilian ships and aircraft to ensure their safety, providing logistical support in rear areas and near combat areas, engaging in transport activities near combat areas, providing medical care in or near combat areas, supplying and storing materials such as ammunition that are intimately linked to combat operations, giving rear support to U.S. forces engaging in an economic blockade and implementing searches in this context, providing information based on patrols, surveillance, reconnaissance, and other intelligence activities, and supporting U.S. forces in locations away from combat zones with supplies, equipment, storage, transport, communications, and medical care. See ibid., pp. 201–02.

14. For an analysis of the bureau's role in interpreting the constitution, see Nakamura Akira, *Sengo seiji ni yureta Kempō dai kyū jō: Naikaku Hōseikyoku no jishin to tsuyosa* (Tokyo: Chūō Keizaisha, 1996).

15. Asagumo Shimbunsha Henshu Sokyoku, ed., *Bōei Handobuku—Heisei 8-nenban* (Tokyo: Asagumo Shimbunsha, 1996), pp. 452–53.

16. "Yukensha no kahansu 'sansei': Okinawa kichi seiri-shyukushō to kenmin toyo," *Asahi Shimbun*, September 9, 1996, pp. 1–3, 22–23.

17. Asō Iku, "Beigun kichi no hito tsubo ji-nushi san-zen nin," *Bungei Shunjū* (October 1996), pp. 118–29; and Hatake Motoaki, *Okinawa mondai-kiso chishiki* (Tokyo: Aki Shobo, 1996), pp. 179–82.

18. For a critical summary of this process, see Hatake, *Okinawa mondai-kiso chishiki*, pp. 146–89, 248–50.

19. "Okinawa Update," *Japan Policy Research Institute Special Report*, vol. 3 (September 1996), pp. 1–2.

20. Military Base Affairs Office, Okinawa Prefecture, "Military Bases in Okinawa: The Current Situation and Problems, November 1995."

21. Bōei-cho, ed., *Bōei hakusho–Heisei 8-nen ban* (Tokyo: Okura-shō Insatsu-kyoku, 1996), pp. 256–57.

22. *Okinawa no Bei-gun Kichi* (Naha: Okinawa-ken Sōmu-bu Chiji Kō-shitsu Kichi Taisaku-shitsu, December 1993), p. 9.

23. They include the Futenma Marine Air Station, Naha Port, Camp Zukeran, Camp Kuwae, and the Makiminato Service Area.

24. "Hondo to no kakusa—nao ishiki heranu kichi ni kibishii me," *Asahi Shimbun*, morning edition, May 12, 1997, pp. 1, 10.

25. "Asian Executives Poll," *Far Eastern Economic Review*, vol. 139, October 3, 1996, p. 30.

26. Gaimushō Daijin Kanbō Kaigai Kōhō-ka, "Bei-koku ni okeru tai-Nichi yoron," photocopy, April 1996. The Japan Ministry of Foreign Affairs commissions Gallup to conduct this survey annually.

27. "Hondo to no kakusa—nao ishiki heranu kichi ni kibishii me," *Asahi Shimbun*, May 12, 1997, p. 10.

28. "Mushiri torareru 'Omoiyari yosan,'" *Sentaku*, May 1996, pp. 58–61.

29. Article 51 of the UN Charter states, "Nothing in the present Charter shall impair the inherent right of individual or collective self-defence if an armed attack occurs against a Member of the United Nations, until the Security Council has taken measures necessary to maintain international peace and security." The preamble of the 1960 U.S.-Japan Security Treaty contains the following clause: "Recognizing that they have the inherent right of individual or collective self-defense as affirmed in the Charter of the United Nations." See Defense Agency, Japan, *Defense of Japan 1996*, p. 260.

30. Nakamura, *Sengo seiji ni yureta kempō kyū-jō*, pp. 178–79. During the deliberations, Kishi's own foreign minister, Fujiyama Aiichiro, gave a different interpretation, saying that Japan did not have the right of collective self-defense. But the official interpretation follows that of Kishi in making a distinction between possessing and exercising the right and in arguing that the constitution prohibits only the latter.

31. Asagumo Shimbunsha Henshu Sōkyoku, ed., *Bōei Handobuku—Heisei 8-nenban* (Tokyo: Asagumo Shimbunsha, 1996), pp. 451–52.

32. Nakamura, *Sengo seiji ni yureta kempō kyū-jō*, pp. 182–84.

33. The exchange of notes states, "Major changes in the deployment into Japan of United States armed forces, major changes in their equipment, and the use of facilities and areas in Japan as bases for military combat operations to be undertaken from Japan other than those conducted under Article V of the said Treaty, shall be the subjects of prior consultation with the Government of Japan." For the text of this exchange, see George R. Packard III, *Protest in Tokyo: The Security Treaty Crisis of 1960* (Princeton University Press, 1960), p. 369. Article V deals with American and Japanese obligations in response to "an armed attack against either Party in the territories under the administration of Japan."

34. Nakamura, *Sengo seiji ni yureta kempō kyū-jō*, pp. 186–90.

35. Asagumo Shimbunsha Henshu Sōkyoku, ed., *Bōei Handobuku—Heisei 8-nenban*, p. 436. This 1980 interpretation concerning participation in a UN force was more restrictive than the position of the Cabinet Legal Affairs Bureau in 1961, which was, "If the U.N. police activities are conducted in an ideal form, in other words, when a country that disrupted order within the U.N. system is to be punished, or in the case of establishing a police corps to maintain order, and if a unitary force under the United Nations is created with the participation of personnel dispatched by member countries, [Japan's participation in such a force] would not be an act of a sovereign nation. Also, there is a possibility of a peaceful police force which does not conduct military activities. These possibilities would not pose problems relating to the First Clause of Article 9." See Tanaka Akihiko, "The Domestic Context: Japanese Politics and U.N. Peacekeeping," in Selig S. Harrison and Masashi Nishihara, eds.,

U.N. Peacekeeping: Japanese and American Perspectives (Washington: Carnegie Endowment for International Peace, 1995), pp. 90–91.

36. Nakamura, *Sengo seiji ni yureta kempō kyū-jō*, pp. 188–96; and Asagumo Shimbunsha Henshu Sōkyoku, ed., *Bōei Handobuku—Heisei 8-nenban*, pp. 452–53.

37. Keizai Doyukai Study Group on Security Issues, *Report of the Study Group on Security Issues* (Tokyo, April 1996).

38. *Yomiuri Shimbun*, April 6, 1997, pp. 1, 12–13.

39. The survey was conducted by the monthly opinion journal *Bungei Shunjū*. See Uchida Kenzō, Kunimasa Takeshige, and Sone Yasunori, "Nihon no kiro o tou," *Bungei Shunju*, vol. 74 (August 1996), pp. 94–109.

40. My thanks to Michael O'Hanlon for pointing out this paradox.

Part One

THE STRATEGIC CONTEXT

CHAPTER TWO

American and Japanese Strategic Debates: The Need for a New Synthesis

Mike M. Mochizuki

ALTHOUGH REALISM and liberal internationalism competed with each other during much of U.S. diplomatic history in the cold war, the strategy of containing the Soviet Union provided a synthesis of these two schools of thought.[1] Applied to East Asia, this synthesis meant that the United States would support Japan's economic reconstruction and development and incorporate it into an alliance network to counter the expansion of Soviet-led communism on both geopolitical and ideological grounds. Although Japan at first endured an intense debate between realists and pacifists that made security policy bitterly conflicted, it too achieved a synthesis. A consensus emerged in favor of relying on the United States for military security while concentrating on economic growth and sticking to a security doctrine focused exclusively on defense.

The end of the cold war has reopened the debate in both countries regarding U.S.-Japan relations in the East Asia–Pacific region. In America, realists and liberal internationalists offer very different diagnoses of trends in the region and recommendations about the future of the U.S.-Japan alliance. And not only do they disagree with each other, they disagree among themselves. The Japanese are also engaging in a lively debate between those who would like to normalize Japan as a political-military participant and those who want not only to preserve but to build on Japan's postwar pacifism. As in the United States, however,

43

the disagreements among the normalizers and the pacifists are just as significant as the disagreements between them.

This chapter identifies and summarizes the various clusters of opinion
in the United States and Japan, assesses the debate, and analyzes its
transpacific linkages. Despite the diversity of strategic perspectives
among analysts and most opinion leaders in both countries, there is
remarkable agreement about the wisdom of continuing the security partnership. The crucial policy issue is not whether to continue the security
alliance, but whether the terms of the alliance need to be changed and in
what way. I contend that instead of choosing between realism or liberalism or between Japanese normalization or pacifism, the optimal strategy
is to develop a new synthesis based on the most attractive features of the
different perspectives. Such a strategic synthesis would enable both
countries to reconsolidate public support for the alliance while contributing more actively to regional security and peace. Finally, the
chapter sketches the implications of the synthesis for policy toward
Korea and China.

The American Debate

On the whole the discussion within the American realist tradition
about U.S. security policy toward Japan in particular and East Asia in
general has been much more fully developed than that in the liberal tradition. Despite the frequent incorporation of "liberal" rhetoric in official
statements about the U.S.-Japan alliance and East Asian security, surprisingly few American analysts have attempted to develop a specific
liberal program for restructuring it or for promoting security in the
region.

Varieties of Realism

Realists share many assumptions about international politics: that
nation-states are the significant actors in an international system, that their
foreign policies are based on calculations of power and national interest,
that security is the paramount national interest, and that relations among
them are essentially anarchical because of the absence of world government. But despite these shared assumptions, American analysts in the
realist tradition differ widely in their policy prescriptions. Their recom-

mendations vary from maintaining the status quo, to making modest adjustments, to a more thorough restructuring to achieve strategic U.S.-Japan reciprocity, and finally even to terminating the formal alliance.

ENGAGED BALANCING. The most influential realist perspective that falls within the existing policy framework supports a U.S. strategy of *engaged balancing*. The United States needs to be militarily engaged in East Asia to maintain a stable balance of power because the states in the region will have difficulty achieving a stable equilibrium among themselves. As Henry Kissinger has noted, the East Asian security environment is structured not according to a community of shared values but according to the pursuit of national interests and an equilibrium of power: "Wilsonianism has few disciples in Asia."[2] In particular, relations between Japan and China are fraught with tensions because of history, geopolitical rivalry, and mutual distrust. The strategic challenge for the United States, then, is to "help Japan and China coexist despite their suspicions of each other." Meanwhile Japan does not want to see a conflict between China and the United States that will force Tokyo to make strategic choices, nor does China want to see a break in the U.S.-Japan security relationship that could free Japan to become a great military power. This assessment leads Kissinger to conclude, "Good American relations with China are . . . the prerequisite for good long-term relations with Japan, as well as for good Sino-Japanese relations. It is a triangle which each of the parties can abandon only at great risk. It is also an ambiguity with which the United States is not totally comfortable, since it runs counter to the American tendency to label nations neatly as either friend or foe."[3]

In addition to maintaining a stable regional power balance, the United States should prevent not only the rise of a hostile regional hegemon, but also the emergence of a coalition of states hostile to the United States. Consequently, according to Michael Armacost, the United States should "cultivate better relations with the key nations of Asia—Japan, China, Russia, Indonesia, and others—than they enjoy with one another."[4] In other words, engaged balancing embodies a circular logic: the United States needs to be engaged militarily in the region because the East Asian states will compete geopolitically in such a way that they cannot establish a stable equilibrium on their own, but U.S. interests are also served if the East Asian states are unable to manage their relations in a cooperative manner *without* the help or presence of the United States.

The option of preserving an equilibrium without a permanent military presence in East Asia and without formal alliances (in the way Britain balanced power in continental Europe during the nineteenth century) is not viable because Americans are unlikely to be skillful at shifting alignments in response to changes in the regional power balance.[5] The more effective course would be to see the security relationship with Japan as a valuable asset for maintaining a stable equilibrium through reassurance in the post–cold war world.

A termination of the alliance or a drastic reordering of its provisions would upset the current balance, according to advocates of engaged balancing. Ending the security commitment to Japan or dramatically reducing U.S. forces stationed there could make the Japanese so insecure that they might build up their military capabilities, which could cause other states in the region to respond in kind. Even if Japan did not respond in this way, its neighbors might think it would, and they would be likely to strengthen their military power. Such a preemptive reaction would then likely provoke Japan into improving its own military capabilities.

U.S. pressures to get Japan to assume a bigger military role in the region could trigger comparable reactions and counterreactions. For example, the Chinese would be likely to consider such a restructured U.S.-Japan alliance threatening and would therefore assume a tougher security posture. But at the same time, the security linkage with Japan would give the United States a sensible way to hedge against the possibility of an emerging Chinese threat.[6] Prudence therefore suggests continuing the U.S.-Japan security relationship pretty much as it exists today.

Proponents of engaged balancing, however, differ slightly from one another about the challenges facing this bilateral alliance. Henry Kissinger, for example, predicts an inevitable resurgence of Japanese nationalism. After the demise of the Soviet Union, American and Japanese national interests are unlikely to remain identical. As Japan gradually strengthens its military capabilities, it will become more interested in improving its freedom of maneuver vis-à-vis the United States. Given the domestic problems associated with its aging population and stagnating economy, Japan "might decide to press its technological and strategic superiority before China emerges as a superpower and Russia recovers its strength." Eventually, it might even choose to arm itself with nuclear weapons. According to Kissinger, just maintaining the status quo with Japan will require active diplomacy, especially given the economic frictions between the two countries, cultural obstacles, and the tedious consensual decisionmaking style of the Japanese.[7] Kissinger would have no qualms with the present policy of reaffirming the U.S.-Japan security relationship and keeping 100,000 troops forward deployed in East Asia. But he might be concerned about the Pentagon's interest in expanding Japan's military role because an overly enthusiastic Japanese response to U.S. pressure would upset the Chinese and the fragile regional power balance.

Michael Armacost is more concerned that under the current security arrangement, Japan may not be willing and able enough to cooperate adequately with the United States in a severe regional crisis such as one on the Korean peninsula.[8] Without some modest adjustments, the alliance may not survive the test of crisis irrespective of (or precisely because of) the pivotal role Japan might have played in U.S. strategy. This raises but leaves unanswered the critical question of how the alliance can evolve to survive a crisis without upsetting the regional equilibrium.

BALANCING AGAINST CHINA. While proponents of engaged balancing emphasize the importance of maintaining a balance between Japan and China, other American realists advocate forming a new balance of power system in Asia to counter the rise of China.[9] Given its enormous population and geographical size, rapid rate of economic growth, and authoritarian political system, China poses a much greater threat to U.S. interests than does Japan. Some even conclude that the United States must work with Japan and other states (especially democratic ones such as South Korea and even Taiwan) to contain Chinese expansionism. It therefore makes sense to urge Japan to broaden its defense role and become a more active ally.[10] The quest for strategic reciprocity between Japan and the United States should not cause concerns that Japan will develop the military capabilities that might eventually feed into an autonomous and nationalistic strategy toward the United States. The threat from China, these realists contend, will surely steer Japan to align with the United States. Furthermore, there is no need to worry over possible Chinese protests about extending Japan's military role under the umbrella of the U.S.-Japan alliance. Seeing that the alliance is solid and understanding the constraints of power, Beijing will have no choice but to restrain itself. Otherwise it would risk the emergence of a regionwide coalition with the United States and Japan at its core to contain China.

Could a hard-line American policy toward China cause tensions with Japan and other Asian states? Advocates of such a position acknowledge that Tokyo and other regional capitals may grumble in the short term but not for long: Chinese expansionism poses the greatest threat to the rest of Asia. If these critics have any complaint about the Pentagon's current policy, it is that defense officials are too circumspect about balancing forces against China and too timid in getting Japan to do more militarily. For them, the notion that a policy of engagement would lead to stable U.S.-China relations is a pipe dream.

OFF-SHORE BALANCING. Although the above two strands of realist analysis accept the existing parameters of U.S. defense policy, others in the realist tradition recommend a thorough transformation of U.S. security ties with East Asia by adopting a strategy of *off-shore balancing*. Given America's relative immunity from external threats, the off-shore balancers believe it should encourage its allies to do more on behalf of their own security, even if this means some strategic independence from the United States.[11] Entangling alliances are unnecessary, and America's involvement should be limited to times when effective power balancing does not emerge. In arguing that America should be the balancer of last resort, rather than the balancer of first resort, advocates of this strategy are much more optimistic than are the proponents of engaged balancing that the rivalry among regional powers will produce a stable equilibrium in a timely fashion, even without active reassurance from the United States. Moreover, they see as inevitable the emergence of autonomous great powers no matter how intense the American effort to constrain allies strategically. In fact, unleashing allies from U.S. security paternalism may be the most efficient way to encourage balancing against potentially hostile emerging powers. Accordingly, Ted Galen Carpenter of the Cato Institute has advocated terminating the U.S.-Japan security pact and withdrawing all U.S. forces from Japan within five years. Similarly, his colleague, Doug Bandow, proposes a military pullout from South Korea.[12]

Echoing the general logic of this view, Chalmers Johnson with the Japan Policy Research Institute emphasizes the intimate link between economics and security. Preoccupied with containing the Soviet threat, the United States supported and tolerated Japanese mercantilism in return for access to bases in Japan. As a consequence America sacrificed its economic interests, and Japan became a one-dimensional state pursuing economic expansion with a vengeance. Not only was the security relationship designed to contain the Soviet Union, but it was predicated on a mistrust of Japan as a security partner. In Johnson's opinion the Pentagon's East Asian strategy report freezes the cold war order and obstructs the emergence of a more balanced, reciprocal U.S.-Japan relationship.[13] This strategy reinforces Japan's unhealthy dependence on American security and prolongs the situation in which the United States provides regional security while Japan and the other East Asian states reap the lion's share of the economic benefits the security makes possible.

To remedy this warped state of affairs, Johnson recommends a variety of changes. The security treaty with Japan should be renegotiated to make it more mutual and less asymmetrical. Japan's participation in regional security matters should be normalized through revision of its constitution. The United States should withdraw all ground forces from Japan and the rest of East Asia while strengthening U.S. naval capabilities in the region. The United States should guarantee the security of Korea and Vietnam as buffer states in a power-balancing system consisting of China, Japan, and Southeast Asia as the principals. Finally, the United States should explicitly link its participation in sustaining an East Asian power balance to being provided greater economic access to the region's markets.[14]

Johnson is critical of recent efforts by Washington and Tokyo to redefine the bilateral alliance. In his view the 1996 Joint Security Declaration between President Clinton and Prime Minister Hashimoto, coming as it did immediately after the crisis in the Taiwan Straits, amounts to a dangerous drift toward containing China. Instead of allowing the U.S.-Japanese alliance to turn into an alignment against China (more as a result of policy drift than a deliberate strategic choice), Johnson believes that the two countries should work together to influence and adjust to the rise of Chinese power so that China will evolve in a "peaceful, nonhegemonic direction."[15] But to the extent that he favors Japan's normalization as a participant in security matters, Johnson is unclear about how the development can unfold without antagonizing China.

DISENGAGEMENT. In applying his controversial "clash of civilizations" thesis to East Asia, Samuel P. Huntington of Harvard University also warns of a collision with China. But unlike Johnson, Huntington considers Chinese hegemony in East Asia inevitable. His analysis yields a policy conclusion in favor of disengagement remarkably similar to the off-shore balancing strategy. According to Huntington, the region's rapid economic growth will inevitably move the balance of power across the Pacific as East Asian states translate their wealth into stronger militaries

and as they resist with greater self-confidence U.S. pressures to liberal-
ize commercial access. Not only will conflicts between the United States
and the East Asian societies intensify, but China will reassert its traditional hegemony as U.S. involvement in the region inevitably decreases.

In this context, Japan is likely to applaud the growth of Chinese power
rather than balance against it. Although East Asia is likely to be more
stable and less prone to conflict under Chinese hegemony, the United
States would be compelled "to accept what it has historically attempted
to prevent: domination of a key region of the world by another power."
The logic of this analysis might suggest that the United States should
remain strategically engaged in East Asia even after the remaining cold
war conflict (a divided Korea) is resolved. America should restructure
the alliance with Japan to balance and contain China, as the engaged balancers and those who would contain China might argue. For Huntington,
however, this strategy's costs and the risks of war are high. He implies
that the only attractive option is to cede East Asia to Chinese dominance
(his "abstention rule") and to negotiate a modus vivendi between the
Chinese hegemonic system and the West (his "mediation rule").[16]

Liberal Explorations

Clinton administration officials, including the president himself, have
frequently referred to liberal ideas in discussing East Asia–Pacific security. The spread of democracy in the region should be a priority of
security policy because "democracies are demonstrably more likely to
maintain their international commitments, less likely to engage in terrorism or wreak environmental damage, and less likely to make war on each
other."[17] Regional economic prosperity and interdependence hold the
promise of creating a Pacific community. Multilateral security discussions can help prevent arms races and competing alignments. But compared with the realists, liberal analysts have yet to lay out a policy
agenda on security in East Asia and the U.S.-Japan alliance. Their contribution so far has been more tentative explorations than fully developed
arguments.

Applying the liberal thesis that democratization ultimately will
produce peace in East Asia poses difficult dilemmas for U.S. policy.
Twenty years ago democratically elected governments in East Asia were
rare compared with other regions in the world. Japanese democracy
stood out as an exception, and even this was the imposition of a victori-

ous power on a defeated nation. But now democratic processes have taken root in South Korea and Taiwan, have been replanted in the Philippines, and are beginning to operate in Thailand.

But it is not at all clear how the United States should promote this trend and assist the democracies to become more stable and resilient. Enlarging the number of democracies confronts the problem of balancing this policy goal with immediate security and economic interests. The dilemma is especially difficult with respect to China. The prodemocracy movement in China in the spring of 1989 indicated significant popular support for political liberalization. But too much pressure on the Chinese government to improve its human rights record might undermine efforts to elicit Beijing's cooperation on security matters and could even compromise the cultivation of norms favoring such cooperation among the Chinese political elite. Taiwan's democratization poses another choice. Should the United States strengthen the security link because Taiwan has become a democracy if the policy risks encouraging Taiwanese moves toward independence and antagonizing China? Or should the United States keep security commitments to Taiwan ambiguous enough to placate China and discourage Taiwan's initiatives toward independence with the effect of subordinating the objective of promoting democracy abroad to other strategic imperatives?

Despite the Clinton administration's call for collaboration with democratic allies, the mode of collaboration possible between the United States and Japan to help spread democracy in East Asia is far from clear.[18] In contrast to the spirited injection of values and ideology in U.S. foreign policy debates, the Japanese take a more detached geopolitical and geoeconomic view emphasizing that economic development must precede democratization. Consequently, while the United States continues to restrict economic ties with Burma, Japan wants to provide economic assistance and encourage private investment in this authoritarian country not only to promote Burma's economic development but also to balance China's influence there. Given Japan's formidable economic influence in East Asia, an effective U.S. policy of democratization in the region is unimaginable without the cooperation of Japan or at least an understanding that Tokyo will not undermine Washington's efforts.

A more fruitful strand of liberal thinking on security policy is the concept of *cooperative security*. In contrast to the realists' emphasis on deterring aggression by preparing for military confrontation, proponents of cooperative security seek to devise "agreed-upon measures to prevent war and to do so primarily by preventing the means for successful aggression from being assembled."[19] Unlike many Japanese pacifists, however, American liberals in favor of cooperative security are not prepared to dismantle the military component of bilateral security arrangements and rely on a regional collective security system. First, they distinguish between collective security and cooperative security. Whereas collective security is "an arrangement for deterring aggression through military preparation and defeating it if it occurs," cooperative security is "designed to ensure that organized aggression cannot start or be prosecuted on any large scale."[20] Second, they believe that the U.S. military presence in East Asia and the U.S.-Japan security relationship is the foundation for promoting cooperative security arrangements in the region. Echoing realist arguments about balancing and reassurance, Janne E. Nolan of the Brookings Institution suggests that weakening the American security commitment to Japan might lead Tokyo to abandon its nonnuclear policy. Moreover, pressuring Japan to strengthen its military capabilities and to move away from its strictly defensive military doctrine might provoke other states in the region.[21] But from the perspective of cooperative security, what then should be the agenda to move beyond simply sustaining bilateral security arrangements with East Asian allies and maintaining a forward-deployed military presence in the region?

Harry Harding has argued for a multilayered and multifaceted approach in applying cooperative security principles to the East Asia–Pacific region.[22] First, there should be efforts to secure compliance from the states in the region with existing international regimes that are designed to check the proliferation of weapons of mass destruction and encourage cooperation in the development of other global regimes to limit the spread of other arms. Second, ad hoc forums and initiatives could be launched to address specific subregional issues such as the Cambodian peace settlement, establishment of a nuclear-free zone on the Korean peninsula, force reductions and redeployment on the Chinese-Russian border, and a modus vivendi in the Taiwan Strait. The U.S.–North Korean nuclear accord of 1994 fits into both categories of cooperative security initiatives. Using the incentives of supplying oil and building light-water reactors in North Korea, the Clinton administration persuaded Pyongyang to remain a party to the Nuclear Non-Proliferation Treaty, to freeze its nuclear program, and to agree to stringent international inspections. The accord's implementation and the establishment of the Korean Peninsula Energy Development Organization (KEDO) present an opportunity to broaden discussions with Pyongyang to include the reduction of military tensions, normalization of diplomatic relations, economic cooperation, and a process for reconciliation of North and South Korea.

The third element in a multifaceted approach to cooperative security is to develop multilateral security dialogues and institutions. Their purpose would be to improve transparency and mutual confidence, cultivate multilateral norms to govern military deployments so as to create a "defensive-intent regime," and even develop peaceful mechanisms for dealing with international disputes.[23] Although the Bush administration feared that such multilateral initiatives might weaken bilateral alliances and become a pretext for an American withdrawal from the region, the Clinton administration has embraced them as a complement to America's bilateral security links with various East Asian states.[24] The United States now participates in the ASEAN Regional Forum (ARF), which was formed in 1993 as the only government-level, multilateral security dialogue encompassing the entire Asia-Pacific region. Whereas substantive discussions with concrete policy implications will take a long time to emerge in official forums such as ARF, nongovernmental dialogues such as the Council for Security Cooperation in the Asia Pacific (CSCAP) provide an opportunity to explore new options without the risk of derailing existing state policies. Drawing on his own experience in developing the concept of cooperative security, U.S. Secretary of Defense William Perry himself came out in favor of a forum for defense ministers in the region. Because ARF is primarily a conference of regional foreign ministers, a defense ministers' dialogue might be more effective in engaging issues related to military transparency and exchanges and other confidence-building measures.

As for Northeast Asia, the Institute of Global Conflict and Cooperation (IGCC) at the University of California in San Diego has sponsored since 1993 a nongovernment forum called the Northeast Asia Cooperation Dialogue (NEACD) with official observers. Participants have come from the United States, Japan, China, Russia, and South Korea; North Korea has so far refused to join. The NEACD has discussed common principles to govern state-to-state relations in the region and such possible mutual reassurance measures as multilateral military exchanges, defense information sharing and transparency, and coordinated responses to emergencies and disaster relief.[25]

Notwithstanding the participation of South Korea, the Americans involved in the NEACD tend to see this forum as encouraging the construction of a great-power concert for Northeast Asia. Like Kissinger, they see the incipient rivalry between Japan and China as having long-term destabilizing consequences for the region. But unlike Kissinger's remedy in which America balances between the two states, the American organizers of the NEACD believe that the United States can help mediate between Japan and China. Of course, China presents an understandable security problem for Japan, given Beijing's military modernization program, its reluctance to make transparent its military policies, and the country's future political uncertainties. But Japan is also a problem for China. Japan's unwillingness or inability to deal with its militaristic past to the satisfaction of China and other East Asian states provokes suspicions about its long-term intentions. If it does not first resolve the problem of history, any attempt by Japan to expand its military participation in regional security, even within the framework of the U.S.-Japan security treaty, could worsen Sino-Japanese relations.

An alternative and more radical way of dealing with the incipient Sino-Japanese rivalry from a perspective of cooperative security would be to integrate China gradually into the U.S.-led security system rather than trying to mediate between China and Japan. This approach considers the danger in East Asia as stemming not only from military competition between China and Japan but also from a possible confrontation between China and the U.S.-Japan alliance. According to John Steinbruner and William Kaufmann of the Brookings Institution, the U.S. alliance system in both Europe and East Asia enjoys a preponderant military advantage over major powers outside it, such as China and Russia. The integration of Germany and Japan into this alliance system has institutionalized security cooperation so deeply that neither country is perceived to be either an immediate or potential threat. Extending this cooperative regime to China and Russia would enable the major powers to lower the costs and risks of traditional security measures. This integration would take place by establishing force deployment standards and operational rules that would systematically reassure all member states that "no military establishment will initiate an attack on any other." Given the superior military and technological capabilities of the United States and its allies, such an option should be much more attractive to China and Russia than the alternative of engaging in an arms competition. And if reliable restraints on military development by potential adversaries could be established, the United States could prudently diminish some of its current military advantage.[26] Presumably, if this idea were applied to East Asia, it would imply not only reductions of U.S. forces there, but also restraints and even reductions in Japanese defense capabilities.

For the time being its sweeping and complex nature places the Steinbruner-Kaufmann approach to cooperative security on the margins of defense policy discussions in the United States. But Robert Manning of the Progressive Policy Institute has proposed a less ambitious initiative to promote regional security cooperation. Despite Japan's firm commitment not to manufacture, possess, or deploy nuclear weapons and the transparency of its nuclear energy programs, Manning argues that its plutonium reprocessing and breeder reactor plans, along with its stockpiling of plutonium, have provoked distrust from China and both Koreas about Tokyo's nuclear ambitions, especially given the legacy of Japanese militarism and its formidable capabilities in defense and space technology. Now that there is a huge world surplus of uranium and commercial breeder reactors have become economically irrational for the foreseeable future, Japan could dramatically reshape the security environment in a more cooperative direction by deferring its nuclear fuel cycle program to reprocess spent fuel for reuse in nuclear reactors for an extended period (fifty to seventy-five years) while continuing basic research and development. If it were to do this, Manning believes that Japan and the United States could initiate a regional regime for nuclear energy cooperation that would bolster nuclear nonproliferation and safety at a time when more and more Asian states are turning to nuclear power for their energy needs. Such a regime could also facilitate the institutionalization of Northeast Asian countries' consultation and cooperation on other security-related issues.[27]

Although the concept of cooperative security places priority on preventing military confrontation, it acknowledges that force might have to be used as a last resort: "[a] fully developed cooperative security framework would include provisions for collective security as a residual guarantee to its members in the event of aggression."[28] But under a cooperative security regime, this use of force would be executed multilaterally as part of an international coalition. This idea has profound implications for U.S. defense planning. Rather than equipping and organizing defense forces for unilateral military responses to aggression, the United States would reconfigure its defense forces so that they would complement the military capabilities of other states belonging to the network. To improve the ability to act militarily in concert with others, the United States would have to share intelligence and develop "commonly agreed-upon guidelines for intervention." If these adjustments are made, it would be possible to reallocate the security contributions among allies for greater equity and efficiency. And the United States would be able to reduce its overseas bases and troop deployments significantly.[29] The full application of this concept to the U.S.-Japan security relationship would ultimately require that Japan move away from its exclusively defensive military doctrine so that it could participate in the collective use of force as a last resort to repel aggression. But this logic of collective security is at odds with the tendency of some cooperative security advocates to oppose expanding Japan's military role beyond the defense of its home islands.[30]

The Japanese Debate

In Japan the cold war strategic synthesis was built on three policy pillars. First, the 1960 Mutual Security Treaty between Japan and the United States established the terms of Japan's alliance with the United States. Japan would provide U.S. access to military bases on its territory in exchange for America's commitment to defend Japan and maintain the security of the Far East. Japan did not assume an obligation to cooperate with U.S. forces on behalf of regional security beyond contributing to its own defense and permitting American use of military facilities in Japan for Far East security missions. Second, Japan defined its military policy in strictly defensive terms. It interpreted Article 9 of its constitution as consistent with the right to individual self-defense but not with the right of belligerency. Although acknowledging that Japan has an inherent right to collective self-defense as well as individual self-defense under international law and the UN Charter, the Japanese government argued that the constitution prohibits the exercise of the right to collective self-defense. Finally, Japan's cold war orthodoxy mandated that it maintain a balanced self-defense force that lacked offensive capabilities and that it develop an autonomous defense industrial base.

The breakup of the Soviet Union reopened the debate on security policy and raised fundamental questions about whether the cold war orthodoxy was still appropriate or adequate. Although Japan no longer had to worry about being embroiled in a catastrophic Soviet-American military conflict, the country's strategic value to the United States could diminish, causing Washington to become tougher in trade disputes and even to consider deemphasizing its security commitment. The shock of the Persian Gulf crisis and war of 1990—91 challenged Japan to think beyond the defense of its own territory. The clumsiness of its response provoked international criticism and wounded its national pride. International lack of recognition for its huge financial contribution showed Japanese leaders and citizens the inadequacy of checkbook diplomacy. Tensions over North Korea's nuclear program and the uncertainties about the North Korean regime have given greater urgency to considering how Japan should deal with regional security crises. Even the prospect of Korean reunification stirs Japanese apprehension about the future of relations with Korea, America's security presence, and the regional security order. More recently, the March 1996 crisis in the Taiwan Straits over China's missile test and military exercises provoked concerns about China and Japan's involvement in the Taiwan question.

In addressing the implications of these developments for security policy, the Japanese debate has focused on conceptions of national identity more than on theories about international politics. The primary intellectual cleavage is between those who would like to normalize Japan as a major international power and those who would like Japan to build on its postwar pacifist tradition and remember the tragic and bitter lessons of pre-1945 militarism. But within each camp, there are also significant differences. Leaders of opinion disagree about how Japan should be normalized, and pacifist commentators differ among themselves about how Japan should contribute to international security.

The Normalization of Japan

The vision of Japan as a normal nation has three versions: a Japan that participates in a collective security system centered on the United Nations, a Japan that exercises its right to collective self-defense as part of an alliance with the United States, and a Japan that is redefined as primarily an Asian power.

PARTICIPATION IN COLLECTIVE SECURITY. Reform politician Ichiro Ozawa, who originally popularized the term *futsu no kuni* or *normal nation*, wants a country that can take a more active part in UN-sanctioned collective security operations. His experience as secretary general of the ruling Liberal Democratic party during the Persian Gulf crisis convinced him that Japan would become internationally isolated if it stuck to what he called one-country pacifism (*ikkokoku heiwashugi*). In his best-selling book, *Nihon Kaizō Keikaku* (*Blueprint for a New Japan*), Ozawa argued that Japan should "willingly shoulder those responsibilities regarded as natural in the international community."[31] Although many of his critics charged that he wanted to revise the postwar constitution, he has insisted that Japan can contribute vigorously to international security through the United Nations within the existing constitutional framework.

Ozawa and his like-minded colleagues in the New Frontier party emphasize the common ground that the Japanese constitution, the Japan-U.S. Security Treaty, and the UN Charter share. The preamble of the constitution refers to Japan's intention to cooperate with other nations to "preserve [its] security and existence" and its desire to "occupy an honored place" in international society. Article 9 states the Japanese people's aspiration for "an international peace based on justice and order." Ozawa sees these words as affirming Japan's responsibility to "defend justice, order, and peace in international society." The Japan-U.S. Security Treaty explicitly commits both countries "to strengthen the United Nations so that its mission of maintaining international peace and security may be discharged more effectively."

By interpreting both the constitution and the security treaty in this way, Ozawa believes that the Japanese self-defense force can and should move beyond its current policy of an exclusive defense strategy (*senshu bō'ei senryaku*) and participate in UN peacekeeping activities on both an ad hoc basis and as part of a UN standing force. His use of the phrase *peace-building strategy* (*heiwa soshutsu senryaku*) suggests that Japan could even participate in UN "preventive or enforcement measures" under Chapter 7 of the UN Charter. What the present constitution prohibits is "the use of military force abroad by the Japanese government *based on its own decision*" (Ozawa's emphasis). By implication, Japan can actively participate in the use of force overseas if such action has the imprimatur of the United Nations and comes under UN command. To reassure those who fear that Japan's participation in UN security activities might eventually lead to remilitarization, Ozawa does favor eventually adding a third paragraph to Article 9 to stipulate that Japan may have a self-defense force for peace-building activities, maintain a UN reserve force for action under UN command when requested, and participate in action by the UN reserve force under UN command. But in the meantime, the constitution should not restrict the participation of self-defense forces in UN security activities, provided that these forces come under UN command.[32]

At the time his book on reforming Japan first appeared in spring 1993, Ozawa saw no conflict between strengthening the bilateral security relationship with the United States and promoting Japan's involvement in UN security activities because he expected Washington (especially under the Clinton administration) to support "an expanded United Nations role in the maintenance of peace and stability." Ozawa's hope is that "America would work with the United Nations on all matters of international importance" and would refrain from acting "only with its own interests in mind." But if the United States were to tire of "bearing its burden in international society" and act unilaterally, thereby weakening the United Nations, Ozawa believes that Japan should thoroughly revise its foreign policy. Barring such a development, Japan should strive to reform the United Nations and encourage the United States to work actively with this international body.[33]

Regarding policy toward Asia, Ozawa acknowledges the need for Japan to recognize its wartime responsibility so as to gain the trust of its neighbors. While continuing to maintain the alliance with the United States as the cornerstone of its foreign policy, Japan should give greater priority to its East Asia–Pacific diplomacy. According to Ozawa, through multilateral diplomacy Japan should "develop a new security framework that can respond to the power vacuum that would be left by an American withdrawal."[34]

THE RIGHT TO COLLECTIVE SELF-DEFENSE. In contrast to Ozawa's collective security concept, the second version of Japanese normalization emphasizes the concept of collective defense for reinvigorating the alliance with the United States.[35] Most Japanese analysts who subscribe to a realist perspective of international politics question Ozawa's expectations for a UN-centered collective security system. Even if the United States did wish to work within the UN framework on security issues, other permanent members of the UN Security Council might block effective UN action by using their veto power. For example, China might wield its veto during an Asian crisis on the Korean peninsula or over Taiwan. Would Japan then be hamstrung from actively cooperating with the United States? Such a possibility requires Japan to look beyond UN-sponsored security activities and consider military cooperation with the United States on its own terms.[36] These realists advocate changing the government's interpretation of the constitution (or even formally amending the constitution) so that Japan can exercise its right to collective self-defense as well as the right to individual self-defense.[37] They also take issue with Ozawa's argument that a regional multilateral security framework should be developed to prepare for a possible U.S. military withdrawal from the region. Rather than anticipating such a withdrawal, Japan should strengthen the U.S.-Japan alliance to ensure the continuation of America's security involvement in the Asia-Pacific region.

The realist advocates of a normalized Japan stress the importance of deterrence, crisis management, and a balance of power for regional security. For them the two greatest security challenges in the region are the uncertainties concerning North Korea (both the military threat it poses and the possibility of the instability and collapse of the regime) and the rise of China. A reinvigorated U.S.-Japan alliance would contribute greatly to deterring both a North Korean attack against South Korea and the Chinese use of force against Taiwan. Despite all the defense burden–sharing efforts of the Japanese government, alliances face their greatest tests during crises. According to realists, no amount of host-nation support or checkbook diplomacy will satisfy the United States if American lives are being sacrificed in an East Asian crisis that is critical to Japanese interests while Japan stands idly by because of its constitutional constraints. At the very least, Japan should be willing to provide rear area support to American troops. Some realists would ultimately like Japanese soldiers to stand shoulder to shoulder with U.S. forces in the defense of common interests.[38] Others believe that relaxing existing restrictions on overseas military deployments should take place conditionally to mitigate the fears that some East Asian states have about Japan's potential remilitarization.[39]

With the rise of China as a regional and global power, advocates of collective defense believe the best way to ensure stability in the East Asia–Pacific region is to balance China with a strong U.S.-Japan alliance. According to Hisahiko Okazaki, one of Japan's leading geopolitical analysts, Japan should play a role in American power balancing in East Asia analogous to the one that Britain plays for the United States in Europe. Japan should serve as America's most reliable partner in U.S. East Asia strategy. Although acknowledging that Japan is "not in a position to interfere in resolving the Taiwan question," Okazaki asserts that if China and the United States were to collide over this issue, Japan would have no choice but to cooperate with the United States to sustain the bilateral alliance.[40]

Most Japanese realists, however, oppose a strategy of containment toward China. In a June 1996 report the Japan Forum on International

Relations insisted that "any policy of 'containment' would likely result in a self-fulfilling prophecy, forcing China back onto the path of isolationism."[41] China is more an irredentist power than an expansionist power with imperial designs such as the Soviet Union. If nationalism drives China to be become territorially more assertive, this is likely to be limited to Taiwan, the South China Sea, and possibly Siberia. As long as China's growing military power can be balanced through a robust U.S.-Japan alliance (and if need be through a coalition with other states on China's periphery), both Japan and the United States should have no qualms about assisting China's economic development and its integration into the world economy.

To achieve such a balance of power, Japan does not need to expand its military capabilities. All that is required is for it to recognize that it can exercise its inherent right to collective self-defense and establish the government mechanisms for effective crisis management. A Japan normalized in this manner would not mean that it would become a heavily armed state that is strategically independent. Rather the aim is to make it into a dependable ally of the United States.[42] The regional order that would emerge would then be what some have called a "nonantagonistic balance of power" that includes China and encourages Beijing to exercise self-restraint.[43]

Whether one supports the collective security or collective defense versions, the campaign to normalize Japan has paralleled an effort to revise the current constitutional regime, either by reinterpretation or formal revision. This revisionist agenda, however, differs greatly from agendas of the past. Before, conservatives who wanted to revise the postwar constitution had reactionary ambitions. They believed that the document written by U.S. occupation officials went too far in changing the best features of the Meiji constitution. Therefore, in addition to altering or deleting the controversial Article 9, they advocated such points as upgrading the status of the emperor or inserting references to indigenous social values. But now the most prominent advocates of constitutional revision seek to make the Japanese political system better able to realize the values embedded in the democratic constitution. In November 1994 the *Yomiuri Shimbun*, Japan's largest newspaper, took the lead in this debate by proposing a set of amendments and using its media empire to publicize them.

The *Yomiuri* constitutional revision calls for a new chapter titled "Security" (*anzen hoshō*) to replace the existing chapter titled "Renunciation of War" (*sensō no hōki*). This security chapter would transpose virtually unchanged the first paragraph of Article 9 in the present constitution. The only revision would be to change the word "renounce" in the clause "the Japanese people forever renounce war as sovereign of the nation" to "will not recognize." But the second paragraph, which now states that "land, sea, and air forces, as well as other war potential, will never be maintained" would be deleted. In its place, the *Yomiuri* recommends including clauses that affirm Japan's commitment not to "manufacture, possess, or use . . . inhuman, indiscriminate weapons of mass destruction," recognize "the maintenance of an organization for self-defense," grant the prime minister the supreme authority to command the self-defense forces, and prohibit national conscription into the self-defense organization.

The newspaper's proposal also adds a chapter on international cooperation that articulates Japan's aspiration for eliminating from the earth "human calamities caused by military conflicts, natural disasters, environmental destruction, economic deprivation in particular regions, and regional disorder." Based on this aspiration, the *Yomiuri* draft states that "Japan will actively cooperate with the activities of established international organizations," and "when necessary, will be able to dispatch civil service personnel and provide parts of the self-defense organization for the maintenance and promotion of peace and for humanitarian support activities."[44] A constitutional revision along the lines suggested by the *Yomiuri Shimbun* would permit the overseas deployment of self-defense forces in peacemaking and peace enforcement operations as well as peacekeeping and humanitarian operations.

Although most advocates of normalizing Japan would support most of the *Yomiuri* recommendations, many doubt that a formal revision of the constitution is politically possible any time soon. They fear that a crisis on the Korean peninsula or elsewhere in East Asia might not wait until domestic conditions become favorable for such a change. Therefore, even while supporting constitutional revision in the long term, many advocate changing the current interpretation of the constitution in the interim.

AN INDEPENDENT STRATEGY. The third and final version of Japanese normalization advocates that Japan should pursue a strategy more independent of the United States and redefine its national identity in more Asian terms.[45] Proponents of this view want the constitution rewritten to reflect indigenous values as well as permit Japan to assume responsibility for its own defense. A prevalent theme has been the economic and social decline of the United States and the West and the rise of Asia. Rather than blindly following the American lead or Western models, Japan should replant its roots in Asia. As the world moves toward a tripolar structure based on North America, Europe, and East Asia, it is naive to think that Japan can and should play a mediating role between East and West. It should instead clearly articulate its position of being a member of the East. Although relations with the United States would still be important, it is much more natural for Japan to emphasize its relations with the East Asian states, given the common Tōyō (Eastern) philosophy and civilization they share.[46] According to these "Asianists," Japan's strategic mission should be to create an Asian coprosperity sphere by promoting regional economic development. One step in realizing this vision would be to establish a yen bloc.[47]

Regarding security policy, these nationalists want to transform the alliance with the United States into a more equal and symmetrical relationship. In contrast to the Anglo-Japanese alliance of the early twentieth century, the U.S.-Japan security relationship has perpetuated Japan's status as a "semipermanently occupied" nation. The idea that Japan is a free rider of U.S. security policy is therefore a myth. In reality, U.S. forces are in Japan to keep it from becoming a sovereign nation in a true sense as well as to promote U.S. strategic interests beyond Japan. To change this situation, Japan must eventually revise the constitution and acquire a real military to defend itself.[48] As a first step, the self-defense forces should participate fully in UN peacekeeping operations, and the number of U.S. bases should be reduced throughout Japan, not just on Okinawa. For example, Ishihara Shintaro has called for the return of Yokota Air Force Base.[49]

The Asianists are the least willing to deal with Japan's militarist past to make the other East Asian states more receptive of Japanese power and influence. Japan should not be preoccupied with this history, they contend, because many countries in the region are now willing to put aside the past and are looking to Japan for more international leadership. In their opinion the version of the Pacific war perpetuated by the Tokyo war crimes trial is inaccurate and biased against Japan, and reports of Japanese atrocities in World War II are grossly exaggerated.[50]

The major shortcoming of the Asianist version of Japanese normalization is the absence of any clear analysis or prescription about the future of Sino-Japanese relations. Asianism might imply a partnership between China and Japan to the exclusion of the United States, but proponents say little about how Japan might develop such a relationship. And they do not seem to recognize that their interpretation of history will complicate the creation of a stable Sino-Japanese relationship.

Post–Cold War Pacifism

After Japan's inadequate response to the 1990–91 Persian Gulf crisis provoked criticism that it engaged in a selfish, purist brand of one-country pacifism, progressive intellectuals, journalists, and politicians began to recast their pacifist beliefs and policy prescriptions to contend that Japan should contribute more actively to international peace. This effort has created two strands of thought: one in favor of transforming Japan into a "global civilian power," and the other in favor of a reconstituted form of pacifism.

The most influential concept has been that of Japan as a civilian power, an idea first introduced to a Japanese audience by the *Asahi Shimbun* journalist Yoichi Funabashi.[51] In attempting to adapt postwar pacifism to the security realities of the post–cold war world, this vision probably has the greatest support among the general public. Instead of normalizing Japan, Funabashi and those who share his outlook argue that the country should build on its tragic historical experience with militarism and strive to internationalize its domestic norms about security and the use of military force. The postwar constitution should not be seen as an impediment to greater Japanese participation in international affairs, but as an embodiment of ideals that all states should work toward and that Japan should take the lead in promoting. As the only country to suffer from a nuclear attack, Japan should become more vigorous in efforts to prevent nuclear proliferation and support nuclear arms control and disarmament. With nations' increasing economic interdependence and the end of the cold war, the need to rely on traditional balance of power will attenuate and an opportunity to cultivate cooperative approaches to security will emerge. Consequently, policymakers should emphasize nonmilitary, multilateral means to increase international security.[52]

For Funabashi, the Asia Pacific Economic Cooperation (APEC) process, a multilateral conference and incipient organization to promote regional economic liberalization and integration, "can support Japan's emergence as the first true 'global civilian power.'" He acknowledges that the Asia Pacific region still operates according to the rule of the jungle, lacks regional institutions such as NATO or the European Union, suffers from the absence of mature civil societies, and manifests large differences in income, culture, and tradition within the region. Nevertheless, with the focus on economic development and the growth of the middle class, APEC can contribute to a sense of community in the region. Japan should seize this opportunity by overcoming its notions of exceptionalism and coming to terms with its militarist past so that it can become an effective bridge between the East Asian and Western nations. Specifically, Funabashi recommends that economic liberalization should be the first policy priority and that Japan should lead the way by liberalizing its own markets and advocating unconditional most favored nation treatment. But he warns against following Asianist tactics, such as the concept of the East Asian Economic Caucus, that exclude Western nations.[53]

Despite their belief in the beneficial effects of economic interdependence on security, advocates of civilian power recognize that in the current era of transition and uncertainty the security alliance between Japan and the United States must be maintained. Drawing on the lessons of the premature dissolution of the Anglo-Japanese alliance in 1922, they believe that the U.S.-Japan alliance should not be replaced with the untested alternative of a multilateral security arrangement for the East–Asia Pacific region.[54] But the U.S.-centered bilateral security arrangements established to deal principally with the Soviet threat are no longer sufficient to manage the multiple and broadly defined threats of the post–cold war era. Multilateral forums on security are increasingly necessary to foster mutual trust. According to one analyst, rather than limiting them to one institution, the aim should be to create a variety of security forums patterned in concentric circles that might include a Pacific 5 group of the five industrial democracies in the region and a North Pacific Security Conference as well as the ASEAN Regional Forum.[55]

Notwithstanding the consensus in favor of keeping the U.S.-Japan alliance, analysts advocating civilian power differ among themselves about how the relationship should evolve. Some would like it to move toward an alliance that excludes permanent stationing of U.S. military forces on Japanese territory (jōji chūryū naki Ampō).[56] Others believe that without the military bases, the United States would have little incentive to continue its defense commitments to Japan. Nevertheless, they still believe that the number of U.S. troops and bases in Japan could be reduced to lighten the burden on local communities, especially Okinawa.[57]

Although many recoil at the thought of Japan cooperating militarily with the United States in a crisis outside the homeland, some do believe that the self-defense forces should support U.S. military operations in regional contingencies within the constraints of the constitution and the current government's interpretation proscribing the exercise of the right of collective self-defense. Former Prime Minister Kiichi Miyazawa, who is known for his dovish views and his vigorous support of the postwar constitution, has said that the self-defense forces should not refrain from cooperating with U.S. military forces during a regional crisis simply because of the prohibition on exercising the right of collective self-defense. If a danger should emerge that critically affects Japan's defense, then Japan should cooperate with U.S. forces as an extension of the right of individual self-defense. But the iron law that Japan must preserve is that of not using military force in foreign countries.[58]

To develop a stable and cooperative balance of power among the United States, Japan, and China, Funabashi argues that while America and Japan cultivate a closer relationship in the context of this triangle, both "must try swiftly to include China in their deliberations." Otherwise China will view the U.S.-Japan alliance a means of containment.[59] Although sympathetic to China's quest to develop its economy and to overcome centuries of humiliation by outside powers, advocates of civilian power have become more critical of China following its nuclear weapons tests in 1995–96. To stabilize Tokyo's relationship with Beijing, Jitsuro Terashima of Mitsui Bussan (one of Japan's largest trading companies) has proposed that Japan follow four principles: develop a clear posture for resolving the matter of Japan's militarist past; maintain a harmonious relationship with China by cooperating with its modernization and supporting its participation in international society; be firm about Japan's nonnuclear policy by opposing nuclear tests by all nations (including China), promoting nuclear disarmament, and getting out from under the American nuclear umbrella; and refuse to intervene in the Taiwan-China dispute even if China and the United States confront each other over it.[60]

The second perspective stemming from Japan's pacifist tradition is more idealistic than the concept of civilian power. For example, a group of nine scholars convened by the Iwanami publishing house has recommended transforming the self-defense force from its current structure as a traditional military force into an armed organization similar to the police or coast guard. This "minimum defensive force" (*saishogen bōgyōryoku*) would be a "democratized" unit whose aim would be to protect the lives and property of Japanese citizens and whose geographic scope would be strictly limited to Japan's land, airspace, and territorial waters.[61]

Although the concept would seem dangerously idealistic to a realist, the Iwanami group appears to be addressing the pacifists who have heretofore opposed on constitutional and philosophical grounds any kind of armed force. Its aim is to convince these "pure pacifists" that there is a defense force that can be legitimate under the current constitution and consistent with pacifist principles. The *Asahi Shimbun* echoed the views of the Iwanami scholars when it contended that Japan should be a con-scientious objector nation that contributes to international society in exclusively nonmilitary ways. Accordingly, the ground self-defense force should be reduced by half, and deployment of such advanced weapon systems as the Aegis naval systems and P-3C antisubmarine warfare aircraft should be scaled back. The mission of this restructured force would be restricted to stopping armed attacks on Japan. Japan would refrain from acquiring weapons that can be used to attack other countries, deploying military forces overseas, or exercising the right of collective self-defense.[62]

For Japan to contribute actively to international peace, the *Asahi Shimbun* favors establishing a separate Peace Support Corps (*Heiwa Shi-en Tai*) limited to humanitarian and economic operations. Japanese paci-fists are skeptical that the use of military force or the deployment of armed peacekeepers will resolve regional conflicts effectively. These operations could even aggravate a problem. So even though the United Nations should be central to Japan's diplomacy, neither the Iwanami scholars nor the *Asahi Shimbun* want Japan to participate in UN security activities that have a strong military component. Japan should set an example of what and how much can be done without the military.

Unlike traditional pacifists, the neopacifists acknowledge the benefi-cial effects of the bilateral security treaty, especially the clauses for eco-nomic cooperation and the settlement of disputes by peaceful means. They even admit that the treaty has helped to restrain Japanese rearma-ment and make other Asian states receptive to Japan's emergence as a regional economic leader. But they are critical of relying on the existence of the treaty to reassure the region about Japanese intentions. If Japan is truly to be trusted, it must address more sincerely its militarist past. Unfortunately, many of the prodefense politicians are the least willing to admit the wrongs Japan committed against other Asians. Therefore, until the nation can clear this hurdle, revising the constitution to clarify its international role will be misconstrued and may even become a destabilizing factor in the region.

For the new pacifists, there is ultimately a tension between the U.S.-Japan alliance and the creation of inclusive cooperative security arrangements. Japan and the United States should therefore amicably reduce the military functions of the alliance and recast the relationship into a political, economic, and cultural partnership. U.S. military forces should gradually be removed from Japanese territory. Only by transforming the relationship in this manner can Japan pursue an omnidirectional peace strategy as a truly sovereign nation.[63] In place of the security alliance, Japan should take the lead in developing a multilateral collective and cooperative security system for the East Asia–Pacific region that can impose sanctions and perform peacekeeping functions.[64]

Critical Assessment

In a general sense the strategic debates in the United States and Japan parallel each other. The American realists and the Japanese normalizers tend to focus on deterrence, crisis management, and the balance of power. American liberals and Japanese pacifists tend to emphasize tension reduction, crisis prevention, and the promotion of cooperative security.

But specifics of the debates do not precisely match. The Japanese proponents of enabling Japan to exercise its right to collective self-defense appear to converge with American commentators who tend to be hostile toward China and find its emergence as a great power threatening. But most of the Japanese advocates of collective self-defense do not support a containment policy toward China. Instead, they urge balancing Chinese military power through a stronger U.S.-Japan alliance while continuing to support China's economic modernization. They would find excessive the confrontational rhetoric of some American analysts who would like to pressure China hard on human rights and trade liberalization as well as contain it militarily.

Similarly, American realists who support a strategy of engaged balancing would not be comfortable if Japan began to favor exercising the right of collective self-defense like a normal power. They would be concerned about the reactions from China and other Asian powers and perhaps even the rise of Japanese strategic autonomy. The so-called off-shore balancers in the United States, who would like to terminate the current security arrangement, would be the most supportive of Japan's normalization.

There are also differences between American liberals and Japanese paci-fists. American liberals are much more willing to consider the use of force (albeit multilaterally) for humanitarian purposes as well as to repel aggres-sion. Most Japanese pacifists remain reluctant to use force except for self-defense in the strictest sense and are even unwilling to dispatch military forces overseas as part of a multilateral collective security operation. U.S. liberals in favor of humanitarian intervention or collective security would thus have to turn to someone such as Ichiro Ozawa, who is considered to be a hawkish on defense matters in Japan and who favors Japan's normaliza-tion via the ability to exercise the right to collective security. Although most American liberals are highly critical of Japan's nuclear fuel cycle program, which involves stockpiling plutonium, recycling spent fuel, and building breeder reactors, most Japanese proponents of the civilian power vision are surprisingly supportive of their government's nuclear energy policies despite their implications for compromising nuclear nonproliferation and confidence building on security matters in East Asia. Only the hard-core pacifists in Japan openly challenge these policies.

What is remarkable about the debates in both the United States and Japan, however, is the consensus for continuing the bilateral security relationship after the collapse of the Soviet Union. In Japan, even the nationalistic Asianists and the traditional pacifists recognize, albeit somewhat reluctantly, the benefits of the security arrangements for the time being. In the United States, only the off-shore balancers—still a dis-tinct minority—openly advocate an abrogration of the security treaty in the near future. For most American analysts, off-shore balancing is too risky because it assumes that a stable power equilibrium will quickly materialize after U.S. disengagement. Such a strategy would also mean that the United States would forfeit its status as a global power.

But despite the breadth of support for the alliance among opinion leaders of each country, the depth of support in the body politic cannot be taken for granted. Although there are hardly any influential political voices in the United States calling for termination of the alliance and drastic military withdrawal from East Asia, this may be more a result of the low costs and risks the engagement currently imposes on Americans.

If, however, a crisis were to occur in East Asia that risked significant numbers of American lives and imposed a major economic burden, questions about the wisdom of U.S. defense commitments would likely spring up, especially if Japan did not meet American expectations about what an ally should be willing to do. In Japan, the sharp drop in public support for the security relationship after the fall 1995 Okinawa rape incident also suggests the fragility of Japanese popular commitment to the alliance.

The apparent consensus about the value of the alliance also breaks down under the weight of the diversity of reasons now put forth to justify it. Instead of simply pointing to a common threat as in the past, opinion leaders on both sides of the Pacific now articulate different rationales:

— to preserve a balance between Japan and China,

— to check Japan's nuclearization and remilitarization,

— to balance against, constrain, or even contain the rise of China's power,

— to prevent the emergence of a hostile hegemonic power or a coalition of powers in East Asia,

— to create a maritime partnership to maintain power balances on the East Asian continent and to secure navigational freedom,

— to protect and promote democratization and economic liberalization,

— to maintain or improve access to each other's markets and technology, and

— to serve as the foundation for a cooperative and collective security regime.

Having a long list of reasons to maintain the alliance is not a bad thing in itself, especially since many of them do not necessarily conflict with each other. Nevertheless, some rationales do point to different priorities, and in a few instances suggest contradictory policies. For example, those who want to balance against or contain China would favor expanding Japan's defense capabilities and missions, while those who consider the alliance a cork in the bottle would oppose such a course. Consequently, policymakers have tended to paper over the differences by defining the alliance primarily in terms of dealing with uncertainty and preserving stability. But this vague characterization of purpose serves as neither a useful guide to concrete policy nor a convincing argument for the American and Japanese publics.

The disagreements lurking in the consensus become more visible when one considers whether the alliance should be preserved in its present form or whether the terms should be altered. Those who want to preserve the status quo are thinking primarily of checking the expansion of Japan's defense capabilities and activities, not triggering a slide toward American isolationism, perpetuating America's dominant role in the alliance, or not provoking China, South Korea, or Japan's other neighbors. Those who seek to alter the terms of the alliance furnish the following arguments, some of which contradict each other:

— to prepare the alliance to handle regional security crises more effectively,

— to balance against or contain China,

— to forge a more equitable distribution of burdens, responsibilities, and power in the alliance,

— to reduce the presence of U.S. forces in Japan, and

— to harness the alliance to help construct a regional security order based on cooperation rather than confrontation.

Because there is so little agreement about whether to change the alliance and if so in which direction, U.S. and Japanese policymakers have by default adopted an incremental approach to prepare it for the post–cold war era.

From a policy perspective, the critical task is not to choose one school over another. Political dynamics in the United States preclude a strong domestic consensus in favor of a policy that is primarily either realist or liberal. Similarly, the Japanese people could not support a policy that strictly followed either the normalization or the pacifist path. A better approach would be to choose the parts of each perspective that make policy sense for East Asia and create a new strategic synthesis that would help resolve the conundrums that complicate both American and Japanese security policy.

In the absence of a clear geopolitical and ideological adversary, the support of the American public for overseas security commitments appears predicated on minimizing costs and risks and mobilizing the active support of other nations, especially allies. But in East Asia, a military crisis in Korea or a confrontation with China would be costly and risky for the United States; and as things stand, active support from Japan is by no means assured. Under such circumstances, one way to sustain the realist policy of keeping militarily engaged in East Asia would be to embrace the liberal agenda of cooperative security to lower the costs and risks of traditional security remedies and to institutionalize multilateral action to deal with aggression.

Japanese security policy faces a somewhat different dilemma. Although an expansion of Japan's defense role along the lines envisaged by the normalizers would help tighten the military alliance with the United States, it could provoke China, the Koreas, and other East Asian states. The solution would be for Japan to deal more forthrightly with its militarist past, as the pacificists have urged, and perhaps even change its nuclear energy policies to reassure the rest of the region about its long-term intentions while it normalizes itself as a participant in regional and international security activities.

An effective U.S.-Japan coordinated strategy requires considering East Asian security in terms of both challenges and opportunities. In light of the challenges posed by continuing military confrontation in the Korean peninsula, uncertainties about the North Korean regime, the future of Taiwan, and the rise of China, deterrence, crisis management, and balance of power continue to be relevant. But at the same time, the end of the cold war, the regional emphasis on economic development, and the preponderant military advantage of the U.S. alliance system present an opportunity to reduce tensions, prevent crises, and promote cooperative security. The difficulty will be to fashion a workable balance between these two sets of imperatives. Rather than reflecting on the appropriate balance in the abstract, it would be more productive to consider the focus points for American and Japanese security interests in the region: Korea and China.

Korea

The possibility of a military conflict in Korea suggests that Japan should, as the proponents of normalization insist, embrace both collective self-defense and collective security. Only then will it be possible for U.S. and Japanese forces to develop guidelines on defense cooperation that will have meaning at the operational level and that can shape defense planning on the basis of complementarity. But the continuing military confrontation in the Korean peninsula has also prompted U.S. and Japanese defense officials to oppose major changes in the U.S. military presence in Japan. They argue that a U.S. troop reduction before resolution of the confrontation would worsen an already volatile situation. But as the chapters by Satoshi Morimoto and Michael O'Hanlon demonstrate, strictly from a military operations perspective, the combat marine forces in Okinawa could be withdrawn without undermining military deterrence or the ability to respond to a crisis or aggression. In fact, if Japan were to recognize that it could exercise its right to collective self-defense, provide rear support for U.S. forces, and facilitate the rapid deployment of U.S. troops into and out of Japan (especially Okinawa and western Japan), the response capabilities of the alliance would be improved even if the marines were withdrawn from Okinawa. The alliance would also be on firmer political ground and less vulnerable to Pyongyang's diplomatic efforts to drive a wedge between Washington and Tokyo.

In addition to preparing for a crisis, there is an opportunity to reduce tensions over Korea. Given the dire economic situation in North Korea, the great danger may be a collapse of the Pyongyang regime rather than an all-out military attack on the South. A weak or collapsing regime could initiate frequent sabotage attacks against South Korea, heightening the danger of miscalculation and inadvertent conflict. A precipitous collapse of the North Korean state would also create chaos that could trigger massive refugee flows and increase the possibility of military clashes, especially if South Korean forces moved northward to restore order. In light of these dangers, the United States, Japan, and South Korea share an interest in minimizing violence even while preparing for violent events.

Here it would be appropriate to consider the use of cooperative security policy to entice North Korea to discuss and implement confidence-building measures, reduce military deployments, and improve North-South relations. After normalizing relations with both Russia and China, South Korea is in a much more advantageous diplomatic position than North Korea. Pyongyang's desire to normalize relations with both Washington and Tokyo is therefore understandable, not only to get economic and food aid but also to equalize its diplomatic status vis-à-vis Seoul. From North Korea's perspective, stable relations with the United States are the key for preserving the security of its regime and gaining access to economic assistance. But normalization of relations with Japan offers the attraction of getting billions of dollars in aid as reparations for Japan's colonial occupation of Korea. In short, Washington and Tokyo have powerful inducements to elicit Pyongyang's cooperation on such matters as closing its ballistic missile program or curbing its ability to inflict a devastating military attack on Seoul.

Of course, North Korea's propensity to provoke crises to increase its diplomatic leverage will complicate efforts to reach verifiable cooperative security agreements. But another stumbling block is whether discus-

sions between North Korea on the one hand and the United States and
Japan on the other can precede or should follow progress in the North-
South dialogue. Without a great deal of trust in American and Japanese
intentions, South Korea will insist that progress in North-South relations
precede moving ahead on U.S. and Japanese normalization of relations
with North Korea. In light of its diplomatic isolation, Pyongyang will
resist moving ahead on relations with Seoul without clear indications of
progress on normalization with at least Washington and perhaps even
Tokyo. This situation will therefore require taking small steps on both
fronts.

To give the United States and Japan some flexibility in advancing this
diplomatic engagement, the improvement of U.S.-South Korean and
Japanese-South Korean relations is essential. Toward this end, the United
States should initiate a security dialogue with the Republic of Korea that
would be comparable to the dialogue it started with Japan in 1994. The
purpose would be to redefine the U.S.-South Korean alliance by con-
firming America's support for Korean reunification and laying the basis
for a security partnership between the United States and Korea after
reunification. At the same time, Japan should work to improve its relations with South Korea by dealing more forthrightly with its militarist
history. To the extent that good Korean-Japanese relations will be critical to Northeast Asian stability after Korean reunification, Washington
should help to improve relations between Tokyo and Seoul.

China

Beijing reacted to the 1996 U.S.-Japan Joint Declaration on Security
by charging that it represented a policy of containing China. For American and Japanese analysts who favor a hard line toward China, the reaction was predictable and should not stop the United States and Japan from
moving forward on bilateral defense cooperation for regional security.
Insofar as the governments of both countries have an interest in engaging
China, however, Beijing's harsh reaction exposed the limits of American
and Japanese diplomacy. U.S. and Japanese officials have traveled around
the region to explain that the declaration was not directed against any particular country, but rather against regional instability. They have also
explained that the proposed modest changes in the bilateral arrangements
are intended to make the alliance burdens more equitable and more sustainable domestically. But because the 1996 declaration was announced

just a month after the crisis in the Taiwan Strait, China's interpretation is not surprising. That many Japanese opinion leaders who vigorously support a stronger U.S.-Japan alliance and Japan's exercising its right to collective self-defense are sympathetic to Taiwan's efforts to gain greater international recognition has fueled Chinese suspicions.

Since President Nixon's opening to China in 1972, Chinese leaders have essentially viewed the U.S.-Japan security relationship as a positive contribution to regional stability because it restrains Japan's remilitarization. But in the past year, Chinese analysts appear to have been reassessing their view. Although their first preference continues to be a U.S.-Japan alliance that restricts Japan's security role to defense of the homeland, they are beginning to consider a Japan strategically independent of the United States as being better for Chinese interests than a Japan willing to perform regional security missions as a stronger ally of the United States. In rejecting a policy of containing China, some Japanese opinion leaders have advocated a "nonantagonistic" balance of power among the United States, Japan, and China whereby China would be "subsumed" into the East Asia–Pacific region while its status as a major power would be respected.[65] But in light of the fervor with which mainland Chinese are committed to preventing Taiwan's independence, a nonantagonistic balance of power is impossible as long as China believes that American and Japanese policies jointly and separately are encouraging Taiwan to move toward independence. No amount of diplomatic rhetoric about the need to check regional instability will allay China's suspicions about the evolution of the U.S.-Japan alliance unless Washington and Tokyo can reassure Beijing that they do not explicitly or implicitly support Taiwan's steps toward independence.

The United States and Japan have a critical interest in a peaceful solution to the Taiwan question. Practically, such a solution would mean prolonging the status quo until China evolves politically in such a manner that the union of China and Taiwan would become acceptable to the Taiwanese. A military conflict with China over Taiwan would represent for the United States a dangerous confrontation with a nuclear power. It is far from clear that Americans would want to risk such a war even to defend democracy in Taiwan. Such a conflict would also pose an impossible choice for Japan and has a much greater chance of breaking the alliance than another Korean war.

Unfortunately, the logic of deterrence is not an adequate guide to prevent war over Taiwan. Deterrence theory would recommend that the

United States make an explicit and firm commitment to defend Taiwan. But such a declaration would negate the one-China policy that has been the basis of U.S.-China relations and put the United States and China on a collision course. It would also likely encourage Taiwan to push ahead with its diplomatic initiatives for independence, which could in turn provoke China to attack. To make deterrence work, the United States would have to reconfigure its alliance network in East Asia to counter Beijing as China's military power grew. It is doubtful that Japan would join such a effort. And certainly, Beijing will do what it can to drive a wedge between Washington and Tokyo.

An alternative would be for the United States to state explicitly that it does not have a commitment to defend Taiwan. But to make such a declared policy would be politically impossible for any U.S. administration, given Taiwan's democratization, America's economic stake there, and Taipei's vigorous lobbying activities in Washington. Even if the United States were to adopt such a policy, the problem would not be solved. Rather than encouraging Taiwan to improve relations with the mainland, it could choose to develop nuclear weapons. Even worse, such a policy might embolden Beijing to use military intimidation against Taipei.

By default, the United States has chosen ambiguity. In declaring its interest in peaceful unification, Washington is signaling to Beijing that without explicitly contradicting the one-China policy it *might* defend Taiwan if attacked. But strategic ambiguity reassures Taiwan just enough to allow it to continue a policy of creeping independence but does not clearly deter China's option to seize Taiwan by force. The legacy of the March 1996 Taiwan crisis has been twofold. First, it has given China's military modernization program a focus: to develop the military capability to prevent Taiwan's independence even if the United States intervenes on Taiwan's behalf. Second, America's dispatch of two aircraft carriers to the area has weakened Taipei's incentive to be more conciliatory toward Beijing. Both results suggest a dangerous drift toward American confrontation with China. Unless Washington and Tokyo seize the diplomatic initiative to develop a workable modus vivendi regarding Taiwan, a revitalization of the U.S.-Japan alliance will only reinforce this trend. What is needed now is diplomatic clarity to supplement the current military ambiguity.

The United States and Japan should therefore publicly and unequivocally oppose not only a formal declaration of independence by Taiwan but also any unilateral efforts to move toward independence. In addition, Washington should renew its commitment to abide by the August 1982 communiqué restraining and reducing arms sales to Taiwan. In response, China should clarify and redefine its concept of "one China, two systems" so that the two systems imply not only different economic systems, but also different political systems. In other words, China should recognize Taiwan's democratization. At the same time, Beijing should accept Taipei's representation in international economic organizations. If Beijing agrees to do these things, Tokyo and Washington should urge Taipei to renounce its diplomatic campaign to gain regular membership in the United Nations or its efforts to move toward independence. The purpose of these diplomatic moves would be to encourage China and Taiwan to resume their cross-strait dialogue, reduce tensions, and further economic links as steps to eventual reconciliation.

Achieving a modus vivendi on Taiwan should make it possible to engage China constructively on other security matters—nonproliferation, arms transfer, military transparency—even as the United States and Japan deepen their bilateral defense cooperation. At this juncture, major power relations in East Asia could move toward a traditional balance of power following a competitive logic or toward cooperative security. Strengthening the U.S.-Japan alliance into a more reciprocal partnership would give it the luxury of being able to pursue either option effectively. With such a strategic advantage, the United States and Japan could with very little risk propose to China a cooperative security regime along the ambitious lines proposed by Steinbruner and Kaufmann involving restraints on Chinese military development in exchange for some reduction in America's military superiority. Such an offer would certainly challenge in a fundamental way the realpolitik assumptions of Chinese leaders. But even if they rejected the cooperative security initiative, the U.S.-led alliance would be in the enviable position of almost surely winning in a military competition with China. This prospect just might lead Chinese leaders to change their assumptions. Such a possibility, no matter how slight, makes the quest for cooperative security worth trying.

Notes

1. Henry Kissinger, *Diplomacy* (Simon and Schuster, 1994).
2. Ibid., p. 826.

3. Ibid., pp. 828–29.

4. Michael H Armacost, *Friends or Rivals? The Insider's Account of U.S.-Japan Relations* (Columbia University Press, 1996), p. 246.

5. Ibid., pp. 245–46.

6. Thomas J Christensen, "Chinese Realpolitik," *Foreign Affairs,* vol. 75 (September-October 1996), pp. 40–45, 48–49; and Thomas L. McNaugher, "U.S. Military Forces in East Asia: The Case for Long-Term Engagement," in Gerald L. Curtis, ed., *The United States, Japan, and Asia* (Norton, 1994), pp. 207–12.

7. Kissinger, *Diplomacy,* pp 828–29.

8. Armacost acknowledges this danger. See *Friends or Rivals?*, pp. 247–48.

9. Examples of this view include Charles Krauthammer, "Why We Must Contain China," *Time,* July 31, 1995, p. 72; and Gideon Rachman, "Containing China," *Washington Quarterly,* vol. 19 (Winter 1996), pp. 129–39.

10. Richard Bernstein and Ross H. Munro, *The Coming Conflict with China* (Knopf, 1997), pp. 219–20.

11. In addition to Christopher Layne, other minimal realists include Doug Bandow and Ted Galen Carpenter of the Cato Institute, Michael Lind, Benjamin Schwartz of the World Policy Institute, and Alan Tonelson (formerly with the Economic Strategy Institute).

12. Ted Galen Carpenter, "Paternalism and Dependence: The U.S.-Japanese Security Relationship," Policy Analysis, Cato Institute, Washington, November 1, 1995; and Doug Bandow, *Tripwire* (Washington: Cato Institute, 1996).

13. Office of International Security Affairs, *United States Security Strategy for the East Asia–Pacific Region* (Department of Defense, February 1995).

14. Chalmers Johnson and E. B. Keehn, "The Pentagon's Ossified Strategy," *Foreign Affairs,* vol. 74 (July-August 1995); Chalmers Johnson, "Korea and Our Asia Policy," *National Interest,* no. 41 (Fall 1995); and Johnson, "The Okinawa Rape Incident and the End of the Cold War in East Asia," JPRI Working Paper 16 (Japan Policy Research Institute, February 1996).

15. Chalmers Johnson, "Containing China: The United States and Japan Drift toward Disaster," *Japan Quarterly,* vol. 43 (October-December 1996), pp. 10–18.

16. Samuel P Huntington, *The Clash of Civilizations and the Remaking of World Order* (Simon and Schuster, 1996), pp. 218–38, 316.

17. Strobe Talbott, "Democracy and the National Interest," *Foreign Affairs,* vol. 75 (November-December 1996), p. 49.

18. Ibid., p. 58.

19. Janne E. Nolan, "The Concept of Cooperative Security," in Janne E. Nolan, ed., *Global Engagement: Cooperation and Security in the 21st Century* (Brookings, 1994), p. 5.

20. Ibid.

21. Janne E. Nolan, "Cooperative Security in the United States," in Janne E. Nolan, ed., *Global Engagement: Cooperation and Security in the 21st Century* (Brookings, 1994), pp. 520–21.

22. Harry Harding, "Cooperative Security in the Asia-Pacific Region," in Janne E Nolan, ed., *Global Engagement: Cooperation and Security in the 21st Century* (Brookings, 1994), pp. 441–42.

23. Ibid., pp. 442–43.

24. In the Bush administration, Secretary of State James Baker was particularly skeptical about multilateral security processes in the East Asia–Pacific region and preferred strengthening the network of bilateral security arrangements—what he termed "spokes in the fan." See James A. Baker III, "America in Asia: Emerging Architecture for a Pacific Community," *Foreign Affairs*, vol. 70 (Winter 1991–92), pp. 1–18. But toward the end of the Bush presidency some officials such as Deputy Secretary of State Lawrence Eagleburger became more supportive of multilateral approaches. My thanks to Michael Armacost for making this point.

25. *IGCC Newsletter*, vol. 12 (Spring 1996), p. 10–11, and vol. 12 (Fall 1996), p. 1, 3.

26. John D Steinbruner and William W. Kaufmann, "International Security Reconsidered," in Robert D. Reischauer, ed., *Setting National Priorities: Budget Choices for the Next Century* (Brookings, 1997), pp. 174–75. Steinbruner and Kaufmann suggest the following specific measures that would be part of this cooperative security regime: reducing active forces to lower levels and preserving them in a state of readiness to preclude an effective surprise attack, keeping nuclear weapons off alert status, prohibiting intimidating concentrations and provocative activities of conventional forces, jointly determining and operating any deployment of wide-area ballistic missile defense systems, and continually exchanging information "to document compliance with the deployment standards and operational rules, to make violations more visible, and to stimulate timely reactions to detected violations."

27. Robert A. Manning, "Futureshock or Renewed Partnership? The U.S.-Japan Alliance Facing the Millennium," *Washington Quarterly*, vol. 18 (Autumn 1995), pp. 97–98; and "PACATOM: A Nuclear Cooperation Regime as Asian CSBM," paper prepared for a meeting of the Council for Security Cooperation in the Asia Pacific, April 1996.

28. Nolan, "Concept of Cooperative Security," pp. 5–6.

29. Nolan, "Cooperative Security in the United States," pp. 516, 518–19.

30. This tension is evident in Janne Nolan's presentation of the cooperative security concept. See Ibid., pp. 516–21.

31. Ozawa Ichiro, *Blueprint for a New Japan: The Rethinking of a Nation* (Tokyo: Kodansha International, 1994), p. 94.

32. Ibid., pp. 106–07, 109–11, 119–21.

33. Ibid., pp. 106–07, 115.

34. Ibid., pp. 135–37.

35. Some of the prominent Japanese realists are Masamichi Inoki (professor emeritus of Kyoto University and advisor to the Research Institute for Peace and Security), Kenichi Ito (president of the Japan Forum on International Relations), Shinichi Kitaoka (professor at Rikkyo University), Satoshi Morimoto (senior researcher at the Nomura Research Institute and former official in the Ministry of Foreign Affairs), Masashi Nishihara (professor at the National Defense Academy), Hisahiko Okazaki (former Japanese ambassador to Saudi Arabia and Thailand), Seizaburo Sato (professor at the Saitama University Graduate School and research director of the Institute for International Policy Studies), Toshiyuki Shikata (professor at Teikyo University and retired lieutenant general of the ground self-

defense force), Tadae Takubo (professor at Kyorin University), and Akio Watanabe (professor at Aoyama Gakuin University).

36. Hisahiko Okazaki, "Japan Should Awake to Right of Collective Self-Defense," *Daily Yomiuri*, July 4, 1994.

37. Recent articles advocating constitutional reinterpretation include Inoki Masamichi, "Kūsō-teki heiwashugi ni ketsubetsu o," *This Is Yomiuri*, vol. 7 (July 1996), pp. 128–37; Sase Masamori, "'Shūdan-teki jieiken' kaishaku no kai," *Voice*, no. 223 (July 1996), pp. 128–49; Shiina Motoo and Okazaki Hisahiko, "Shūdan-teki jieiken rongi o nigeru na," *Chūō Kōron*, no. 1340 (July 1996), pp. 62–69; and Sato Seizaburo, "Clarifying the Right of Collective Self-Defense," *Asia-Pacific Review*, vol. 3 (Fall-Winter 1996), pp. 91–105.

A group within Ozawa's New Frontier party known as the New Frontier Party Security Diet Members' League (Shinshintō Anzen Hoshō Gi-in Renmei Yūshi) has proposed such a change in constitutional interpretation in its draft policy titled "Security Policy Outline for the New Century: New Thinking on Security and Defense." Because of strong opposition from some segments of the New Frontier party, this policy outline has not become part of the party's official platform.

Keizai Dōyūkai, the influential Japan Association of Corporate Executives, has also endorsed reinterpreting the constitution so that Japan can exercise its collective self-defense right. See Keizai Doyukai, "Report of the Study Group on Security Issues," April 8, 1996.

38. Shikata Toshiyuki, *Kyoku-to yuji* [Far East Crisis] (Tokyo: Kuresuto Sha, 1996)

39. For instance, the Asian Forum Japan has proposed four principles to preserve Japan's nonaggression stance while enabling it to participate in cooperative security activities (including overseas military deployments) in Asia: Diet approval and monitoring of Japanese participation in cooperative security operations, respect for the judgments of international organizations (especially the UN Security Council) regarding whether a given act is "aggressive" or "self-defensive," joint action with China, South Korea, and other Asian countries, and prohibition of the dispatch of Japanese ground forces to Asia except for traditional peacekeeping operations. The Asian Forum Japan is a network of mainstream international relations specialists with close ties to the large conservative parties, especially the Liberal Democratic and New Frontier parties. See Asian Forum Japan, *A Call for a Multilateral Strategy for Japan* (Tokyo, May 1995), pp. 106–09.

40. Okazaki Hisahiko, "Ajia no ashita to Nichi-Bei dōmei," *This Is Yomiuri*, vol. 7 (December 1996), p. 209.

41. Akio Watanabe, Kikuchi Tsutomu, and Yamanouchi Yasuhide, *The Perspective of Security Regimes in the Asia-Pacific Region* (Tokyo: Japan Forum on International Relations, 1996), p. 31. Founded in March 1987, the Japan Forum is a private membership organization composed of influential members of the business, academic, political, and journalistic communities and structured in a manner similar to the Council on Foreign Relations in the United States.

42. Okazaki Hisahiko and Nakajima Mineo, *Nihon ni Ajia senryaku wa aru no ka: Genso no Chugoku—yuji no kyokuto* (Tokyo: PHP Kenkyūjō, 1996), pp 79–80; and Okazaki Hisahiko and Chalmers Johnson, "Tokushū—Setogiwa no Nichi-Bei

dōmei: Nihon no ego ni Amerika no iyaki," *This Is Yomiuri*, no. 67 (September 1995), p. 116. Okazaki disagrees with Joseph Nye's implication that Japan as a normal country would necessarily be Japan with an independent military capability. See Joseph S. Nye Jr., "The Case for Deep Engagement," *Foreign Affairs*, vol. 74 (July-August 1995), p. 96.

43. Watanabe, Kikuchi, and Yamanouchi, *Perspective of Security Regimes in Asia-Pacific Region*, pp. 29–31.

44. *Kempō: 21 seiki ni mukete* (Tokyo: Yomiuri Shimbunsha, 1994), pp. 46–47, 53–54.

45. Prominent commentators holding these opinions include Jun Etō (literary critic and professor at Keio University), Shintarō Ishihara (author and former conservative Diet member), and Shoichi Watanabe (professor at Sophia University).

46. Ishihara Shintaro and Mahathir bin Mohamad, *"No" to ieru Ajia* (Tokyo: Kobunsha, 1994), pp. 36–40, 44–45.

47. Ibid., pp. 224–31; and Watanabe Shoichi, "'Ajia kyō-en ken' e no michi," in Kyu Eikan and Watanabe Shoichi, eds., *Ajia kyō-en ken no jidai* (Tokyo: PHP Kenkyūjo, 1994), pp. 169–86.

48. Etō Jun, *Hoshu to wa nani ka* (Tokyo: Bungei Shunjū, 1996), pp. 39–41.

49. Ishihara Shintaro, *Kaku are sokoku* (Tokyo: Kobunsha, 1994), pp. 108–09, 137–42.

50. Watanabe Shoichi and Komuro Naoki, *Onozukara kuni o tsubusu no ka* (Tokyo: Tokuma Shoten, 1993).

51. Yoichi Funabashi first referred to "global civilian power" in two English-language articles: "Japan and the New World Order," *Foreign Affairs*, vol. 70 (Winter 1991–92), pp. 58–74; and "Japan and America: Global Partners," *Foreign Policy*, vol. 70 (Spring 1992), pp. 24–39. He developed the concept in more detail in *Nihon no taigai kōsō: Reisen go no bijon o kaku* (Tokyo: Iwanami Shoten, 1993). Funabashi acknowledges his debt to Hanns W. Maull for originally coining the term "civilian power" in "Germany and Japan: The New Civilian Powers," *Foreign Affairs*, vol. 69 (Winter 1990–91), pp. 91–106.

52. Japanese commentators who generally support the substance of Funabashi's concept of global civilian power include Hisayoshi Ina (editorial writer for *Nihon Keizai Shimbun*), Terumasa Nakanishi (professor at Kyoto University), Shunji Taoka (editorial writer for *Asahi Shimbun*), and Jitsurō Terashima (director of the Washington, D.C., office of *Mitsui Bussan*).

53. Funabashi Yoichi, *Asia Pacific Fusion: Japan's Role in APEC* (Washington: Institute for International Economics, 1995), pp. 246–51.

54. Ibid., pp. 252–53.

55. Ina Hisayoshi, "Kokusai kankei no atarashii tenkai to Nichi-Bei anzen hosho taisei," *Gaikō Forum*, kinkyu zōkan (June 1996), pp 109–11; and Ina Hisayoshi, "A New Multilateral Approach for the Pacific: Beyond the Bilateral Security Network," Washington: Foreign Policy Institute, 1993. Ina's concept of a Pacific 5 group would encompass Australia, Canada, Japan, South Korea, and the United States. His North Pacific Security Conference would include Canada, China, Japan, North Korea, Russia, South Korea, and the United States.

56. Taoka Shunji, *Senryaku no jōken* (Tokyo: Yūhi-sha, 1994), pp. 264–70; and

Terashima Jitsurō, "'Shin-bei nyū-a' no sōgō senryaku o motomete," *Chūō kōron*, vol. 4 (March 1996), pp. 32–35.

57. Maehara Seiji, "Nihon ni dekiru bōei kyōryoku," *Voice*, no 226 (October 1996), pp. 178–87; and Maehara, "Japan's Security Policy: A Time for Realism," *Japan Digest*, December 11, 1996, p. 5. A member of the Japanese House of Representatives, Representative Maehara chairs the Democratic party (Minshutō) Security Affairs subcommittee.

58. Kiichi Miyazawa, "Kokumin no mae de yuji rongi o," *Asahi Shimbun*, May 3, 1996, p. 10.

59. Funabashi Yoichi, "Bridging Asia's Economics-Security Gap," *Survival*, vol. 36 (Winter 1996–97), pp. 112–13.

60. Terashima Jitsurō, "Nichi-bei-chū toraianguru-kuraishisu o dou seigyo suru ka," *Chūō Kōron*, vol. 9 (August 1996), pp. 37–41.

61. Kozeki Shoichi and others, "Ajia-Taiheiyo Chi-iki Ampō o kōsō suru," *Sekai*, no. 602 (December 1994), pp. 25–28.

62. Asahi Shimbun Ronsetsu I-inshitsu, ed, *Kokusai Kyōryoku to Kempō: Asahi Shimbun wa teigen suru* (Tokyo: Asahi Shimbunsha, 1995), pp. 39–46.

63. Noda Eijirō, "Jiritsu heiwa gaikō e no michi," *Sekai*, no. 630 (January 1997), p. 116. A retired career diplomat, Noda served as Japanese ambassador to India and is currently vice chairman of the Japan-China Friendship Assembly Hall (Nit-chū Yūkō Kaikan). His views certainly fall outside the mainstream thinking of the Japanese Foreign Ministry.

64. Asahi, *Kokusai Kyōryoku to Kempō*, p. 54.

65. Watanabe, Kikuchi, and Yamanouchi, *Perspective of Security Regimes in Asia-Pacific Region*, pp. 30–31.

CHAPTER THREE

The Security Environment in East Asia

Satoshi Morimoto

IN THE YEARS since the end of the cold war, international society continues to search for a new order in a context of uncertainty. The important characteristics of international society today can be understood from three perspectives.

First, with the collapse of the cold war structure and the emergence of new threats to security, most states are increasing their national power. But because they vary in their stage of development and their position in the international system, they also differ in how they are going about it. The United States is concentrating on reducing its budget deficit, reforming domestic social programs, and restructuring its defense capabilities. Most of the modern nation-states in the East Asia–Pacific region that are undergoing an industrial revolution are autocratic and tend to stress economic development, exemplifying the slogan "rich country, strong military." Finally, Africa, the Middle East, the Persian Gulf, South Asia, and Central and South America have many countries that lag behind in state development. They have governments of dubious legitimacy or political systems that are far from being democratic. Although these countries focus on maintaining their political regimes and increasing agricultural production, many are politically and economically unstable.

Second, two contrasting dynamics seem to be operating internationally. One is the tendency toward hegemonic behavior as a way of increasing national power. Some countries seek regional hegemony by pursuing a rich country, strong military strategy. Others are trying to increase their influence by exerting political, economic, and military leadership in the region. The United States clearly follows this tendency, as demonstrated by its pursuit of a strategy of enlargement—increasing the number of democracies—and engagement—maintaining a military presence and security commitments in crucial regions. The other dynamic is the development of multilateral cooperation in political-security and economic affairs. Although multilateralism is not a recent phenomenon, what is distinctive now is the progress in political-security cooperation along many dimensions. Not only the collapse of the cold war structure but also disappointment about the ineffectiveness of the United Nations in dealing with regional crises have contributed to this trend. What stands out is multilateral security cooperation at the regional level.

Third, to the extent that the world is assuming a unipolar structure centered on the United States, America's will and capacity to engage in international affairs will become even more critical to establishing and maintaining peace. Although most Americans seem interested only in domestic problems, maintaining order in East Asia in this era of uncertainty depends on U.S. leadership. And essential to the effective exercise of this leadership will be the extent to which the United States can make the most of its alliances. Unfortunately, since the cold war the rationales and objectives of these alliances have become ambiguous. Americans would like to describe them as based on common values, but alliances must serve the national interests of their respective members. They are not relationships designed to foist the values of one country on another. What, then, is the purpose of alliances now and how can they be harmonized with multilateral cooperation? These are the critical questions that confront the United States and other major powers.

With these matters in mind, I examine the security environment of the East Asia–Pacific region. In recent years peace and prosperity appear to be firmly planted. The region's economic development has been remarkable, and there have been no major conflicts since the resolution of the Cambodian conflict. No other region has developed as fast economically or displayed such stability in the 1990s. But historically, as states develop economically, they often face serious internal contradictions and also cause regional power balances to shift. These developments may make conflicts among them more likely. The East Asia–Pacific region harbors many of these potential problems.

The region also contends with residues from the cold war, exemplified by the tensions between North and South Korea and between China and Taiwan. Socialist regimes in addition to those in Pyongyang and Beijing continue to survive. Nationalism is on the rise, and some states appear to be seeking regional hegemony. China's future and problems in its neighboring areas such as the South China Sea are of critical concern. The region faces pervasive security challenges: weapons purchases from foreign countries, arms buildups as part of military modernization, territorial disputes (especially disputes over territorial sovereignty in ocean areas and resulting threats to navigational freedom), difficulties maintaining domestic stability (including observing human rights and achieving smooth transitions between regimes), and the problems related to achieving adequate food supplies, maintaining environmental integrity, and controlling energy use. Ethnic and religious conflicts mar some areas. Transitions of leadership in developmental authoritarian regimes, shifts in the regional division of labor, and patterns of economic management inherent to socialist regimes can also complicate regional economic development.

The Role of Great Powers

The manner in which the great powers (Russia, China, and the United States) are involved will be an important factor for peace and stability in the East Asia–Pacific region.

Preoccupied with its domestic political and economic disorder, Russia has been unable to develop an integrated policy toward Asia; but its will and interest in participating in matters there remains strong. Although Russia cannot help secure Asia's stability, it is to be hoped that it will not become a destabilizing factor. Russia still deploys formidable military capabilities in the Far East, including the northern territories claimed by Japan. Although its military activities in the region have subsided, it has recently commissioned an Akula-class nuclear powered attack submarine in the Far East and is continuing to deploy fourth-generation fighter aircraft. In effect, the Russian military is improving its capabilities qualitatively even while making quantitative reductions.[1]

During the past several years, major accidents—Russian forces have dumped nuclear waste in the Sea of Japan and fired at Japanese fishing vessels—have happened because of the deterioration in the discipline of

Russian Far Eastern military units. These acts pose a serious cause for concern for the other countries in Northeast Asia. And there are suspicions that Russia has provided nuclear technology to Iran, sold conventional arms to China and Malaysia, and supported the Shiite Islamic faction in the Afghanistan conflict. Perhaps the best way for the East Asian countries to deal with Russia is to encourage it to achieve domestic political stability and resolve internal conflicts such as the Chechen conflict, then to take a more active and constructive role in Asia.

China's politics and economy will have a fundamental effect on the prospects for peace in the region. The country's advances in the South China Sea, the modernization of its naval and air forces, and the development of its nuclear forces have caused some alarm among its neighbors. If more resources gained from economic development are allocated to strengthening military capabilities, China will become a threat to its neighbors.[2] Of keen interest will be its political evolution after Deng Xiaoping, especially whether Jiang Zemin can consolidate his power and exercise political leadership. The Fifteenth Chinese Communist Party Congress, scheduled for fall 1997, is likely to witness the retirement of the old guard and confirm a generational change in the leadership. Given this change, to what extent will the political influence of the People's Liberation Army expand or contract? As China sticks to its diplomatic doctrine of autonomy and independence, the future of relations with Taiwan is especially worrisome. Although China should be prevented from destabilizing the region, it is not a power than can be either contained or moved through external pressure. Therefore, rather than exclude it, the countries of the region should invite China into a variety of forums, articulate at every level their common fears and concerns regarding its activities, and give warnings and raise critical issues.

As for the United States, Americans have been engaged in a comprehensive review of their nation's diplomatic and security policies, reassessing and redefining U.S. national interests; clarifying the criteria for U.S. foreign engagement, military intervention, and participation in UN peacekeeping operations; and reexamining the responsibilities and missions of the U.S. military and the military force necessary to protect American interests. In July 1996 the Commission on America's National Interests released a report that ranked four priorities.[3] Among them was America's vital interest in preventing the emergence of a hostile, hegemonic power in either Asia or Europe. China has the potential to become just such a power. In pursuing this national interest, the report argues, maintaining strategic relationships with allies, including Japan, is important to America's security.

The absence of explicit criteria for U.S. intervention in Somalia, Haiti, Bosnia, and other troubled countries has made it difficult to mobilize public support for foreign activities. Policymakers are therefore trying to devise clear criteria for military intervention. In *American Military Intervention: A User's Guide*, released in May 1996, the Heritage Foundation suggested five criteria: intervention is necessary to protect U.S. national interests, U.S. military capabilities are suited to perform the mission, American political and military objectives can be effectively achieved, the support of Congress and the public can be obtained, and the conditions for a successful U.S. military operation can be established.[4] Concerning the function of the U.S. military, the Commission on Roles and Missions of the Armed Forces, created by Congress in November 1993, released its report in May 1995 covering integrated forces and operations among the army, navy, air force, and marines; improved air defense, missile defense, intelligence, transport, and bombing capabilities; and active support for UN peacekeeping operations and humanitarian missions.[5]

In addition to these matters, a revolution is under way that will transform U.S. military operations in the next generation.[6] Advances in electronic technologies will give information functions and operations completely new characteristics. There was a hint of this during the Persian Gulf War. U.S. satellites and AWACS planes located Iraqi Scud missiles and relayed the data instantly via space-based controls to the Patriot missile defense systems deployed in Saudi Arabia. Satellites continuously provided the U.S. ground force command in Saudi Arabia with information about enemy troop movements. Combat will increasingly involve operations that integrate ground, naval, and air forces; and even an extremely small unit may be able to affect the direction of an entire military operation.

As military units become equipped with advanced electronic weaponry, long-range missiles, and artillery with superior accuracy and firepower, combat in the sense of traditional battles will become less frequent. One example of this kind of weaponry is the recently publicized robotic warship. Known as the arsenal ship, it would have on board more than 500 large computerized missiles but would require a crew of fewer than fifty. Although it is difficult to predict whether such an advanced warship will in fact be developed, changes in military technology will change the nature of combat. A desire to maximize combat efficiency and minimize human casualties drives the development of such weapon systems.

Mobilizing popular and congressional support for lengthy military operations that may involve large numbers of casualties for American military personnel has become virtually impossible. Therefore, at the early stage of a military operation, the focus will be on checking and impeding the enemy's movements and on launching air and missile attacks. A ground operation will not commence until the likelihood of casualties has been minimized. During the Persian Gulf War, the United States carried out an intensive air campaign for the first thirty-eight days. Although 400,000 troops participated in the ground war after that, combat deaths did not exceed forty. In the case of the UN operation in Somalia, Congress began to call for the withdrawal of U.S. forces after only twenty-four combat deaths. Although there has not been a single U.S. casualty from hostile fire in the Bosnian peace operation so far, a congressional resolution calling for the withdrawal of U.S. forces would be likely if casualties were to exceed twenty. To put it differently, society's demands are accelerating the transformation of military operations.

Since the end of the cold war the United States has emphasized the pursuit of its national interests in the East Asia–Pacific region. Nevertheless, by sustaining strategic alliances and a military presence of about 100,000 troops, it appears to remain committed to preserving peace in the region.[7] This commitment is an important stabilizing force, and therefore most of the regional states welcome it.[8] But insofar as U.S. foreign policy entails a strategy of selective engagement that emphasizes U.S. national interests, America is unlikely to become a global policeman.

Stability in the region and good political and economic relations with its various states are critical to America's own prosperity and national interests. In particular, the alliance with Japan is essential. With the loss of U.S. military bases in the Philippines, the flexibility and response times of forward deployments have been affected, increasing the importance of bases in Japan. While keeping its deterrence system based on its alliance relationships intact, the United States now welcomes multilateral security dialogues with countries in the region. These forums, however, are meant to support, not replace, this deterrence network.[9]

The Korean Peninsula

The situation in the Korean peninsula continues to pose one of the most acute security problems in the region. Although stability there ultimately hinges on relations between North and South Korea, much of the current concern focuses on developments within North Korea—the direction of the Pyongyang regime's evolution (especially of Kim Jong-Il's leadership), military buildups and threatening manuevers, and economic problems (especially the food shortage). Even if Kim Jong-Il is able to consolidate his leadership, the impact of domestic economic conditions on the regime must be carefully watched. Predicting the way the North Korean regime might collapse is of course difficult. Although providing food and energy supplies may temporarily extend its life, the long-term effects of such assistance for stability in the Korean peninsula must be weighed. At the very least, one must take into account whether this aid will help the North Korean military and how it might affect U.S.–South Korean and Japanese–South Korean relations.

North Korea's light-water nuclear reactor project based on the October 1994 and June 1995 agreements with the United States should proceed under the control of the Korean Peninsula Energy Development Organization (KEDO). To ensure the success of this multilateral organization, as many countries as possible should be encouraged to help fund it. Improvements in relations with North Korea should be contingent on further clarification of suspicions that its nuclear programs have been processing spent fuel for use in developing nuclear weapons. Pyongyang's long-range missile program is also disturbing because of the threat it poses for Japan.

Given the manifold causes for concern that North Korea engenders—even while the light-water nuclear reactor project proceeds—a robust deterrence system must be maintained, especially in light of the possibility that disorder will erupt there. Security consultations and cooperation among Japan, the United States, South Korea, China, and Russia are critical. Although Japan should take steps to encourage dialogue between North and South Korea, the promotion of Japanese–North Korean relations should always give priority to Japanese relations with South Korea. The reunification of Korea has the potential to reshape the strategic configuration in Northeast Asia. It is in the interest of both Japan and the United States not to have a reunited Korea align with China. But even if the new Korea were to maintain its alliance with the United States, most of the U.S. military forces there would probably be withdrawn. What must be prevented, however, is a situation in which a reunited Korea poses a threat to Japan. Therefore, it is essential from Japan's perspective to promote security cooperation between it and South Korea *before* the reunification process moves forward.

Developing a Regional Framework

If the problems I have outlined are to be resolved satisfactorily, political stability and economic development and prosperity in the region must be maintained. Although the European practice of constructing regional institutions may ultimately work, it would not be realistic for the East Asia–Pacific region for the foreseeable future. Thus the priority should be to deal skillfully with particular destabilizing political and security factors and prevent the growth of conflicts. During the past several years, this view has been winning greater support, suggesting the emergence of a new regional consensus.

The past few years have witnessed the rapid development of a framework for discussing political-security issues in the region, beginning with an agreement at the January 1992 ASEAN (Association of Southeast Asian Nations) summit to make the ASEAN Post-Ministerial Conference the forum for exploring issues. A historic agreement was reached in July 1993 to establish the ASEAN Regional Forum (ARF). The first ARF meeting was held in July 1994 in Thailand. Brunei hosted the second in August 1995 and Indonesia the third in July 1996. Dealing with Asian political and security problems in the context of ARF is certainly a desirable development.[10] The July 1996 meeting was especially fruitful, with frank discussions on the situation in the Korean peninsula, political conditions in Myanmar, the competing territorial claims over islands and shoals in the South China Sea, nuclear tests, and banning antipersonnel land mines. Intergovernmental sessions on confidence-building measures were also held, and these talks resulted in a public declaration.[11]

In addition to ARF, there is, of course, the Asia-Pacific Economic Cooperation (APEC) process to deal with regional economic questions. The Asia-Europe Meeting (ASEM) was created to bring together Asian and European leaders, and the concepts of an East Asian Economic Caucus (EAEC) and an ASEAN Free Trade Agreement (AFTA) continue to be discussed. Although these modes of regional cooperation have as their objective the stability and prosperity of East Asia and the Pacific, it will take time for them to develop into full-fledged regional organizations. As these forums evolve, one of the more challenging tasks will be harmonizing two very different approaches to regional peace and stability: the promotion of international cooperation through multilateralism and the maintenance of a balance of power system.

To summarize, the major problems facing the East Asia–Pacific region can be grouped into three areas. First, regional development and economic growth must not become a destablizing force. For the past several years, economic growth in the region has averaged 6 to 7 percent a year, with the growth rate peaking in 1994. The real growth rate for the region surpasses that of the rest of the world. The economic development of China and the ASEAN states has been especially remarkable and has generated much interest within the region about how to build on this dynamism. The challenge will be to prevent economic development from buffeting political-security relationships. Therefore, it is terribly important that a regional framework for resolving political and security problems be constructed as soon as possible. As a precursor to such a framework, broad-ranging dialogues on political-security issues must be promoted.

Second, the root of many of the destabilizing political factors in the region lies in the underdevelopment and fragility of political and societal structures, coupled with political pluralism. Domestic problems can complicate leadership transitions and relations with other countries. China, North Korea, and Indonesia are now either undergoing or about to undergo a leadership change.[12] The evolution of Chinese politics and economics will have important implications for Sino-American relations, relations between China and Taiwan, and Hong Kong. And Russia's direction is as murky as ever. In addition, with political liberalization and the growth of the mass media, the people in many East Asian states are becoming more interested in democratization, human rights, and social welfare. This trend is likely to become a driving force in the domestic politics of many of them. Finally, nationalism has erupted in some countries and could have far-reaching effects in the international arena.

A third major problem is that most of the countries in the region are strengthening their military capabilities, and many are acquiring modern weaponry.[13] Territorial disputes in the South China Sea, on the Korean peninsula, between China and Taiwan, and elsewhere are serious and destabilizing. A number of states are trying to expand their political influence. In this dynamic the direction of China's politics and military and U.S. strategy toward East Asia will be especially critical in shaping the prospects for regional stability.

During the past several years, China has not only posted annual economic growth rates exceeding 10 percent, but has also increased its military expenditures by 15 to 20 percent a year—Beijing claims that the increase has been due to inflation. Although the breakdown of its defense budget remains unclear, China has been modernizing its naval and air forces by purchasing Russia's most advanced fighter planes and constructing a new class of warships. It has continued nuclear tests and is trying to modernize its nuclear warheads for land-based missiles and those that can be launched from nuclear submarines. As its naval and air power grows in the South China Sea, it is occupying the Spratly Islands and strengthening its operational capabilities in the area, thereby provoking concerns among most East Asia–Pacific countries. Beijing has not disavowed the possibility of using force against Taiwan and has used coercive pressure by conducting missile tests near Taiwan waters. Confident that it will become a regional superpower, China is expressing a new nationalism concomitant with its economic growth.

How to deal with China is a common concern for all countries in the region. Because only the deterrence capabilities of the United States can respond effectively to Chinese tendencies, maintaining America's presence in East Asia is critical to regional peace and stability.

Japan's Posture in the East Asia–Pacific Region

Japan has already contributed immensely to regional development by providing 60 to 70 percent of its official development assistance to East Asian countries. Economic interdependence between Japan and the newly industrializing economies in the region and the ASEAN states has expanded to such an extent that relations among these countries are now even more vital than before.

As Japan's status in international society has risen, many of the East Asia–Pacific countries are beginning to expect it to build on its economic power and exercise more political influence and leadership on behalf of regional stability and prosperity. Of course, the people of these countries have not forgotten what Japan did in Asia in the first decades of this century. Nevertheless, many believe that relations with Japan should look toward the future, not dwell on the past. Countries in Southeast Asia are especially concerned about what they perceive as dwindling American interest in relations with East Asia and the rise of China. They occasionally express their wish to let Japan respond to China. Whatever ideas the East Asia–Pacific countries may have about Japan, as a major power in the region it must become a more important force for stability.

In responding to regional expectations, Japan should ascertain its national interests and develop an appropriate policy. Its national objective in East Asia should be to become an indispensable force for promoting regional development and stability. Insofar as it shares universal values with other advanced countries, Japan may be able to take a conciliatory position among the regional countries regarding world economic matters. Although Japan's economic aid and cooperation have contributed to the region's development, it is important that such efforts be favorably evaluated by all the countries in the region as well as being in Japan's national interest. In particular, Japan must strive to make its technical assistance efforts, development assistance programs, and foreign investments a critical part of East Asia's future development.

Maintaining and strengthening the Japan-U.S. alliance will be the way Japan can become an indispensable leader in the eyes of the region. It can contribute most by sharing with the United States the values of freedom, democracy, and market economics and by cooperating on security and economic policy issues. Japan and the United States together have far greater importance than any other country in political and economic matters related to the region. U.S.-Japanese cooperation is indeed absolutely vital for regional peace and prosperity.

Japan decided to enter its alliance with the United States at the time it signed the San Francisco Peace Treaty in 1951 and agreed to the previous Japan-U.S. Security Treaty. After that it established its self-defense force and then moved to revise the original bilateral security treaty. Although at the time the new security treaty was ratified Japan experienced what came to known as the "1960 antisecurity treaty disturbance," prosperity and peace have been maintained for half a century because of the alliance. History has certainly shown that this choice was the correct one.

The Japan-U.S. alliance was important in the East Asia–Pacific region in politics, economics, and security. The security arrangements contained the Soviet threat in the Far East, and bilateral political and economic cooperation contributed to the stability of international society as a whole. The alliance also made possible Japan's postwar economic growth.

With the weakening of the military threat from the former Soviet Union, new dangers have emerged. Regional conflicts and arms proliferation are posing serious challenges to national security. The Japanese public's attitude toward security matters remains one-country pacifism. But as countries experience a harder time defining their security objectives, the view that multilateral security cooperation should be promoted is gaining popularity.[14] Although the United Nations has been unable to resolve regional conflicts effectively by itself, its peacekeeping activities have begun to be constructive. Consequently, more people in Japan are beginning to argue that the functions of the United Nations should be strengthened.

In the post–cold war security environment, many countries are reassessing their security policies. The security of individual states is becoming more deeply linked to the security of international society as a whole and the security of particular regions. Japan is no exception. Although the alliance with the United States remains the pillar of Japanese security policy, Japan must now contribute more actively not only to the peace activities of the United Nations, but also to multilateral security forums in the region. Japan is now pursuing a security policy that emphasizes both its alliance with the United States and multilateral cooperation.

Maintaining good relations with other countries in the region is therefore an important element of Japan's security policy. This objective raises the question of how to use the existing regional forums, especially APEC and ARF. Although Japan has supported these dialogues, where should it go from here? In the long term a regionwide security organization may be inevitable, but at this point a consensus does not exist in East Asia and the Pacific for establishing such an entity. Therefore, it would be better to build incrementally on the existing forums. At some point ARF could be integrated into APEC, creating a comprehensive framework to deal with economics, trade, politics, and security. As a non-ASEAN member of these dialogues, Japan can help develop a regional framework that bridges politics and economics. But for the time being, it should concentrate on collaborating with the ASEAN states to maintain regional stability and prosperity.

An agreement was reached at the second ARF meeting, held in 1995, to pursue security cooperation in three stages: confidence building, preventive diplomacy, and elaboration of approaches to conflicts. In the first stage, Japan and Indonesia are chairing the working group on confidence-building measures. Other working groups are focusing on peacekeeping operations, search and rescue efforts, and disaster relief coordination. Japan should make specific constructive recommendations in each of these sessions. For example, in terms of confidence building, it should make policies to improve transparency, such as establishing a registry for conventional arms transfers and publishing defense white papers, a priority. It should also put forward proposals to ensure safe navigation in the South China Sea, advance regional cooperation for peacekeeping operations and disaster relief, and promote security dialogues in Northeast Asia, including the Korean peninsula. Such proposals, of course, should be discussed thoroughly with the United States and the ASEAN states on a bilateral basis as well as in the context of ARF.

Notes

1. Japan Defense Agency, *Bō'ei Hakusho* (Tokyo: Okura-shō Insatsukyoku, 1996), pp. 45–55.

2. Ibid., pp. 55–62.

3. Commission on America's National Interests, *America's National Interests* (Washington, 1996).

4. Heritage Foundation, *American Military Intervention: A User's Guide* (Washington, 1996).

5. Report of the Commission on Roles and Missions of the Armed Forces, *Direction for Defense* (Government Printing Office, 1995).

6. Stephen J. Blank, "Preparing for the Next War: Reflection on the Revolution in Military Affairs," *Strategic Review*, vol. 24 (Spring 1996), pp. 17–90.

7. "Japan-U.S. Joint Declaration on Security—Alliance for the 21st Century," April 17, 1996. See the appendix for the full text.

8. Robert Scalapino, "The U.S. Commitment to Asia," in Desmond Ball, ed., *The Transformation for Security in the Asia/Pacific Region* (London: Frank Cass, 1996), pp. 68–73.

9. Commander in Chief of Pacific Forces, Testimony to the U.S. Congress (February 16, 1996).

10. Ministry of Foreign Affairs, *Gaikō Seisho* (Tokyo: Okura-shō Insatsukyoku, 1996), pp. 20–21.

11. "Declaration of the ARF Chairman," Jakarta, Indonesia, July 23, 1996.

12. Robert Scalapino, "National Political Institutions and Leadership in Asia," *Washington Quarterly* (Fall 1996).

13. For representative discussions of the military buildup see Paul Dibb, "Asia Is Strengthening Its Military Capabilities," *International Herald Tribune*, November 26, 1993, p. 6; Murai Tomohide, "Ajia wa naze gunbi kyōka o isogu no ka," *Ekonomisuto*, December 1, 1992; and Panitan Wattanayagorn and Desmond Ball, "A Regional Arms Race?" in Ball, ed., *Transformation of Security in the Asia/Pacific Region* (1996), pp. 147–74.

14. According to an opinion poll conducted jointly by the *Asahi Shimbun* and Louis Harris in late October 1995 in both the United States and Japan, the share of American respondents giving a favorable assessment of the Japan-U.S. Security Treaty had increased from 44 percent in April 1992 to 57 percent. The percentage of the Japanese respondents who believed that the bilateral pact was beneficial to Japan fell from 52 to 42 over the same period. Nevertheless, 76 percent of the Americans and 64 percent of the Japanese support maintaining the treaty.

CHAPTER FOUR

Economic Interdependence and Security in the East Asia–Pacific Region

Takuma Takahashi

ALTHOUGH most of a decade has passed since the fall of the Berlin Wall, the East Asia–Pacific region still has remnants of the cold war structure. The kind of communist regimes that have disappeared from eastern Europe still retain some power in East Asia. The influence of Russia in East Asia has been declining, but China, given its nuclear tests in 1995–96 and its missile launching in the Taiwan Strait on the eve of Taiwan's presidential election, looks as if it is aiming to establish hegemony in the region. China claims that it is simply trying to modernize its nuclear forces to acquire a secure second-strike capability before joining a comprehensive test ban regime as well as to protect its claim to Taiwan. East Asia also has nations—continental China and Taiwan, North and South Korea—that remain divided along cold war lines. The border between North and South Korea is the most fortified in the world, with a million military personnel. It is not surprising, therefore, that the security regime in the region also still reflects the cold war structure.

The East Asia–Pacific region has, however, witnessed phenomenal economic growth in the past twenty years. Growth has brought stability, and stability has brought more growth. The increasing economic interdependence among the nations in the region has strengthened regional security. Thus as Satoshi Moriomoto has pointed out in chapter 3, the concept of balance of power is by itself no longer an adequate security framework. An appropriate security structure must be eclectic and include the concept of interdependence. Views of liberals and realists must be taken together to find the real picture of the international political conditions in the region. Moreover, we need to carefully consider how much weight should be allocated to realist views and how much to liberal views to construct a workable security process. In some cases these views are consistent and complementary, but in others there are striking contradictions.[1]

Security Implications of Regional Economic Development and Interdependence

Realists looking at East Asia today see the potential for instability and conflict looming large. Some find an analogy with the situation in the nineteenth century, when the countries of Europe engaged in a series of devastating wars despite the expectation of economic growth and the increase in their interdependence that came from industrialization. The same could well happen as East Asia industrializes. However, on balance the pattern of economic growth and interdependence in the region mitigates the potential for geopolitical rivalry and conflict. The outlook for regional security is much better than realists seem to think. Nevertheless, there are still some potential security problems and challenges associated with economic development.

The East Asia model of economic growth supports stability in the region in various ways. First, the benefits of economic growth have been widely and equally distributed. Severe socioeconomic stratification was a major cause of war in nineteenth and early twentieth century Europe, as leaders engaged in external exploits to divert the attention of dissatisfied domestic social groups.[2] But East Asia's development dictators, the authoritarian leaders in the industrializing countries of the region, have adopted a policy of egalitarian or shared economic growth. The most important direct causes in this adoption were the leveling effects of World War II, the sweeping influence of American democracy, and the response to postwar revolutionary movements. Land reform promoted by the U.S. occupation army triggered Japan's egalitarian economic growth. Independent farmers were motivated to improve productivity and behave as entrepreneurs. Land reform has been achieved in other East Asian countries, the latest example being Vietnam under Doi Moi. Agricultural land reform in various countries of the region was instrumental in creating equal opportunity and triggering economic growth.[3]

Although there has been a sweeping leveling of society throughout the region since World War II, it is best to distinguish the egalitarianism in the north from that in the south. In Northeast Asia the small-farmer system began in the fourteenth century, whereas in Southeast Asia social equality has been introduced only in the past fifty years as an affirmative action against the severe division of the society and as a way to promote economic growth triggered by the agricultural sector. Thus the education system reforms in Northeast Asian countries are grounded in a long tradition. Social reforms in Southeast Asia are related to a recently acquired egalitarianism designed to mitigate racial conflict. In Malaysia, for example, conflict between native Malays (bumiptra) and overseas Chinese, who as the agents of the colonial masters had accumulated the financial and technical means to control the distribution system and other resources, led to a rebellion by the Malays in 1969.

Even China may not be an exception to this pattern. After the Cultural Revolution left the rural areas exhausted and widely disaffected with the Communist party, Deng Xiaoping's agricultural reforms and promotion of village enterprises led to dramatic economic progress. This progress generated great support for Deng among the rural people and allowed him to stick to his overall program of reforming and opening up China's economy even as it began to create imbalance between the urban and rural sectors.

A second difference in circumstances between East Asia and nineteenth century Europe is that now the economic costs of war far outweigh the benefits. At the same time, the benefits of pursuing economic growth through peaceful, nonaggressive means are great. Today's East Asian countries have expectations of faster future economic growth than their counterparts in Europe a century ago. The industrialization of Europe proceeded slowly. The agricultural population declined only gradually, taking more than a hundred years to fall below 20 percent of the total population.[4] By contrast Japan exhausted its agricultural labor in fifty years and South Korea did so in twenty-five.[5] The speed of transformation and economic growth was possible because of East Asia's access to the stock of technologies, its ability to create new technologies, and phenomenal trading opportunities. East Asian economies, especially Southeast Asian countries and the southern part of China, became major exporters of a variety of home electronic products because of the flood of foreign direct investment they received from other parts of East Asia. As these areas have acquired technologies and marketing skills, they have established their own technological development bases and marketing channels for exports.

The increasing volume of East Asian trade makes a striking contrast to the growth in merchandise trade when European countries experienced their greatest military conflicts. For the period 1870 to 1913, the average annual growth rate of real world trade was 3.4 percent (3.2 percent for Europe). From 1985 to 1994 real world trade increased about 1.7 times (6 percent a year) and trade volume in the East Asian region (excluding Japan) increased almost fivefold.[6] Countries that enjoy growing prosperity brought about by peaceful exchange are not about to seek prosperity by appropriating another's territory. Against the general belief that today's prosperity is generated from international trade and investment, it is unlikely that a government would start a war to seek prestige or score other gains.

A third difference is that the pattern of stratified economic growth, which is growth at different rates, in East Asia should lead each country to economic maturity in a way that does not create friction with others. The ultimate end of the growth will be the convergence of all nations in the region to the standards enjoyed by industrialized economies. East Asian countries will develop a horizontal and vertical division of labor like that achieved in the European Union. A horizontal division of labor, or intrasector trade among countries emphasizing production in similar economic sectors, is a product of the society that emerges with the formation of an affluent middle class. A vertical division of labor, or intersector trade, was characteristic of Europe early in the century. It would have been unthinkable for a German to choose to buy a French-made car while a Frenchman bought a German-made car. In the framework of the horizontal division of labor, affluent democracies do not have incentives to fight each other, although they do have incentives to capture the tastes of people in neighboring countries.

It is certainly in Japan's national interest to be surrounded by prosperous and peaceful countries rather than by poor and unstable ones. The per capita GNP of the newly industrialized economies (NIEs) has already reached the standard of the member countries of the Organization for Economic Cooperation and Development, and the era of Japan's being the only industrial country in Asia has ended. South Korea is now not only a leader in such industries as steel, iron, and shipbuilding but also one of the world's most competitive producers of microchips. Using its position as the leading assembler of personal computers, Taiwan has developed a world-class electronics and software industry. East Asia has an integrated network for selling parts, mostly to Japanese multinational corporations, built on the foundation of investment in parts production and assembly facilities. A horizontal division of labor has already formed in such electronics products as color televisions and videos; Japanese imports of these products have increased. These developments indicate that economic integration will deepen.[7]

However, for the time being East Asia's growth pattern will continue to have four strata. Each layer comprises countries with similar levels of per capita GNP that took off ten to fifteen years after the countries in the previous stratum (figure 4-1): Japan took off first, followed by the NIEs, the ASEAN-4, and finally China. An advantage of this pattern is that countries in one stratum can look to those in the previous stratum to find successful policies and appropriate models to adopt. They can thus shorten their development time. Another advantage is that the economies are complementary to, or at least not highly competitive with, each other because their industrial structures vary according to their stage of development (a vertical division of labor). This pattern also tends to allow countries to enjoy absolute gains.

Since China added the fourth stratum by reforming its socialist economic system, socialist Vietnam has joined ASEAN, which was originally an anticommunist organization. Today, the region is experiencing a reverse domino effect, belying the cold war fear that communism would spread throughout East Asia. In Europe the core economies have failed to incorporate in their growth structure the peripheral, former communist countries, which are smoldering in civil war and ethnic strife.

The stability of East Asia's stratified growth depends on the expectations of the region's countries, especially those in the lower strata. Vietnam seems to have accepted its place in the fifth stratum, but other countries could be less willing to conform. An extreme case might be North Korea, which has yet to join the East Asian economic growth spiral. With a per capita GNP less than one-tenth that of South Korea, North Korea feels a desperate need to catch up to avoid being engulfed by its rival, as was East Germany. This desperation has led it to demand face-saving concessions while accepting aid from the United States and Japan. North Korea's recent threat to develop nuclear weapons is the same coercive brinksmanship that it used in negotiations with the Soviet

Figure 4-1. *Asian Countries' Stages of Economic Development Compared with Japan and South Korea, 1995*[a]

Per capita GDP, U.S. dollars

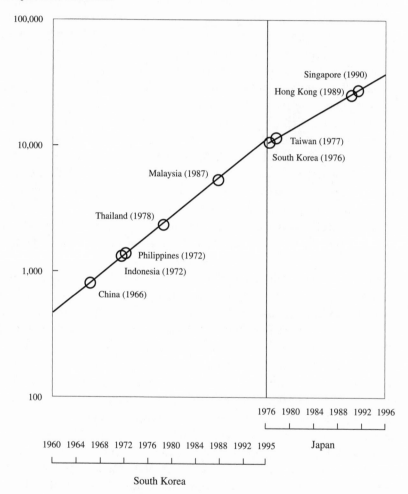

Source: Nomura Research Institute.
a. U.S. GNP deflator used to translate Japanese and Korean historical per capita GDP to 1995 prices.

Union and China during the cold war. To maintain regional stability, East Asian countries that are more economically advanced should help their less developed neighbors so that a sharp decline in expectations of future growth or excessive expectations do not lead to aggressive behavior.

A fourth factor supporting stability in East Asia is the attitude of the developing economies toward the developed ones. East Asian economies emphasize maintaining good relations with the developed economies to ensure continued growth through access to new technologies and markets. The region is not burdened by the anticolonial movements and conflicts that have plagued other developing regions. Instead, it is now trying to induce direct investment from the developed economies. This is sharply different from the time when developing countries were driven by the theory of dependence. G. A. O'Donnell demonstrated the limitations of an economic development plan based on import substitution with the experiences of Brazil and Argentina.[8] In both countries economic development came to a halt when import substitution had progressed to a certain level. At that point the military, bureaucrats, and technicians formed a bureaucratic-authoritarian government that sought protectionism.

East Asian economies adopted more liberal policies based on openness and interdependence. They recognize that they can acquire advanced technologies through trade, direct investment, and foreign aid even if they cannot develop them indigenously. Their capacity to absorb new technologies will increase as they accumulate management know-how and improve their educational systems and infrastructure. They are willing to spend funds on development and applied research to create differentiated products and to produce efficiently. Foreign direct investment flows encourage indigenous labor to stay at home, which helps each country to accumulate production skills and strengthen its competitiveness.

As East Asian countries seek access to new technology in developed countries, competition from these developing economies has led the industrial countries to try to protect their advanced technologies by strengthening intellectual property rights and taking other measures. These actions have not stopped the transfer of technology, however, because multinational companies continue to invest in the developing economies as long as they present new opportunities, and these investments bring new technologies. Improvements in information and telecommunications systems as well as the migration of scientists and engineers will facilitate the continued diffusion of technology. Thus the network among the developed and the developing economies will strengthen economic interdependence.

This interdependence has been further facilitated by the Asia-Pacific Economic Cooperation (APEC) promotion of foreign direct investment and trade. When China tried to use access to its markets to attract more direct investment, the other East Asian countries responded through the APEC forum to include China in APEC's regional liberalization program. To confront the challenge posed by China's huge markets, the members of ASEAN agreed on a brand-to-brand complementation policy in which industrial products, including automobile parts, produced in different ASEAN countries, move freely among member countries. Thus the countries would become more attractive to foreign multinational corporations. The countries recently integrated complementation policy and extended the concept in the ASEAN Industrial Cooperation Policy (AICO). Thus they have come to learn that economic openness and regional interdependence can be a force to protect the common economic interests of all countries in the region.

In a fifth difference with nineteenth century Europe, the flexible financial market mechanisms in East Asia are much more conducive to international stability than the gold standard. The modern fluctuating exchange rate system mitigates competition among nations and regions, and contemporary international financial markets provide access to outside funds and impose outside control. East Asian countries that have high per capita incomes tend to have lower inflation rates than those with low per capita incomes (figure 4-2). This difference is due not so much to countries' abilities to control inflation but to preferences regarding how much to protect the standard of living that they have already attained. Lower-income countries, with underdeveloped fiscal systems, have greater incentives to use the inflation tax (or simply print money) as a source of public revenue. Countries that have lower per capita incomes also tend to accommodate higher inflation so that they can gain a competitive edge over other countries. However, official development assistance loans or external debt provide incentives not to accommodate higher inflation and to keep the liability from inflating due to currency depreciation.

Under the gold standard, mechanisms such as the inflation tax and Office of Development Assistance (ODA) loans were not available. To accumulate capital, European countries had to seek opportunities to exploit their colonies. The United Kingdom's huge current account sur-

Figure 4-2. *Inflation and Economic Development, 1982–94*[a]

Inflation rate (percent)

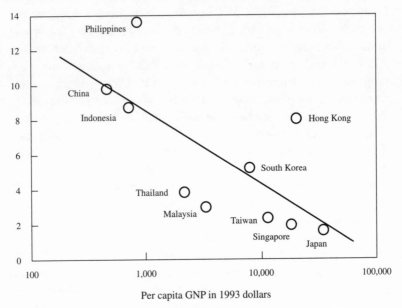

Per capita GNP in 1993 dollars

Source: Nomura Research Institute.
a. Inflation rate shows 1982–94 average annual increase in CPI.

pluses or external investments, which fluctuated between 3 and 7 percent of GNP, simply reflected the difference between haves and have nots. At the start of World War I, the size of the German economy had surpassed that of the United Kingdom although Germany owned 13 percent of the total stock of overseas investments compared with Britain's 43 percent. This disparity is believed to have driven the two countries to war.

The rigid exchange rate of the gold standard also aggravated the rivalry between Germany and the United Kingdom. In 1885 trade between the two countries was more or less balanced, but Germany ran a trade surplus of DM 150 million in 1900, and its surplus increased to DM 560 million in 1913, probably because of the difference in the industrial structures of the two countries.[9] Despite such a marked trade imbalance, the currency exchange rate was fixed under the gold standard. In contrast, the modern flexible system has allowed the yen-dollar exchange rate to appreciate more than 100 percent as the trade imbalance between the United States and Japan expanded from 1971 to 1995.

A sixth factor supporting stability in the East Asia region is the improvements in industrial technology and commercial markets. The technologies of the nineteenth century were heavy consumers of materials and energy. Competition for natural resources led to international conflict as countries tried to make themselves invulnerable to outside economic and political pressure. In comparison, electronics and other industrial technologies today are energy saving and resource efficient. Furthermore, better-organized markets and more smoothly functioning price mechanisms reduce the chance of severe political competition or military confrontation among countries in quest of energy and new markets.

Even so, the need for energy and natural resources has the potential to cause regional instability. Consider what could happen if China were to face a food or power shortage that threatened its economic development. But the potential for instability would be considerably reduced if China could satisfy its food and energy demands through trade. Then it would not feel the need to conquer new territory.

The last argument for regional stability is that the strength of territorial claims in East Asia is much weaker than in nineteenth century Europe. Before European colonial domination of the region, East Asia had not known the concept of territoriality, especially with regard to the periphery. For example, when fifty-four Ryukyuans were killed in Taiwan in 1871, an official of the Qing dynasty told a Japanese diplomat that the Taiwanese people were "outside of civilization" and so the emperor would not punish them.[10] In most of East Asia, borders have been drawn according to the Western mode, but some areas remain untouched. There are at least fifteen maritime, border, or island sovereignty disputes on-going in the region. These could result from the absence of a concept of exclusive territory until recent times. Many of these disputes involve China, but at least five are among ASEAN countries.[11] In any case, East Asians appear willing to subsume the issue of sovereignty, at least for territory in peripheral areas, in the expectation of joint development. Japan has been following this concept since it successfully applied to the former Soviet Union to negotiate an exclusive economic zone for fishery rights.

Recently, it has become more difficult for Japan to carry out this strategy.[12] Increased nationalism has led some East Asian countries to seek advantage over others. There have been more and more claims and counterclaims under the Law of the Sea, which defines the sovereignty of the continental shelves. But while nationalism is fanning territorial disputes, the region has begun to develop the institutions to resolve or control them. China had long refused to join multilateral discussions on territorial issues. Nevertheless, through the ASEAN Regional Forum the ASEAN states persuaded it to come to the negotiating table to discuss the soveriegnty of the Spratly Islands, a regional flash point because of potential deposits of minerals and oil. The cooperative framework of APEC and the deterrent effect of the U.S. presence help to keep China from bullying smaller countries in the region.

Despite all the arguments that interdependence and economic growth mean stability rather than instability, the development of East Asia still presents problems for regional security. Some problems arise from increased energy demands; others arise from democratization as East Asian economies achieve high growth.

Energy and Security

Kent Calder contends that potential international conflict over energy resources will emerge as continued economic growth in East Asia increases energy consumption by improving living standards, concentrating people in cities, and causing a general energy shortage.[13] I do not agree. The imbalance of demand and supply will not be so severe as Calder predicts, and territorial disputes in the Spratly Islands and elsewhere will not materialize. The International Energy Agency (IEA) expects the oil-equivalent per capita consumption of energy to grow to 1.1 tons in China and 1.2 tons in East Asia as a whole by 2010.[14] Nearly half the increase in the world's future energy consumption will be in East Asia. However, East Asia's projected 550 million oil-equivalent tons of additional energy consumption will not cause a shortage because innovations in oil drilling techniques and the operation of new oil fields in the North Sea and central Asia will expand petroleum production. Nevertheless, I do share Calder's view that both the United States and Japan, which are the two largest oil importers and have a common interest in maintaining a stable global economic and political climate, should carefully monitor such potentially divisive regional energy-related issues as the security of sea lanes, environmental degradation, and nuclear proliferation.

Rather than the adequacy of global energy supplies, the acute problem is East Asia's growing dependence on the Middle East to meet its energy demands. For instance, Japan imports 70 percent of its oil from this region, and South Korea imports 80 percent.[15] Even China now relies on the Middle East for more than half its oil imports. The political situation of the Middle East is uncertain. Many of the oil-producing Persian Gulf countries have feudal regimes that maintain their political legitimacy through distribution of their oil revenues. But some of these states are now running short of these revenues and may encounter domestic political conflict unless they undergo thorough political reforms.[16] In addition conflicts could easily flare up between Iran and Iraq or Israel and its Arab neighbors.

The heavy reliance on Middle Eastern oil by Northeast Asian countries, including Taiwan, also poses a problem of ensuring the security of oil import routes and sea lanes. Thus the territorial dispute over the Spratly Islands demands attention not only because of potential energy deposits in the South China Sea but also because of the need to maintain safe maritime passage. Joint naval patrols by the United States and Japan, as proposed by Michael O'Hanlon in chapter 6, would serve not only to deter large-scale aggression but also to demonstrate the solidarity of the two principal maritime powers of the region. China's agreeing to discuss the Spratlys was certainly a positive development.

The alternatives to Middle Eastern oil have their own problems. Pollution, particularly for China, is one. China is likely to fill its current 20 percent shortfall in electrical output by burning more coal. According to an International Energy Agency estimate, China's carbon dioxide emissions will double between 1990 and 2010. The increase of 27 billion tons will almost equal the incremental emissions of all OECD countries.[17] Asia's share of world carbon dioxide emissions will climb from one-fifth to one-third. Air pollution from China and neighboring countries will affect Japan's environment; and the increase in carbon dioxide emissions will accelerate the global warming process.

China and other developing countries blame the environmental deterioration on the massive energy consumption of developed countries and argue that they have the right to develop their economies. Nevertheless, if China is to continue its economic growth, it must realize savings in terms of energy consumption per GNP.[18] In both Taiwan and Japan economic growth was stymied for a time by environmental problems. The current situation in China is no better than that Taiwan faced some years ago. When China's per capita income reaches a level that would support widespread motorization, it is hard to envision this occurring unless the gasoline engine were replaced by a more efficient, less polluting power source. Through its official development assistance programs, Japan has provided China with desulfurization equipment for coal thermal power and it has applied to sell relatively simple environmental systems. The United States could also provide instruction in oil drilling techniques and coal liquefaction technologies.

China's continued economic growth will inevitably require some technological breakthrough in energy generation by the developed economies, and it must learn to seek advice from them. With the initiative of Germany and the northern European countries Europe has succeeded in undertaking collective action to alleviate regional environmental problems. It is likewise appropriate for Japan to advocate an Asian initiative to integrate the region's various efforts to improve the environment. Such a program could be modeled on Germany's 30 Percent Club to reduce sulphur oxide emissions in both west and east European countries.

Nuclear power generation may be a more attractive option than burning coal, but of course it has its own problems. The Chinese government is pinning a lot of hope on nuclear power to meet its energy needs. So are other East Asian countries. Although the developed nations plan to reduce reliance on nuclear power, East Asian countries have plans for nuclear generation plants throughout the region. Nuclear power appears more attractive than other alternatives for developing economies. High-quality, safe facilities could be provided by a nuclear power plant consortium consisting of American and Japanese firms, but it is inevitable that East Asian countries will rely heavily on cheaper, domestically developed nuclear power generation.

In addition to safety, the region's enthusiasm for nuclear power generation raises the danger of nuclear proliferation. Civilian and military uses of nuclear energy are linked at two critical points in the nuclear fuel cycle: the uranium enrichment process and reprocessing of the spent uranium. Reprocessing generates plutonium, which forms the core of a nuclear bomb.

Although Japan has made it clear to the public that it has no intention of pursuing the military applications of nuclear power, other countries may still suspect its intentions. Ratification of the Nuclear Non-Proliferation Treaty was by itself a clear sign that Japan has no intention to become a nuclear power. To clarify its position further, Japan should take the initiative to establish PACATOM, a regional nuclear energy organization similar to Euratom in Europe, to ensure safety and promote security.[19]

Expansion of the Korean Energy Development Organization's function to the East Asian region, as the Philippines has advocated, might be another option for PACATOM. Because the most urgent security matter facing the region is the future of the Korean peninsula, where the interests of the United States, Russia, China, and Japan intersect, the expansion of KEDO could be a good starting point for reducing the level of tension.

Although the Geneva Agreement has provided the basis for defusing potential confrontation over the North Korean nuclear program, fundamental difficulties in how to address the geopolitical problems of the peninsula will remain with or without reunification. Korea was the battlefield of East Asia in the nineteenth century and it became the first battlefield of the cold war. Moreover, under the Strategic Arms Reduction Treaty, Russia has to dismantle more than 2,000 nuclear weapons a year, generating a flow of both enriched uranium and plutonium. Therefore PACATOM should include, among other countries, the United States, Russia, China, and North and South Korea. It should address such problems as establishing standards that are higher than those of the International Atomic Energy Agency, cooperating on the storage and management of spent fuel, establishing a system to recycle waste, and promoting joint energy efficiency and resource development projects to alleviate a possible energy shortage.

Democratization and Security

In addition to energy-related issues, East Asian countries face the difficult problems of transitional democracy. The strong performance of the economies in the region will inevitably bring the democratization of their political systems. Democracy should be encouraged to promote security: no democracies have ever fought a war against each other, given reasonably restrictive definitions of democracy and of war.[20]

However, examining European development in the past two centuries, many people have pointed out the limits of this statement and the subjectivity of the concept of "democratic peace."[21] The idea of democratic peace is formulated in terms of two concepts: norms and checks and balances.[22] In mature democratic states, acceptable means to resolve conflict include adjudication and bargaining; the use of force is to be avoided.[23] Checks and balances mean that ex ante and ex post constraints operate on renegade leaders.[24] Not satisfied with these explanations, Henry Farber and Joanne Gowa undertook a statistical analysis of the correlation between wars and polities and found that democratic peace is a phenomenon that emerged only after World War II.[25] I contend that the absence of military conflict between mature democracies results from the horizontal division of labor brought about through trade among affluent economies. This conforms with the conclusion of Farber and Gowa. However, while they focus on the coincidence of peace with the cold war political regime, I focus on economic causality.

Political analysts suggest that countries in the transitional phase of democratization become more aggressive and prone to war because their political systems are not yet equipped with appropriate norms and checks and balances. Some assert that these governments are even more aggressive than authoritarian governments. Economic development in East Asia will inevitably bring political development, and the transition to democracy could be a difficult process with the potential to cause problems in international security.

Why is the likelihood of war increased during democratization? Edward Mansfield and Jack Snyder contend that although well-institutionalized democracies place ultimate authority in the hands of the average citizen, a transitional democratic government may not have control over foreign policy and may tend to expose its country to the risk of preventive wars based on the narrow interests of a group of privileged people.[26] The authors attributed Japan's propensity for aggression in the early twentieth century to the fact that although the electoral franchise was widened in the Taisho period, the choice of who would govern was left to the oligarchs who had founded the Meiji state.

If ultimate authority is in the hands of the average citizen, who bears the costs of war, nations virtually never fight each other. Among transitional democracies, Mansfield and Snyder found that democratization was least likely to lead to imprudent aggression where the old elites saw a reasonably bright future for themselves in the new social order. For example, nineteenth-century British aristocrats with their wealth invested in commerce and industry had many common interests with the rising middle classes, while Germany's Junker land-owning elite had a stake in using state-backed protectionism and political repression to maintain social position. Britain remained relatively peaceful while Germany became an aggressor.

In virtually every East Asian country, economic development has been achieved under a more or less authoritarian government. Democratization has been characterized by the gradual relaxation of this development dictatorship. Just as the countries fall into different strata according to economic development, they also manifest different levels of democratization. This indicates that there is a trade-off between governability and democracy during economic development.

Perhaps the key relationship in this political development is the one between the formation of a middle class and democratization. East Asia's egalitarian industrialization took place in the absence of old elites (although socialist countries have their own party and military elites). Having the common goal of egalitarian economic growth, development dictators paid close attention to the interests of the average citizen. Their political constituency changed from farmers to middle-class urban businessmen as economic development proceeded. Ascendance of the middle class in a society will create the demand for more democratic institutions. One advantage of a stratified growth pattern is that democratization progresses gradually. But development dictators often overstay their welcome. For example, Lee Kuan Yu's strong control was very successful in leading Singapore to surpass its onetime suzerain, the United Kingdom, in per capita GNP. But he and his successors continue to wield tight control over people's behavior, driving many Singaporeans from the prosperous island to seek greater personal freedom. Likewise, Indonesia's Suharto has retained political power too long after his contribution to his country's economic success. Even while enjoying less poverty and higher per capita incomes, the Indonesian people have become fed up with Suharto's paternalistic dictatorship and his corrupt government, especially the influence of Suharto family-related besinesses. They recently mounted a first, though unsuccessful, attempt to end his rule.

The end of the cold war promoted democratization in East Asia. The political impact of democratization depended to a large extent on a country's level of economic development: the greater the development, the greater the impact. But television, the revolution in information technology, and a global economy have introduced additional factors. Today, political events in developing countries are witnessed by the rest of the world as they unfold. This often results in outside influences on the progress of democratization.[27]

In Japan the end of the cold war provided the conditions for ending the monopoly power the Liberal Democratic party had held since 1955. Political scientists Junnosuke Masumi and Robert Scalapino once referred to this situation as the "one and a half party system," but it is better described as a bureaucratic monopoly of policymaking. Since the collapse of the Miyazawa cabinet in July 1993, Japan has had four prime ministers who have each tried to chart a new national direction by reclaiming the politicians' function in policymaking from the bureaucrats.

Among the second-stratum countries Singapore held its first democratic presidential election in 1993. Although president Ong Tengcheong was duly elected, a significant number of voters voiced their criticism of the government. Lee Kuan Yew, the founder of the nation, stepped down as a senior minister and became a target of criticism in Singapore's media, which had previously been strictly controlled.

South Korea also belongs to the second stratum. Kim Young Sam became its first genuinely civilian president since the Park regime took power in a military coup in 1960. In many ways South Korea's new party system is like Japan's under the Liberal Democratic party. President Kim has aggressively urged the prosecution of two former presidents for treason, although some might view this cynically as just a form of political grandstanding. But South Korea has successfully evolved with a minimum of violence from being a military dictatorship to operating under a democratically elected civilian government.

Countries in the third economic stratum may be able to follow the South Korean path, as recent developments in Thailand, the Philippines, Malaysia, and Indonesia suggest. Between 1980 and 1991 military coups were almost annual events in Thailand, with eight successful takeovers and seven abortive attempts.[28] The concept of *tham* (social equity) that pervaded the rural population was a powerful force in Thai politics, giving support to successful coups against corrupt governments. In 1981, however, Thailand introduced a system of government-industry dialogues known as K-R-O, which reflected the drift from *tham* as the economy changed from one based on agriculture to one with expanding export industries. A Thai urban middle class emerged. Meanwhile the military has been kept weak but happy. In this new social and political context, military coups have become difficult to stage, and the election system seems to have taken firm hold. Since the failure of a coup in 1991, the country appears to be moving toward genuinely democratic politics, as attested by successful elections in 1992, 1995, and 1996.

In the Philippines, land reform has been considered a starting point of economic development and democratization. But reform was prevented for many years because public policy was dominated by the interests of a narrow elite under the regime of Ferdinand Marcos. The United States helped the Philippines expel Marcos and establish President Corazon Aquino. Since the election of Fidel Ramos in 1992, the Philippines seems to be on the track to economic development and democratization. There are finally signs that land reform might materialize and the guerrilla activities of leftists will cease. Because the constitution forbids the reelection of the president, Ramos announced he will step down after his current six-year term, although his supporters are trying to amend the constitution to allow a second term.

Malaysia has its own succession problem as Prime Minister Mahathir Mohamad approaches the age of seventy. Malaysia differs from other Southeast Asian states in that the presidential election system of the ruling United Malays National Organization is open. Although Tunku Razaleigh Hamzah, who recently returned to the UMNO, could be a wild card as successor to Mahatir, Anwar Ibrahim, the party's vice president, remains heir apparent.

In Indonesia, questions about President Suharto's health have also raised the issue of political succession. Street demonstrations in 1996 in response to the government's suppression of opposition forces have signaled that the transfer of power after more than thirty years of dictatorship will be far from smooth. Megawati Sukarnoputri, the strongest potential opposition candidate, was forced to drop her candidacy. And the rigidity of the presidential election system prevents the popular election of a new president. But although the military retains considerable influence, the private sector and the bureaucracy have gained overwhelming influence in recent years. In particular, business leaders and bureaucrats maintain good relations with young officers of the so-called Magellan generation. The Indonesian military made the unusual announcement that there would be no coup d'état after Suharto retires, but the struggle for power has intensified among the military leaders, as indicated by unusual riots against Indonesians of Chinese origin. Nevertheless, the expectation in Indonesia is that Suharto will try to exert his influence on the nomination of his successor, and the transfer of power will take place in conformity with the current election system. Indonesia will need more time to make a transition from military dictatorship to presidents who are former military officers to genuine civilian leaders.

China belongs to the fourth stratum of economic development. Given its immense size and central geopolitical position, the evolution of its politics will have profound implications for regional security. Although China's aggressive military behavior on the eve of Taiwan's presidential election raised doubts about whether the civilian communist leaders really control the military, the recently passed national defense legislation appears to formalize civilian control. With the departure of Deng Xiaoping, Chinese leaders will jockey for position and influence. But President Jiang Zemin has been in power for seven years, and Chinese politics has shown considerably less overt friction than it did with the succession to Mao. As the National People's Congress gains more influence, even China may move steadily toward democracy. Promotion of a non-Communist party member, Rong Yiren, to the state vice presidency and the emergence of a multicandidate system in the third-tier election for the National People's Congress may herald both a bicameral system and multiparty politics for China.

East Asian countries are bound to meet unexpected events and incur setbacks during democratization. There is little that the developed countries can do except to create incentives to form ruling coalitions that will promote democratization. Especially for China, whose democratization may occur in the context of sharply expanding economic ties to the West, the steadiness of the Western commercial partnership and security presence is likely to be extremely important in shaping the incentives of protodemocratic coalition politics.

By the same token, the West's interest in human rights should be asserted at appropriate times and through appropriate channels to give other incentives to China. The Japanese do not accept the notion of "Asian values" that was put forth by the development dictators of East Asia in response to the West's demand for instant democratization. The Japanese also share with the West a belief in the universality of human rights. The ideal of human rights is, however, fragile unless it is supported by adequate living standards. As demonstrated in Taiwan and South Korea, democratic political systems emerge in the context of economic and social maturation and the institution of market economies. To facilitate this process, the advanced industrial democracies, especially Japan and the United States, should promote the emergence of a strong middle class by helping to sustain economic development and by encouraging the younger generation to hope for a better government.

Democratization can, however, increase international tension. The direct popular election of the Taiwan president in the spring of 1996 symbolized a new era in Chinese as well as Taiwanese history. The aspirations of many Taiwanese for national independence that accompanied Taiwan's democratization alarmed the Chinese regime into making threatening missile launches in the Taiwan Straits. As long as the internationally acknowledged concept of "one China" prevails, democratic elections in Taiwan will not lead to the birth of a new nation.

Deeper East Asian regional economic interdependence will help the cause of regional security. Thus economic development will follow a path distinct from that of Europe in the nineteenth century. Nevertheless, uncertainties and problems, especially those associated with China, remain as a challenge to security.

Bringing China into the International System

Liberals and realists view the development of East Asia in different ways, and this leads to different perceptions of security. Realists would find the argument that economic development leads to greater security and democratization too optimistic because it leans too heavily on liberal ideas. First, liberals tend to view lean and hungry countries as more dangerous, while realists focus concern on prosperous countries because of their capability to build up their military muscle. Liberals reason that war is always motivated by economics and rarely by prestige. Realists find in normal economic development the dangers of an imbalance of power. Second, because liberals emphasize the importance of international economic cooperation in increasing national wealth and deemphasize the traditional search for added state power as a sensible national objective, they consider that the interdependence brought about by East Asian development will improve the chances for maintaining peace. Realists often point out that greater interdependence can produce political friction as well as amity and can increase the chance of conflict among countries in the quest for wealth. Third, realists more often emphasize that the direction of development in China is uncertain because of its extraordinary size and its position on the fourth stratum. For this reason, I now turn to analyze the security situation with respect to China separately from developments in the rest of the region.

What China has achieved since the mid-1970s is phenomenal. In late 1978 it adopted a reform and open door policy that has allowed it to begin integrating with the global economy and, internally, move toward a market economy. It achieved an economic growth rate of 9.5 percent a year from 1979 to 1995, the highest in the world.[29] Regulation of the economy has been relaxed to a great extent. The share of retail products with market-determined selling prices has increased from 3 percent in 1978 to about 95 percent in 1994. In the same period the share of agricultural product prices under government control decreased from 94 percent to 12 percent. In the industrial sector, state enterprises' share of production has decreased from 80 percent in 1978 to 34 percent in 1995.[30] China has become an increasingly open economy. Its trade volume now exceeds 30 percent of GNP. In just a few years it has accepted foreign direct investment flows almost equivalent to Japan's total accumulation of inward foreign investment during the past fifty years.

Many observers contend that China has already passed the point of no return on the way to becoming a market economy. But despite its success in privatization and the extent to which the economy operates under market forces, the reform of state-owned enterprises will be particularly difficult because these represent not only China's core businesses, but also because they have to honor their commitments to their employees. The state enterprises provide pensions, medical insurance, and other benefits for privileged employees and their families. Institutional reform would require terminating these contracts and replacing them with contracts between the state and individuals, including unemployment insurance. Tax reform was the first step in implementing this plan, but it will take some time to complete.

China's institution of a so-called socialist market economy has brought with it many contradictions. Uneven income distribution has become a threat to the stability of the society. Although 8 percent of Chinese now enjoy an affluent standard of living, another 8 percent are farmers whose income is less than one-fiftieth of those in the top 8 percent.[31] It is true that migration within the country narrows the income gap between the coastal and inland areas: remittances of migrants to their home provinces are not reflected in the provincial GDP statistics. It is also true that the government has tried to stimulate investment in inland areas by applying the flying geese model.[32] But a major discrepancy in income distribution remains.

Apparently there are political limits to how wide the urban-rural income disparity can be allowed to grow. As a development dictator, the Chinese government has to pay attention to its political constituency. Because China will remain an agricultural society for the foreseeable future despite the success of industrialization, the Chinese Communist party leaders should be careful not to provoke rebellion among the peasants, many of whom resent those who have become rich. This realization was behind the party's recent efforts to deal with food shortages and its decision to increase the government budget allocation to rural areas. This concern also motivated the reform of the three-tier electoral system for choosing the party congress. At the village and town level, multiple candidates are now permitted, and competitive elections for village-level officials are being held in four-fifths of Chinese villages.[33]

But how should the government respond to the needs of people in higher income strata and the participants in rapid economic growth? It has become increasingly difficult for the government to respond to the diversified needs of its populace from the rigid platform of the monopolistic Communist party. At the same time, allowing a pluralistic political system would undermine the power of the party.

Communism has completely lost its ideological value among the people. A substitute could be nationalism, which the party fanned at the Sixth Chinese Communist Party Assembly, but encouraging a nationalist ideology might promote dangerous subnationalism in Tibet, Xinjiang, and other restive areas. It could also encourage Chinese ruling elites to pursue excessively narrow and short-run nationalistic interests that might appeal to the masses. Lack of strong leadership can let these kinds of parochial interests run out of control, as they did in bullying Taiwan with provocative military exercises and missile tests in 1995–96.[34] Engaging in territorial disputes and recognizing historical events of national significance, such as Japan's aggression in China during World War II and the ideological dispute with India, tend to aggravate China's relations with its neighbors.

China is struggling to achieve the proper balance between its continental interests and its maritime interests. The continental interests stem from its territorial situation: its border with Russia and Mongolia, the national aspirations in Tibet and Xinjiang, and its rivalry with India. Considering these continental interests, accommodating Taiwan's independence is unthinkable. As a continental state China feels the need to exert its prestige over bordering countries, just as the Middle Kingdom did in the old days. In other words, China's preferred tactic of protecting its continental interests is to command respect and obeisance through patronage and preponderant power.

Despite these problems, China's interests in world trade and in protecting its coastal waters have had the greatest influence on its current situation. Since 1978 these interests have led the government to modernize its economy, society, and institutions by pursuing an omnidirectional foreign policy. China has come to acknowledge itself as an Asian country rather than as the champion of the third world. But if it pursues maritime interests exclusively, focusing on modernizing its economy and society, it will inevitably come under the influence of a catching-up mentality, a kind of inferiority complex, that might collide with the national prestige it derives from its sense of itself as the Middle Kingdom.

Historically, China's continental interests have caused it to focus on its capacity to resist foreign aggression. It has developed an autarchic economic structure not only at the national level but also at the provincial level. It has emphasized the capability of the army rather than that of navy. Reform and the open door policy brought changes to its economic structure, including a new division of labor. Where the Chinese economy was once simply a conglomeration of discrete peripheral economies isolated from each other, under the reform program it is being remodeled into a single national economy by mergers and consolidations and other rationalization measures. Thus the move to an open market economy has brought a new division of labor in China. As a result China has become more sensitive to its maritime interests. However, when it considers itself as a marine power, it perceives that it is surrounded by hostile nations. To free itself from this feeling, China is building up its naval capability and its short-range missiles on the expectation that it might become engaged in a local, high-technology, Persian Gulf–type war.[35] Furthermore, rather than negotiate with ASEAN, it has tried to establish bilateral relations with countries in the region. Chinese leaders have from time to time visited those countries. Jiang Zemin visited Singapore, Malaysia, Indonesia, and Vietnam in 1994, and Li Ruihuan, one of the candidates for the next prime ministership, paid visits to Myanmar, Malaysia, Singapore, and Thailand in 1995. In addition, Chi Haotian has visited the ASEAN countries every year since he was elected defense minister in 1993. Beijing has restored its strategic partnership with Moscow. In its quest of access to the open ocean, China is trying to break out of the constraints it feels from other countries in the region and use the Law of the Sea as an instrument to pursue its territorial claims in the South China Sea and the continental shelf.

Whether China will become a military threat to its neighbors, an adversary to the United States, a systemic challenge to the global order, or a cultural-ideological challenge to the West remains unknown.[36] To give China the proper incentives to join the global order, the United States and Japan must judge its current and future position carefully.

With the demise of the Soviet Union, China is left as the lone global power rival to the United States. It is tempting to substitute Beijing for Moscow and look at the world in terms of the same cold war structure based on a balance of power. Using this framework calls for the United States and Japan to pursue a policy of containing China. But it would be wrong to make this kind of substitution. China in the 1990s is very different from the Soviet Union in the 1950s, 1960s, and 1970s. China has a large population, but it must still concentrate on its economic development instead of military expansion. It presents no strong ideological opposition to the West; it is not a military menace to the West because it is a less competitive nuclear power than the Soviet Union was; and it has decided on its own to establish many economic links with the West. If the adoption of a market system by the former socialist countries of eastern Europe signaled the end of the cold war system, one of the goals of containment has already been achieved. Therefore, the cold war framework and the security policy it implies may not be the best way to look at current issues, particularly those involving China.

The alternative to containment is engagement. From the Western point of view, engagement offers leverage to influence the domestic evolution of Chinese society in a more liberal and open direction. But Chinese leaders resent engagement as a means for the West to bring about a peaceful transformation of China's international and domestic behavior in accordance with rules and norms set by the West. Therefore some observers argue that engagement policy is futile, that China will only cooperate with the international community when it is in its national interest to do so. Others contend that China does accept interdependence and embraces multilateralism so that engagement can work. Engagement has its own logic because the world will shape China more than China will shape the world.[37]

Although supporters of containment condemn engagement policy as naive, wishful thinking, China is more benign than proponents of containment acknowledge.[38] An alternative that takes this reality into account could be called assurance policy. The United States and Japan could provide assurance for both China and the region by adopting a policy that allows China enough time to prepare itself to participate in the international system and become a stable factor in the region and the world. Neither containment policy nor engagement policy allows for China to change on its own, and China will change greatly. Under an assurance policy, China as well as other East Asian nations will be able to concentrate on economic development to pursue a better quality of life. By offering a grace period, assurance should be more acceptable to China than engagement. Assurance policy would encourage China to concentrate on its economic development and evolution into a mature, democratic society through the shift in power within Chinese society that economic development will bring.

As a first step in carrying out an assurance policy, the United States and Japan should look for ways to promote cooperation with China to encourage it to work in a constructive manner in the region. However, the United States and Japan should also be firm about constraining it from using force, as it did on the occasion of Taiwan's presidential election, and deter it from establishing a balance of power structure. The United States and Japan should initiate a trilateral security forum to address such matters as arms restraint, nuclear proliferation, and the future of the Korean peninsula.

The commercial network of the region can aid China as it moves into the international economic system. Singapore and Hong Kong are nodes of the network. In particular, Hong Kong has been the intermediary for Taiwan and others seeking to invest in and export to China. As a colony of the United Kingdom, Hong Kong's legal framework and professional work force have introduced China to British practices. The city has also provided the financial and commercial support to mediate between mainland Chinese business practices and those elsewhere in the world. The reversion of Hong Kong to China will determine the direction of China, whether it results in the "Hong Kongization" of China or the "Sinozation" of Hong Kong. Long-term success would seem to require China's gradual democratization in the manner of Taiwan, but the Chinese government has adopted a short time horizon and concentrates on demonstrating its control over commercial affairs. For example, it has used access to Hong Kong as leverage to force some countries to sever diplomatic relations with Taiwan and to establish China's power in the regional commercial network. Such a shortsighted strategy may not work out. For example, it may trigger a new wave of competition among East Asian cities. Shanghai and Taipei may both emerge as successful financial centers or nodes for container shipping, especially if Hong Kong suffers under ideological pressure from China.

China should move smoothly and naturally into the regional and global network through commercial transactions in pursuit of its maritime interests. So far, overseas Chinese in the ASEAN states and elsewhere have functioned as conduits for foreign direct investment seeking access to China's markets. Hong Kong and Taiwan account for 64.5 percent of the accumulated foreign investment coming into China from 1979 to 1996.[39] The intermediary role of the overseas Chinese was necessary because the Chinese economy does not operate transparently enough to attract direct investment from businesses in rule-based, developed countries. The expanding investment network is integrating China into the global economic order. What Robert Scalapino calls "natural economic territories" have even formed between Taiwan and Fujian Province in China.

Competition and cooperation among East Asian cities could restore the trade network that flourished around the Kingdom of Malacca until the seventeenth century.[40] Today's regional commercial centers are identical to the strategic sites of the old network that functioned well without strong naval support until it was destroyed by the British East India Company. ASEAN countries have shown their eagerness to reestablish such a network by promoting the free trade system discussed at the Asia-Pacific Economic Cooperation meetings. It is not in anyone's interest for such a network to be controlled by any particular entity. Joint oversight would allow it to function well and safely. A new trade network would augur especially well for Okinawa, which is likely to see a reduction in U.S. military bases in the not-too-distant future. As part of its policy to promote Okinawa, Japan could permit it to become a special economic zone, creating a new intermediary for transactions between Taiwan and China. This would alleviate the adverse effect on economic links with Taiwan resulting from the reversion of Hong Kong. Okinawa could once again become a commercial hub for maritime East Asia.

China's membership in the World Trade Organization is an essential step in including it in global trading. Even so, China's size makes the terms of its integration into the international economic system a problem. It is still a developing country with a per capita GNP of only $574, but it is also the world's eleventh largest trading nation, with a highly literate population of 1.2 billion people. The U.S. government has tried to use the preconditions of WTO membership as leverage to reduce America's bilateral trade deficit with China, arguing that the world's eleventh-ranked trader should not be permitted to claim a handicap.[41] Beijing now insists that it has done everything possible and that it deserves to be admitted to the WTO as a developing country. It is understandable for the United States to insist on increased transparency and amending the import rights system.[42] But the U.S. demand that China dismantle its protective trade measures is in effect a demand for instant institutional reform because they preserve and promote its state enterprises, the foundation of its industrial system. Washington insists it will support the entry of China into the WTO as a developed economy.[43] This means that China must reform its market institutions, including its corporate system, before it can be allowed to join.

The Japanese government has urged WTO member countries to allow China to join as soon as possible because it believes China should be bound by international rules. If Beijing expects WTO members to engage in hard-line negotiations to win concessions, it might, to hold on to bargaining chips, simply delay carrying out what it can do immediately. Although China does not like to be ordered about, the Japanese government believes Beijing's behavior demonstrates that it wants to be inside the world order. Therefore, Japan thinks China should be allowed to join the WTO with a relatively short phase-in period, perhaps less than ten years, so that China must at least follow the principles of the WTO. In this way Japan tries to pursue a constructive engagement policy.

China is now demonstrating its intention to be part of the WTO. It is willing to give up, for example, its import permit system to comply with the rules and requirements of the organization. Unless the West takes this opportunity to get China into the world trade system, there is a strong possibility that Beijing will elect to remain outside the WTO indefinitely. This would not be good for either the United States or China. Neither would it be desirable for the future of the world trading system.

Whatever the merits of the U.S. arguments, the reality is that China is still a developing country and should be allowed time to comply with WTO requirements. China was allowed to join the International Monetary Fund in 1980, when its monetary and foreign exchange systems were still undeveloped, and by 1996 it was able to comply fully with the requirements of Article 8 of the IMF Treaty. By welcoming China into the WTO now, with the proviso that it conform to WTO standards within a certain period, the advanced industrial states can apply international rules in a multilateral context to deal with economic disputes with China and stimulate Chinese institutional reforms. Accepting China's WTO membership would boost Washington's policy of engaging Beijing by helping alleviate the suspicion that engagement is merely a means to contain China. Such a move would also have favorable security consequences if the United States could allocate more bilateral negotiating channels to strategic issues.[44]

In part, China's future economic and political stability depends on food. It must feed its people, who account for 22 percent of the world population, by relying on a mere 7 percent of the world's arable land. In 1994 Lester Brown of the World Watch Institute warned of a global food crisis caused by China's food shortage.[45] The warning was strongly challenged by the Chinese government and the academic community. Nevertheless, in 1994 China became a net importer of grain. To ensure its continued development and bolster regional and global security, the more developed nations must address possible food shortages well before a crisis occurs.

During the initial period of economic reform, the Chinese government provided substantial assistance to agriculture and rural areas. But recently it has focused on industrialization to the neglect of investing in agricultural infrastructure and an adequate farm price policy. A 1995 report based on joint research by Japan's Overseas Economic Cooperation Fund (OECF) and the Rural Economics Research Center under the jurisdiction of China's minister of agriculture criticized present policies and estimated that China would have a food shortage of 136 million tons in 2010.[46] This is, incidentally, not far from Brown's 1994 forecast.

Given China's port, storage, and distribution facilities, a shortfall of this magnitude could not be filled sufficiently by imports, even if the United States or other countries had the production capacity. China must be able to feed itself. To cut the shortfall to 65 million tons, the OECF report recommended policies to increase the irrigation rate, improve agricultural infrastructure, and enlist cooperation from abroad. Heeding this advice, China's National Congress for Rural Work Policy, held in January 1996, backed measures to raise total food production to about 500 million tons by the end of this century. The problem will be in implementation. In the meantime, Chinese agricultural prices have risen by 20 percent in 1996 to approach international levels. With the agricultural price structure more in tune with that of the manufacturing sector, China is at last beginning to improve its farming infrastructure and use market mechanisms to increase agricultural production. Now, China must undertake a program, perhaps similar to South Korea's Heavy Chemical Industries program adopted at the beginning of the 1960s, to invest in industrial sectors that will support the further improvement of agricultural output.

Is Japan Ready to Assume a New Role in East Asia–Pacific Security?

Following the demise of the Soviet Union, Japan expected the U.S.-Japan Security Treaty to be reevaluated and feared the downgrading of the U.S. commitment in the Asia-Pacific region. Then the 1990–91 Persian Gulf crisis had an even greater impact on Japan's framework for making security policy. American condemnation of checkbook diplomacy first demonstrated to Tokyo the need for it to act on the values it shared with the United States. This led Japan to reexamine the lopsidedness of the treaty and reflect on such matters as the Acquisition and Cross-Servicing Agreement, whereby Japan provides logistical support for U.S. forces in Japan during peacetime, and the reinterpretation of the constitution to allow the right to collective self-defense. The U.S. condemnation also forced Japan to think about its security in a broader sense than the defense of its own territory or region. This led it to dispatch minesweepers to the Persian Gulf and participate in UN peacekeeping operations.

The Japanese have come to recognize that the security treaty must be redefined to reflect the new situation in the East Asia–Pacific region, along with the uncertainty in the Korean peninsula and the tension in the Taiwan Straits that are remnants of the cold war. The U.S.-Japan Joint Declaration on Security issued at the 1996 summit meeting between President Clinton and Prime Minister Hashimoto pointed the way by outlining the intention of the two countries to work jointly for regional security.

Although maintaining security requires more than military arrangements and agreements, officials on both sides of the Pacific have so far been preoccupied with the technical details of bilateral defense cooperation under the security treaty and the U.S. military presence on Okinawa. Neither the United States nor Japan has yet clearly ranked its policy objectives in East Asia. The United States has many goals, ranging from preventing the emergence of a regional hegemony or a hostile coalition to promoting commercial interests to protecting human rights. But the goals can and often do conflict, making U.S. policy incoherent, inconsistent, and unsystematic. Nor is Japan yet ready to prepare specific proposals for policy coordination. Despite the intention of both countries to extend Japan's responsibilities in the region, Japan has not increased its coordination of regional security policy.

During the cold war, security treaties with the United States connected the countries in the East Asia–Pacific region like spokes to the U.S. hub. The small countries had an incentive to reduce their military spending because the chance of their engaging in wars with each other was slight. Japan's primary security problem in the 1950s was eliminated by the Korean war as the United States and its allies assumed responsibility to deter the threat from the North.[47] The problem of Chinese power never materialized because the Soviet Union pinned China down. Japan endeavored to improve its relations with China because this was in line with the overall strategy of the West. When the United States improved relations with China in 1972, it had two intentions. At the global level it aimed to influence the confrontational balance between the United States and the Soviet Union and to place the United States in a pivotal position in a strategic triangle following the Sino-Soviet split. At the regional level the opening to China helped foster a favorable diplomatic environment for terminating the American military involvement in Vietnam.

The Shanghai Communiqué of 1972, which initiated the process for normalizing U.S.-China relations, eased tensions in the East Asia–Pacific region. This new atmosphere facilitated the end of the Vietnam War, enabled Japan to restore diplomatic relations with China, and allowed China to begin trade with Asian nations. The opening also paved the way for China's 1978 adoption of a reform and open door policy. With the security interests of the West in mind, Japan tried to maintain good relations with China. This was a change. But whatever changes in its approach from the 1960s to the 1980s, we can safely say that all of Tokyo's foreign policy actions were taken within the framework of the Soviet-U.S. rivalry or the U.S.-Japan alliance. Because Japan regarded the security provided by the United States as a sort of public good, it felt no incentive to increase its own efforts at maintaining regional security, although its economy had grown to a significant size. The mutual security system was, in a sense, incentive compatible.[48] Japan had an incentive to rely on the United States as much as possible, while the United States had an incentive to request Japan's contribution to security by financing U.S. activities or making economic concessions.

With the collapse of the cold war system there arose the possibility that small countries might engage each other and, along with this, the probability of an arms race among them. In fact, defense expenditures in East Asia have increased considerably but are still reasonable in proportion to economic growth and have not yet reached the level of an arms race.[49] Although Japan is drawn into the economic vortex of East Asian growth, it must construct its own post–cold war framework for conceiving regional security and use the framework to cope with the new situation in the region.

But neither Japanese foreign policy experts nor the Japanese populace has reached a consensus on the best attitude toward China and other East Asian countries. Japan has yet to formulate a comprehensive security concept for the region because it has relied too much on the U.S.-Japan Security Treaty. After having enthusiastically welcomed China in the 1970s and 1980s, Tokyo now seems to be considering how to treat a China that has shown a hegemonic attitude and, at the same time, how to incorporate China more profoundly in the security framework. During the 1980s, opinion polls showed the average Japanese considered Sino-Japanese relations as relatively good, but the optimism deteriorated after the events at Tiananmen Square. In 1995 Japanese opinion deteriorated further: polls showed for the first time the number of those holding an unfavorable attitude toward China exceeded the number of those retaining a good image. Then came China's nuclear test. In 1996 Japan's disapproval confronted the nationalism of China in the dispute over ownership of the Senkaku (Japan)–Diaoyu (China) Islands. When Japanese rightists tried to construct a lighthouse on one island, demonstrators from Hong Kong and Taiwan flocked to the islands to display their support for China's territorial claims. But in the face of heated sentiments and provocative incidents, the Chinese and Japanese governments have managed to maintain diplomatic relations on an even keel.

How, then, should Japan engage China? The Japanese hold several different views on how China should fit into Japan's new security framework. Some Japanese, seeing China's tendency to hegemony, favor a U.S.-Japan strategic partnership.[50] They point out that an alliance between the United States and Japan is natural, since they are the two largest powers in the region and share the values of the market economy and democracy. Moreover, they see an inherent imbalance between Japan and China because China has 3 million soldiers and its own nuclear weapons, while Japan has to rely on the U.S. nuclear deterrent. They add that China's Middle Kingdom mentality is inherently inimical to Japan, although at present China exhibits no strong ideological antagonism toward Japan. These observers accept that Japan should admit its misdeeds during the past war, but they believe that China should not try to pursue its short-run interest by emphasizing Japan's history. These facts must be accounted for in the geopolitical balance of the region.

Other Japanese advocate that Japan make its diplomatic foundation two strategic partnerships: China-Japan and U.S.-Japan.[51] They assert that Japan should pay due attention to the recent development of East Asian economies. Although they admit that strong ties with the United States are necessary, they make Sino-Japanese relations the pillar of Japan's East Asian diplomacy. They argue that Japan's official development assistance programs such as yen loans are an effective inducement to China to become a stable and predictable country because Beijing has concentrated on economic development and has been willing to accept foreign direct investment. Although China will not become a mature market economy and democracy for some time, Japan would do well to recognize that it has the potential to become as affluent and influential as America. The observers further assert that while the U.S. comprehensive engagement policy toward China is often inconsistent, Sino-American relations could become solidly favorable. In that case, Washington would become much more serious about a cooperative security agenda embracing Japan and China.

Without good U.S. and Japanese contacts among countries in the East Asia–Pacific region, the U.S.-Japan Security Treaty would not function well. In this sense the difference between advocates of a U.S.-Japan strategic partnership and advocates of two strategic partnerships for Japan is not so great. Contacts with China by both the United States and Japan are necessary to reach more constructive common views on the security of the region. Both Japan and the United States have to prepare for a more benign regional security environment, although they have been preoccupied so far with possible adverse events on the Korean peninsula. But the Clinton-Hashimoto summit paved the way to restructure the security treaty to meet regional security needs. As the document stated, this way is to offer cooperation with China to encourage it to take a constructive part in the region's affairs. Even if there is little chance that China will accept the treaty as a public good at this time, the United States and Japan should encourage it to participate in creating a common security order that will serve common security interests.

Japan has maintained its contacts in the region. Even during the cold

war it paid considerable attention to regional development. In 1977
Prime Minister Takeo Fukuda announced the so-called Fukuda Doctrine,
in which he ruled out the possibility of Japan's becoming a great military
power. He advocated solidarity between Japan and the ASEAN countries
and the promotion of social and cultural exchanges in addition to those
in political and economic spheres. In January 1980 Prime Minister
Masayoshi Ohira unveiled his "grand design for the solidarity of the Pan-
Pacific region." Ohira's design was not fully developed because of his
sudden death, but his aides and advisors later published an expanded
version in voluminous books. The design reflected his recognition that,
despite its diversity in history and culture, the region had begun to unify
due to technological progress in telecommunications and transportation.
He advocated a new type of regional cooperation among countries at different stages of economic development and with different cultures, and
he pointed out the possibility of bringing forth a new civilization in the
region.

Ohira's grand design foreshadowed the birth of APEC in 1989. And
the Fukuda Doctrine can be said to have laid the foundation for the construction of the ASEAN Regional Forum in 1993, although Foreign Minister Taro Nakayama's 1991 address was the direct stimulus. These collective bodies exemplify the Japanese way of approaching the region.
Some observers argue that Japan has not adequately addressed the problems and challenges in Northeast Asia by putting the initiative in the
hands of the ASEAN countries. Nevertheless, the institutions have been
instrumental in contributing to confidence building. They should augment
a redirected U.S.-Japan Security Treaty.

The most cynical aspect of the regional security problem is other
East Asians' suspicion of Japan's intentions. They are concerned with
the potential changes in the regional power structure that would result
should China achieve a high level of economic development or Japan
decides to project a military presence. How should Japan address the
suspicion that it might seek to become a military power ? The average
Japanese would answer that the pacifist feelings of the citizens will
never let the country take on a military role. Indeed, most Japanese
rarely consider that their country has the third largest defense budget in
the world or that other countries in the region regard Japan as a potential adversary. This lack of awareness is the direct result of Japan's lack
of open discussions of defense and military problems by the public and
even the Diet.

The East Asia–Pacific region is less institutionalized than Europe, but this does not necessarily mean that it lacks security. It is in a much better position because it can build new institutions rather than having to rely on an old system that is unsuited to the new situation. The U.S.-Japan Security Treaty has established the structure for relationships among the four powers with interests in the region, ruling out bilateral alliances that could bring instability. Japan should give the treaty the central role in providing regional security because of the two countries' common values and common interests.

From this platform the United States and Japan should ensure China and other East Asian nations enough time to catch up with the developed economies and democracies and assume a greater constructive function in the region. Together with South Korea, and using the same supportive, cooperative approach that Japan adopted toward the Chinese food shortage, they should assist North Korea's economic development. The United States and Japan should constrain any adversarial activities by countries in the region. To clarify its position regarding nuclear arms, Japan should establish PACATOM. Although the two countries should encourage security dialogues at the ASEAN Regional Forum, they should also initiate security discussions among China, the United States, and Japan concerning issues vital to Northeast Asia and the East Asian–Pacific region as a whole.

At present, Japan is not fully prepared to assume a more active and independent part in regional security. It has been searching for a new image of itself as a nation-state and for a foreign policy direction suitable to the post–cold war era. Ichiro Ozawa, formerly of the Liberal Democratic party, has advocated that Japan take on new military responsibilities. Politicians with opposing views have yet to present alternative nation-state models. The LDP seems to be divided between members who accept Ozawa's normal-country model and those who support the concept of a global civilian power that would expand Japan's contribution in nonmilitary ways.

The LDP appears to be formulating a new political direction by constructing a montage from many points of view. First, it accepted as prime minister the Social Democratic party's Tomiichi Murayama, who admits Japan's misdeeds in World War II. Then it installed as his successor its own Ryutaro Hashimoto, who holds views on the international and domestic political situation that are close to the normal-country model.

Judging from opinion polls, publications, and contact with politicians,

I sense the possibility that this trial and error may eventually lead to a consensus similar to the views of many Japanese who have been trying to reevaluate Japan's post-Meiji history. So far, advocates of a less critical interpretation of Japan's role in World War II and of a better balance between economic and security issues have no formal organization except for a small ad hoc history study group led by Shoichi Nakagawa.[52]

In due course these people will gather into a group, possibly under younger leaders like Sadakazu Tanigaki of the LDP. To the extent that they share a single point of view, it is that they are prepared to admit the misdeeds of Japan during the war. On this point they differ from traditional nationalists who have always believed that Japan does not need to apologize and that it was no more morally culpable for the war than the Western powers. They also differ from the believers in global civilian power in that they accept Japan's assuming a military role in the world. In addition, they agree that there should be a new division of labor for providing regional security. Because they recognize that the contribution of Japanese military power would be limited, they would also like to have it make a much greater contribution in nonmilitary ways. Were this point of view to gain ascendance in Japan's political platform, a newly directed U.S.-Japan Security Treaty would function well. Today's advocates of this view are preparing Japan psychologically for a new relationship with the United States.

Conclusion

Contrary to realists' fears, the phenomenal economic growth in the East Asia–Pacific region offers opportunities for stability through economic interdependence. However, liberals would do well to remember that economic growth might create an imbalance of power. To pursue prosperity and security, effective deterrence and a mechanism for cooperation among countries are needed. The U.S.-Japan security relationship should be structured to help meet these needs. From this platform the United States and Japan should encourage China to participate in the global order. While promoting a cooperative framework, Japan should accept a much greater burden as a provider of public security goods. To avoid some potential pitfalls, it is also very important for both the United States and Japan, but especially Japan, to exert every effort to build confidence among the East Asia–Pacific states.

Notes

1. Richard K. Betts, "Wealth, Power, and Instability—East Asia and the United States after the Cold War," *International Security*, vol. 18 (Winter 1993–94), pp. 34–77.

2. Stephen Van Evera, "Promise for Peace: Europe after the Cold War," *International Security*, vol. 15 (Winter 1990–91), pp. 7–57.

3. Absence of land reform does much to explain why the Philippines has lagged behind other East Asian economies despite its experience as an American colony.

4. P. Deane and A. W. Coles, *British Economic Growth, 1689–1959* (Cambridge University Press, 1962), p. 142.

5. Statistical Bureau of the Prime Minister's Office (Japan), *Census Series* (Tokyo, various years); and Republic of Korea Economic Planning Institute, *Statistical Yearbook* (Seoul, various years).

6. International Monetary Fund, *International Financial Statistics* (Washington, various issues).

7. Robert Z. Lawrence, *Regionalism, Multilateralism, and Deeper Integration* (Brookings, 1996); and Lawrence, Albert Bressand, and Takatoshi Ito, *A Vision for the World Economy: Openness, Diversity and Cohesion* (Brookings, 1996).

8. G. A. O'Donnell, *Modernization and Bureaucratic-Authoritarianism: Studies in South American Politics* (University of California Press, 1979).

9. For example, Henry Clay remarked that Britain had "too many eggs in too few baskets," pointing out that cotton accounted for one-third and coal and steel for one-fifth of total U.K. exports before the war. See "The Place of Exports in British Industry after the War," *Economic Journal* (June-September, 1942).

10. Banno Masataka, *Kindai Chugoku Seiji-Gaikoshi* (Tokyo University Press, 1973), p. 375.

11. Desmond Ball, "A New Era in Confidence Building: The Second-Track Process in the Asia-Pacific Region." *Security Dialogue*, vol. 25 (June 1994), pp. 157–76.

12. Yamauchi Yasuhide, "Kaiyō Regime no Genjō to Nippon no Taiou," *Kokusai Mondai*, no. 438 (September 1996), pp. 47–62.

13. Kent E. Calder, *Pacific Defense: Arms, Energy, and America's Future in Asia* (William Morrow, 1996).

14. International Energy Agency, *World Energy Outlook* (Paris, 1996), pp. 248–53.

15. Nihon enerugi keizai kenkyūshō, *Enerugi Tōkei (Kaigai-hen)*, p. 12.

16. Vahan Zamoyan, "After the Oil Boom: The Holiday Ends in the Gulf," *Foreign Affairs*, no. 74 (November-December 1995), pp. 2–7.

17. International Energy Agency, *World Energy Outlook, 1996*, p. 60.

18. Marginal energy consumption per GNP is an indicator of efficiency of energy use obtained by dividing the incremental energy consumption (in terms of price and volume) required to increase GNP by one unit. By this measure the United States is a relatively efficient user of energy, even though its per capita energy consumption is unreasonably high. China is just the opposite; it has low per capita consumption and low marginal efficiency as well.

19. Robert A. Manning, "PACATOM: A Nuclear Cooperation Regime as Asian

CSBM," paper presented to the meeting of the Council for Security Cooperation in the Asia Pacific, April 22, 1996.

20. Michael Doyle, "Liberalism and World Politics," *American Political Science Review*, vol. 80 (December 1986), pp. 1151–69.

21. Edward D. Mansfield and Jack Snyder, "Democratization and the Danger of War," *International Security*, vol. 20 (Summer 1995), pp. 5–38; and Ido Oren, "The Subjectivity of the 'Democratic' Peace: Changing U.S. Perceptions of Imperial Germany," *International Security*, vol. 20 (Fall 1995), pp. 147–84.

22. Joanne Gowa, "Democratic States and International Disputes," *International Organization* (Summer 1955).

23. T. Clifton Morgan, "Democracy and War: Reflections on the Literature," *International Interactions*, vol. 18, no. 3 (1993), p. 200.

24. Ex ante constraints are emphasized in T. Clifton Morgan and Sally Howard Campbell, "Domestic Structure, Decisional Constraints, and War: So Why Kant Democracies Fight?" *Journal of Conflict Resolution*, vol. 31 (June 1991), pp. 187–211. Ex post sanctions on leaders are considered more important in Bruce Bueno de Mesquita, Randolf Silverson, and Gary Woller, "War and the Fate of Regimes: A Comparative Analysis," *American Political Science Review,* vol. 86 (September 1992), pp. 638–47.

25. Henry S. Farber and Joanne Gowa, "Polities and Peace," *International Security*, vol. 20 (Fall 1995), pp. 123–46.

26. Mansfield and Snyder," Democratization and the Danger of War."

27. Takahashi Takuma, "Actors on Different Stages Are Playing in the Same Theater," paper prepared for a seminar sponsored by the European Commission, Haiko, Hainan, China, September 1995.

28. Suehiro Akira, *Tai: kaihatsu to minshushugi* (Tokyo: Iwanami shoten, 1993), pp. 6–7; and Tamada Yoshifumi, "Coups in Thailand, 1980–1991: Classmates, Internal Conflicts and Relations with the Government of the Military," *Southeast Asian Studies*, vol. 33 (December 1995), pp. 317–39.

29. C. H. Kwan, "A Rebuttal of Pessimism about the Chinese Economy," *Nomura Asian Focus* (Spring 1997), pp. 2–11.

30. The government-controlled proportion of important materials and parts declined from 100 percent in 1978 to 18 percent in 1994. People's Republic of China, State Statistical Bureau, *China Statistical Yearbook, 1996* (Beijing: China Statistical Publishing House, 1996), pp. 120–22.

31. Tomoyuki Kojima, "Ajia no nakano Nichibeichu-kankei," *Kikan Asteion*, no. 43 (Winter 1997), pp. 30–47.

32. The flying geese model of economic growth refers to the tendency for developing economies to progress by following in the path of successful economies just ahead of them in development. Together the developing countries are arrayed in a pattern similar to a flock of flying geese. The most advanced country produces high-technology products, the ones immediately behind making slightly less sophisticated products from which the leaders have graduated, and so on, with the countries in the rear producing products involving the least technology, such as footwear.

33. Yasheng Huang, "Why China Will Not Collapse," *Foreign Policy*, no. 99 (Summer 1995), pp. 54–68.

34. David Shambaugh, "Containment or Engagement of China?: Calculating Beijing's Responses," *International Security*, vol. 21 (Fall 1996), pp. 180–209.

35. Kojima Tomoyuki, "Chūgoku Gaikō no Ronri" *Shinbouei Ronsō*, vol. 24 (September 1996), pp. 1–16.

36. David Shambaugh, "China's Military: Real or Paper Tiger?" *Washington Quarterly*, vol. 19 (Spring 1996), pp. 19–36.

37. Shambaugh, "Containment or Engagement of China?, pp. 180–209.

38. Arthur Waldron, "Deterring China," *Commentary*, vol. 100 (October 1950), pp. 17–21; Gideon Rachman, "Containing China," *Washington Quarterly*, vol. 19 (Winter 1996), pp. 129–39; and Gerald Segal, "East Asia and the 'Containment' of China," *International Security*, vol. 20 (Spring 1996), pp. 107–35.

39. People's Republic of China Ministry of Foreign Trade and Economic Cooperation.

40. Sakurai Yumio, "Higashi ajia to Tōnan ajia," *Kokusai Kōryū*, (1993), pp. 45–53; and Mizoguchi Yuzo and others, eds., *Chiiki Shisutemu: Ajia Kara Kangaeru*, 2d ed. (Tokyo University Press, 1993).

41. The U.S. calculation of the bilateral deficit is overestimated. See, for example, K. C. Fung and Lawrence J. Lau, "The China–United States Bilateral Trade Balance: How Big Is It Really?" Asia/Pacific Research Center, Stanford University, 1996.

42. Japan also complains about the same things and has submitted to the Chinese government proposals to increase transparency and amend some rules. "Proposals Regarding the Improvement in the Business Environment for Foreign Capitals in China," Tokyo, 1996.

43. Office of the U.S. Trade Representative, *1996 Trade Policy Agenda and 1995 Annual Report of the President of the United States on the Trade Agreements Program* (1996), p. 90; and Office of the U.S. Trade Representative, *Foreign Trade Barriers* (1996), pp. 45–61.

44. Nicholas R. Lardy, "China and the WTO," Policy Brief 10, Brookings, 1996.

45. Lester Brown, "Who Will Feed China?" *World Watch*, vol. 7, no. 5 (1994).

46. Research Institute of Development Assistance, *Prospects for Grain Supply-Demand Balance and Agricultural Development Policy in China* (Tokyo: Overseas Economic Cooperation Fund, 1995).

47. Kosaka Masataka , *Nihon Sonbo no Toki* (Tokyo: Kodansha, 1992).

48. Mancur Olsen and Richard Zeckhauser, "An Economic Theory of Alliance," *Review of Economics and Statistics*, vol. 48 (August 1966), pp. 266–79.

49. Stuart Harris, "The Economic Aspects of Security in the Asia/Pacific Region," in Ball, ed., *Transformation of Security in the Asia/Pacific Region*, pp. 32–51.

50. Among the adherents of this school Hisahiko Okazaki is the most articulate on these points.

51. This group includes many members of the so-called civilian global power school, such as Yoichi Funabashi and Jitsuro Terashima, in addition to scholars such as Akihiko Tanaka. More important, however, it also includes some seventy career diplomats who have specialized in dealing with China.

52. Although many tend to see this group as a sign of political contention within the Hashimoto cabinet, it could herald a more conservative coalition between the rightists of the LDP and Ozawa's faction of the New Frontier party if the Hashimoto cabinet fails to bring about a satisfactory solution to the Okinawa problem.

Part Two

U.S.-JAPAN DEFENSE
COOPERATION

CHAPTER FIVE

A Tighter Japan-U.S. Alliance Based on Greater Trust

Satoshi Morimoto

THE JAPAN-U.S. ALLIANCE is unquestionably critical for the peace and stability not only of Japan but of the entire East Asia–Pacific region. Even in the post–cold war environment, this security relationship serves as the linchpin of America's deterrence strategy in the region and is essential to an effective response if deterrence were to fail. Both Japan and the United States must make this partnership tighter and base it on greater mutual trust. Indeed this is the best way that Japan can contribute to regional stability.

The alliance, however, faces serious challenges. Since the collapse of the former Soviet Union, explaining its purpose has become more difficult, and the number of Japanese who believe they can live without it is increasing. But in the April 1996 Japan-U.S. Joint Declaration on Security, Prime Minister Ryutaro Hashimoto and President Bill Clinton reaffirmed the importance of the relationship and defined it in terms of the common interests and values as it responds to emerging regional conditions. In many ways the declaration marks the most significant turning point for the alliance since the 1960 Mutual Security Treaty.

The Japanese and American people tended to welcome this declaration because of changes in the East Asia–Pacific region during the preceding year and because of the leadership of the Japanese and American governments. The enigmatic behavior of the North Korean military and China's military pressure on Taiwan had demonstrated that the region remains unstable and persuaded many Japanese about the necessity of maintaining the alliance. But the September 1995 rape of an Okinawan schoolgirl by U.S. servicemen had triggered a strong antibase movement in Okinawa with which many Japanese empathized. Prime Minister Hashimoto and President Clinton's decision to return the Futenma Marine Air Station to Japan checked Japanese opposition to the joint declaration.

Now attention has turned to whether the Japanese and American governments can implement the main points of the declaration. This will not be easy. No previous U.S.-Japanese communiqué has posed as many difficult tasks.

U.S. Bases in Okinawa

The first challenge concerns U.S. bases on Okinawa, especially the handling of Marine Corps bases and personnel. Before turning to this problem, one must first clarify the missions of the marines in the context of U.S. strategy and the changing security environment.

The primary mission of the Marine Corps is to establish a bridgehead for a ground campaign by making surprise amphibious landings at critical points. For this purpose the corps has been organized into three types of units: ground, air, and service support. In general, with air units engaging in air strikes and assault units providing support, the ground forces establish a beachhead using landing ships and helicopters.[1]

Currently, the marines have three active divisions and one reserve division, of which the Third Marine Expeditionary Force (MEF) is forward deployed in Japan. The Third MEF consists of the Third Marine Division, the First Marine Wing, and a support group. The Third Marine Division is organized into one infantry and one artillery regiment, making it smaller than the other divisions, which have three regiments each. Normally, the marines stationed in Okinawa engage in training soldiers sent on rotation from the U.S. West Coast. The troops are organized into units of about 2,000 that board amphibious ships dispatched from Sasebo. These units perform their missions either on their own or as part of a carrier mobile unit of the Seventh Fleet.

In distinguishing four stages of military defensive campaigns, the U.S. defense report of 1995 indicates that the responsibility of the marines comes primarily later in a conflict.[2] In the first stage the United States halts the invasion with the assistance of allied and friendly states.

In the second the United States and its allies build their combat power while reducing the enemy's. The third stage encompasses defeating the enemy decisively through air operations, combined naval-ground warfare, and ground combat. The combined amphibious operations of the Marine Corps belong to this stage. The fourth stage is devoted to providing for postwar stability, such as maintaining the cease-fire and cultivating a stable regional environment.

The marines on Okinawa are not adequate by themselves to launch an amphibious operation. The United States would first have to deploy helicopter units and marine regiments from the American West Coast and elsewhere to Japan and train these units for the operation at hand. In the meantime air and naval operations would be launched. The marines would wait for the most appropriate time before beginning their operation. Because the marine bases on Okinawa can receive and train marines from other areas, there is no military necessity to have troops permanently stationed on Okinawa after the reunification of North and South Korea. What is much more important is to ensure that marines dispatched to Japan can freely use facilities there and train and stockpile supplies. By having this assurance, the Commander in Chief, Pacific (CINCPAC) can use the marines in the most flexible and effective manner.[3]

Stationing marines in Japan (primarily on Okinawa) derives from the historical experience of successfully landing on Iwo Jima during the World War II. Stationing marines on Okinawa thus has a powerful symbolic meaning. And if one considers the financial cost to Americans and the amount of Japanese host-nation support, the deployment has been remarkably inexpensive for the United States.[4]

Despite the 1996 agreement to return the Futenma Air Station within seven years, Japan has to find a helicopter base and to transfer some of the Futenma base's functions to other locations. No current facility on Okinawa can accommodate the functions. And although constructing a heliport at Kadena Air Base and Ammunition Storage Site may appear desirable, there is strong opposition from the U.S. Air Force, which administers the base, and from residents of Kadena Town. It would be even more difficult to locate a new U.S. military facility on one of the main Japanese islands. But if this matter is not resolved, the consolidation of bases mentioned in the Japan-U.S. joint declaration will not move forward. What means might there be to break the impasse?

I propose pulling the marines out of Okinawa when Futenma is returned. But for this to occur, at least one rear support base with pre-positioned supplies and equipment necessary for the deployment of marine units would first have to be secured. The marines are indeed critical for regional deterrence. Insofar as those in Okinawa will be crucial to the outcome of a Korean contingency, keeping them deployed on the island is essential to both Japanese and Northeast Asian security until the situation in the Korean peninsula improves. Nevertheless, by the beginning of the twenty-first century, the need to station such forces permanently in Okinawa will diminish, especially in light of the probable revolution in military affairs.

As all marine helicopter units and regiments are removed, arrangements should be made so that marines dispatched to Japan as well as U.S. forces already stationed in Japan can use the facilities in an emergency. During a crisis on the Korean peninsula, U.S. bases in Japan would, of course, still be critical for military operations. In addition, making it possible for U.S. troops stationed in Japan and U.S. military units deployed from the U.S. mainland and bases in other parts of the East Asia–Pacific region to use airports, harbors, and other facilities (especially those in the Kyushu area and the rest of western Japan) flexibly and freely under the administration of the Defense Agency and the Transportation Ministry will give the forces more military options in Korea. If these arrangements are made in advance, marines could be rapidly deployed to Japan and prepare for combat operations. Japan should facilitate such deployments by providing transport and other logistical support.

About 75 percent of the U.S. bases in Japan are concentrated on Okinawa, a share that will not change significantly even after the Futenma base is returned. But if the future structure of U.S. forces in Japan is considered, the importance of Kadena Air Base will grow. Furthermore, Kadena is the largest base for the U.S. Air Force in East Asia. If some of the military units now dispersed throughout Okinawa were to be relocated there, much of the base-related problems on Okinawa would be resolved. The so-called Kanto relocation plan of the 1970s, which involved moving and consolidating bases in the Kanto area, could serve as a model for managing overseas American bases that could be applied to Okinawa.

Even after the departure of the marines and the implementation of a relocation plan, Kadena and some other bases will remain important to Okinawa's economy. The presence of the bases has caused the development of the island to lag behind that of the rest of Japan, with the citizens of Okinawa forced to make major sacrifices in their livelihoods.

Therefore, the Japanese government must provide funding to Okinawans and promote the development of the prefecture. As the central government implements these measures directly through the prefectural government, the Okinawa Development Agency, which is now in charge of regional development, will become unnecessary. Once the realignment and consolidation of the bases begins, the situation in Okinawa should not differ much from that in other prefectures that host U.S. military bases.

My reasoning in proposing the solution is as follows. By the time the Futenma Marine Air Station has been returned at the beginning of the next century, the reunification in Korea is likely to have begun. The military necessity of having marines deployed in Japan as well as U.S. forces in Korea will diminish dramatically. There will be no need to have a marine division stationed permanently on Okinawa. All that would be required are a rear-support unit and some pre-positioned equipment so that deployments can be made from other areas.

This conclusion holds even if the Korean problem is not resolved by the time Futenma is returned. As in the Persian Gulf War, an intense air campaign would be waged at the start of hostilities in Korea. Only after it was possible to minimize casualties would the ground campaign begin. At the earliest, Futenma will not be returned until 2001. By this time it is hard to imagine that American society and the U.S. Congress would permit marines to invade at the beginning of hostilities and allow them to suffer significant casualties. What this means is that while the air campaign is going on, there will be time to deploy marine units from other areas to U.S. bases in Japan.

If the problem of Korea is resolved by the time Futenma is returned, an alternative heliport would be unnecessary. Even if the problem is not resolved, there is no need to invest ¥800 billion for construction of an alternative heliport in Okinawa. An area could be designated within the Kadena Air Base and Ammunition Storage Site for the alternative heliport, and the Kadena airstrip could be used. Although the U.S. Air Force at Kadena is strongly opposed to accepting a new heliport, it is not likely that the Third Marine Division is going to be transferred to Kadena. What about the possibility that after spending large sums on constructing the heliport, conditions change so that the marines do not use this new facility? How would this wasted expense be explained to the Japanese people?

Of course, there are counterarguments. A commitment to withdraw the marines might make other East Asian countries anxious about regional stability and send a wrong message to China and North Korea that the United States is slackening its commitment. Withdrawal might also damage the Japan-U.S. alliance. However, if it is possible to sustain the stable use of U.S. bases in Japan, including Okinawa, U.S. deterrence capabilities would be secure and the long-term trust essential to Japan-U.S. security arrangements would be ensured. Viewing the Okinawa base issue as just a matter of resolving the Okinawa problem is misguided. The most important questions are whether Japanese security can be maintained as conditions in Northeast Asia change and whether the U.S. military can sustain the functions of its bases in Japan. If there were another incident involving U.S. servicemen and Okinawans, use of the bases would become unsustainable.

In April 1997 the legal status of thirteen U.S. military bases in Okinawa became a major political issue in Japan. Although the leases on the land occupied by the bases were due to expire in mid-May, 3,000 of the 32,000 landowners refused to renew them. In addition, Okinawa's governor and various mayors expressed their opposition to mandatory renewal. Consequently, the Japanese government proposed legislation to enable the U.S. military to continue to use the land legally on a provisional basis after the leases expire. Technically, the legislation amended a 1952 "special measures" (tokuso) law that enabled the government to compel the leasing of private land for use by U.S. military forces as part of Japan's obligation in the bilateral security treaty.

The special measures law has been used three times since 1982. Under the procedure it mandates, after the director general of the Defense Facilities Administration Agency submits the necessary documents on behalf of the state's interest in having the U.S. military use the land, a prefectural land use committee appointed by the governor reviews the case and determines the length of the leases and the rental fee. But after the 1995 rape incident, the Okinawa governor and various mayors have complicated this review process by refusing to carry out the necessary paperwork. In the case of the leases that were due to expire in mid-May 1997, delays made it impossible for the review procedure to be completed by the expiration date, forcing the government to submit a revision of the special measures law. Political confusion ensued. The Social Democratic party, which was part of the ruling coalition, opposed the bill, while some opposition parties supported the government. Eventually, the bill passed both houses of the Diet with overwhelming majorities, clearing the way for the 1996 U.S.-Japan summit at which President Clinton and Prime Minister Hashimoto reconfirmed their commitment to the alliance.

Despite this positive result, the whole episode calls into question the rationality of the current procedure for determining land use. As it stands, the law allows a prefectural land use committee appointed by a prefectural governor to hold hostage the U.S. military bases on which Japan's national security depends. To prevent this from happening again, Japan needs to legislate an entirely new legal framework for determining how land and other facilities are provided for U.S. military use. But such legislation will certainly spark an intense national debate as Okinawans and some of the political parties fiercely oppose any fundamental change in the procedure.

The antibase movement in Okinawa continues unabated and has mobilized sympathy among some people living on the main islands. One reason is that the Japanese people cannot fully understand the rationale for the U.S.-Japan alliance after the end of the cold war. The Japanese government must therefore clearly explain the purpose and objectives of the U.S.-Japan security system to the people. But even if the public were to understand the purpose of the alliance, there remains the problem of how to reduce the burden of the U.S. military presence on Okinawa. Although both matters are Japanese domestic problems, they have important implications for whether Japan can provide bases on its territory for U.S. military forces on a stable, long-term basis.

Review of the Japan-U.S. Defense Cooperation Guidelines

The other task mandated by the U.S.-Japan Joint Declaration on Security is to review the Japan-U.S. Defense Cooperation Guidelines. This task is of utmost importance because the new guidelines will shape the direction of bilateral defense cooperation. Drafted in 1978 during the severe conditions of the cold war, the guidelines, based on Article 5 of the Japan-U.S. Security Treaty, outlined the character of defense cooperation under the assumption of an attack against Japan by the Soviet military in the Far East. Given the changes in the East Asia–Pacific region after the end of the cold war, however, what needs to be examined now is the nature of bilateral defense cooperation during a Far East crisis based on Article 6 of the treaty. If Japan cannot cooperate more fully with the United States during a regional crisis, the future of the bilateral alliance will be bleak.

Dealing with crises covered by Article 6 raises difficult legal and political issues for Japan. How would Japan respond to an American request to engage in activities in areas beyond Japanese territorial waters either with U.S. forces or by itself? Under such circumstances, to what extent is Japan permitted to engage in activities that would be an exercise of the collective right of self-defense or could be considered as such? If the United States asked Japan to cooperate in minesweeping operations in international waters during a Far East crisis, the request would raise the problem of whether Japan can legally engage in such operations in a tension-ridden situation. Even if legally permissible, there would be the political issue of whether Japan should undertake such activities.

If the United States asked Japan to rescue and transport the families of U.S. forces and foreigners in Korea during a Korean crisis, Japan would face the problem of whether it can carry out such a mission not only in international waters but also in Korean territorial waters. In this case, a naval escort would be necessary for the transport vessels. Because the potential for using force is great during maritime escort operations, the legal problem goes beyond the matter of providing transportation. A transport operation without a military escort is extremely dangerous, and it is unrealistic to expect that such an operation would be undertaken. The legal question pertaining to these possibilities boils down to whether Japan can and should exercise the right to collective self-defense.

In other instances, the United States might ask Japan to provide support within Japan's own territory, for example, to increase the joint use of base facilities, to provide transportation between bases, or to assume such functions of U.S. forces as guard duty, procurement, and administration. Rather than becoming a legal issue related to the right of collective self-defense, these activities would involve domestic laws related to the Japan-U.S. Status of Forces Agreement and the self-defense force.

From the perspective of strengthening the bilateral alliance, however, Japan should not merely respond to American requests regarding the defense cooperation guidelines. Based on its own independent analysis, it should also actively propose to the United States appropriate modes of defense cooperation in pursuit of Northeast Asian stability and common interests.

In their June 1997 interim report on reviewing the guidelines, Japanese and American defense officials distinguished three different contexts for defense cooperation: "cooperation under normal circumstances, actions in response to an armed attack against Japan, and cooperation in situations in areas surrounding Japan that will have an important influence on Japan's peace and security." For each of these contexts the report identified modes of defense cooperation that are both appropriate and reasonable. The issue of constitutional interpretation, however, still leaves murky the extent to which Japan can really perform tasks such as rear support for U.S. forces that includes supply and transportation, minesweeping, and inspections of ships.

First, Japanese self-defense forces should provide supplies and offer transport services to U.S. forces in the open seas. There should be no restrictions on what items can be supplied or transported. For example, from a military perspective, it would be irrational to argue that it is permissible to supply water to U.S. forces but not ammunition. Agreeing to something that does not make sense militarily could make things worse for the alliance. Second, Japan should perform minesweeping in the open seas. This is a service in which Japan excels and which is critical to its national interest. Third, under the revised guidelines U.S. forces stationed in Japan and those dispatched to Japan should be able to operate freely within and outside Japanese territory during a crisis. To make this possible, Japan should make available the necessary facilities and locations. Fourth, in the context of trilateral defense cooperation (among Japan, the United States, and the Republic of Korea), Japan should provide broad-ranging rear support in intelligence exchange, air defense, patrolling, warning, search and rescue, refugee relief, and medical operations for U.S. and ROK forces. To carry out these tasks effectively, an adequate network must be developed among Japan, the United States and South Korea regarding command, control, and coordination. The performance of these types of military operations beyond its national boundaries will require Japan to develop a new legal and political framework for defense cooperation.

The review of the Japan-U.S. Defense Cooperation Guidelines will inevitably require dealing squarely with exercising the right of collective self-defense. The reason the Japanese government interpreted the constitution as not permitting exercise of the right is that at the time the self-defense force was established, the government chose to legitimize the exercise of the individual self-defense right by denying the exercise of the collective self-defense right. Rather than being based on an interpretation of the text of the constitution, the decision was based on a political judgment. This

judgment has kept Japan's self-defense capabilities to a minimum and contributed to good relations with other countries in East Asia. The fact that
Japan did not become involved in a military conflict for a half century after
World War II also enabled it to sustain this policy. But with the situation in
Northeast Asia becoming more uncertain, Japan must now extricate itself
from a legal interpretation based on a political judgment and make a new
political judgment based on changing circumstances.

If the United States acts to sacrifice its own citizens during a Far East
crisis while Japan stands by, it would be impossible for the two to cooperate adequately and for the alliance to survive. U.S. citizens are unaware
that the legal framework of the alliance, that Japan cannot exercise its
right to collective self-defense, prevents it from cooperating fully. When
the American people become aware of this during a Far East crisis, they
will likely say that such a country is not an ally or demand that the security treaty be abolished. The alliance would be endangered. Japan must
do what is necessary to prevent this from happening.

Japan's Defense Capabilities and Crisis Management System

Japan has preserved its security through Japan-U.S. security arrangements and effective defense capabilities. To respond to the diverse and
complex dangers of today, the defense capabilities must become more
comprehensive and efficient. To preserve territorial integrity and ensure
the safety of citizens requires correcting the shortcomings in current
defense capabilities and acquiring efficient defense systems that are
highly adaptable and technologically advanced.[5]

Japan's defense capabilities must also help promote security dialogues
and confidence-building measures in the region. In this regard, Japan
must be able to respond to large-scale terrorist activities and natural
disasters. It must also actively participate in and cooperate with UN-
centered peacekeeping activities and international emergency relief
operations. In short, the self-defense forces need equipment and training
that are adaptable to complex and diverse conditions.

Although the new National Defense Program Outline approved in
November 1995 will guide the acquisition of defense capabilities, there
are some shortcomings. In particular, it needs a clearer articulation of the
specific military systems that Japan should acquire so that it can complement those of U.S. forces in providing deterrence. For example, intel-

ligence gathering capabilities, including information satellites, need to be improved significantly. This would improve bilateral cooperation in intelligence exchanges. To reinforce maritime operations, Japan should acquire large transport ships, intelligence-gathering vessels, and a small aircraft carrier. These acquisitions would enable it to engage in joint sea-based air defense operations with the United States even in areas where a U.S. carrier task force may not be deployed. For air defense, existing missile defense systems (including theater missile defense) and multi-purpose fighter aircraft are insufficient. Midair refueling planes, for example, would allow Japan to cooperate more fully with U.S. air operations in Northeast Asia.

For the past several years, Japan and the United States have been discussing the acquisition and deployment of theater missile defense systems. TMD raises political, military, economic, and technological issues, including an assessment of the threats that the systems would be designed to counter, their cost effectiveness, the prospects for joint Japan-U.S. technological development, and the overall impact of TMD on Japan's defense systems. But the most critical issue is whether to view TMD as a way of strengthening the Japan-U.S. alliance. On this particular point, both Japanese and American officials are forward looking. Although for the time being the two countries are likely to focus on research and development, TMD acquisition and deployment will become a cornerstone of the future Japan-U.S. alliance.

Being able to respond to regional emergencies is critical for the security of Japan and the region. The best way to deal with Northeast Asian crises is for Japanese and South Korean defense forces to cooperate closely with and support U.S. forces stationed in Japan and South Korea. To this end, a review of the Japan-U.S. Defense Cooperation Guidelines must be completed as soon as possible. As part of this review, Japan should make the necessary legal and political arrangements so that it can expand rear support for U.S. forces. At the same time, the United States and the Republic of Korea should develop a similar defense cooperation guideline. The U.S.-ROK security consultative mechanism that already exists should be used to discuss measures to strengthen bilateral defense cooperation. Based on these two sets of guidelines, the United States, Japan, and South Korea should then promote defense cooperation among the three countries. Without cultivating this sort of trilateral coordination, it will be impossible to have effective cooperation at the operational level during a crisis in the Korean peninsula.

Given its natural protection as an island and its national pacifism since World War II, Japan has little awareness of crises. Public interest in crisis management has therefore been alarmingly low. Although the greatest crisis for a nation is aggression from other countries, states must also respond to natural disasters, attempts to overthrow the government, large-scale terrorism, and other domestic crises. In recent years Japan has faced a number of unexpected incidents—the earthquake off the shore of southwest Hokkaido; the Hanshin earthquake; the sarin gas attack in the Tokyo subway and other incidents related to Aum Shinrikyo; the hijacking of a passenger plane; and the abduction of Japanese nationals overseas. To respond properly to such crises, the state must be able to gather information rapidly and accurately. This information must be relayed in a precise manner, and the government must make effective and timely decisions based on it. Japan sorely needs a crisis management system that delineates the responsibilities and authority of the prime minister, strengthens state intelligence capabilities, and amplifies the vital functions of the prime minister's office and other state agencies.

Moreover, to manage crises as effectively as possible, a system of policy implementation and briefings must be set up so that the state's decisionmaking can be clear to the citizens. This system should have clearly defined lines of responsibility and authority, receive adequate funding, and be based on a firm legal foundation. The Japanese government should also make better use of specialized organizations and experts in managing crises. Crisis management means being prepared for the unexpected and responding effectively to defend the safety of the nation and its people. To make this possible, state institutions and the people must share a comprehensive perspective and cooperate with each other.

Notes

1. Nonaka Ikujiro, *Amerika Kaiheitai* (Tokyo: Chuo Shinsho, 1995).

2. William J. Perry, *Annual Report to the President and Congress* (Department of Defense, 1995).

3. Mike Mochizuki, "Okinawa no Kaiheitai wa tettai subeki da," *Sekai Shuho*, vol. 76 (December 12, 1995), pp. 42–43.

4. Joseph S. Nye, "The Case for Deep Engagement," *Foreign Affairs*, vol. 74 (July-August 1995), pp. 90–102.

5. *National Defense Program Outline in and after FY 1996* (Tokyo: Japan Defense Agency, 1995).

CHAPTER SIX

Restructuring U.S. Forces and Bases in Japan

Michael O'Hanlon

WHEN CHANGES in U.S. force configurations in the East Asia–Pacific region are contemplated, many policymakers emphasize their possible symbolic importance. It is appropriate that they do so; perceptions clearly do matter in international affairs.

For example, the U.S. ground forces based in Korea, although militarily capable, are probably even more important as a demonstration of commitment. Because they would be involved immediately in opposing any North Korean attack and would inevitably suffer casualties, they provide an important tripwire. Pyongyang can therefore hardly doubt the U.S. commitment to South Korea or devise a way to initiate a conflict that stands a good chance of keeping the United States out.

But forces deployed for general reassurance serve a far less obvious purpose, not only in narrow military terms but also from a political and strategic perspective. If providing reassurance is the main reason for keeping the U.S. Marine Corps combat forces on Okinawa, and they are becoming politically damaging within Japan to the security relationship, their presence bears reassessment.

Marine facilities on Okinawa do provide significant military capabilities. They would help the Marine Corps substantially in the event of another major war on the Korean peninsula, and they provide a convenient launching pad for marine patrols with 2,000-troop shipborne units in the Western Pacific. But there are ways to preserve or even augment

149

these benefits without stationing nearly 20,000 marines on Okinawa indefinitely.

My argument begins with a strategic framework similar to that espoused by Satoshi Morimoto in chapter 3. Although all branches of the U.S. military remain important in the post–cold war world, the U.S. Navy and Air Force probably have the most critical roles in the East Asia–Pacific region. As President Nixon stated on Guam in 1969, and as will be an even more compelling argument once Korea is reunified, the United States should avoid ground wars in Asia except under the most extreme circumstances. This view is also consistent with those of George Kennan shortly after World War II; his famous five centers of global industrial strength included three European countries (considering Russia principally a European state for these purposes), the United States, and Japan.[1] The shape of the world economy, and thus the world's latent military potential, has shifted since Kennan's major writings. But most of the new economic activity—Persian Gulf oil drilling, Taiwanese and Indonesian manufacturing, the growth in Latin America and South Asia—does not require protection from U.S. ground forces based in East Asia.

This argument should not be pushed too far. U.S. marines and army forces might, for example, participate in a multilateral peace operation in the region. But modest numbers of U.S. ground troops based on an island hundreds or thousands of miles away from a potential zone of unrest offer only modest benefits for conducting such missions. U.S. marines on Okinawa are relatively few in number, constituting only about 10 percent of the Marine Corps and just over 1 percent of the total active-duty U.S. military. Eight countries in the East Asia–Pacific region have militaries at least ten times larger than the aggregate marine strength on Okinawa. The Okinawa marines represent less than 5 percent of the total number of troops the United States would probably deploy to a war in Korea. They equal about 1 percent of the combined Korean strength on the peninsula.[2]

The number of Okinawa marines that could be quickly deployed with their equipment is smaller yet. There are only enough U.S. amphibious ships based in Sasebo, Japan, to carry about 10 percent, or 2,000, at a time. (Unlike U.S. tactical fighter aircraft, and to some extent navy ships in Japan, Marine Corps ground forces cannot defend most U.S. and Japanese interests in the region from where they are based.) Two thousand marines would generally not be enough to establish even a firm initial foothold in places where hostilities were under way.

The Okinawa-based marines also offer few advantages for light operations with small numbers of troops, given the availability and mobility of army airborne and special forces as well as the army's Twenty-fifth Infantry Division and marine forces based in Hawaii. Admittedly, there are some situations that one could imagine in which the marines' ability to deploy a few hours more quickly than other U.S. units could make an important difference. But these would rarely require more than a few hundred troops to handle.

This survey of U.S. combat capabilities in the region is not intended to denigrate the caliber of the Okinawa-based marines, whose personnel are undoubtedly as proficient as any in today's excellent U.S. armed forces. It is, rather, designed to show that their ability to deploy in strength quickly is limited and that alternatives to them do exist.[3]

Not only are the U.S. Navy and Air Force more likely to be relevant to the defense of U.S. and Japanese interests in East Asia, but they derive great operational benefits from having bases in Japan. (So do the marines' own fixed-wing combat aircraft based at Iwakuni on the main Japanese island of Honshu, although under the options discussed later, they would return to the United States along with marine ground forces and be replaced in Japan by air force aircraft or army helicopters.) As such, ensuring the future access of U.S. ships and fixed-wing planes to existing bases in Japan is much more important than preserving a marine ground combat–oriented force on Okinawa that, if beneficial, is not critical.

To maintain a permanent aircraft carrier presence in the Western Pacific, for example, requires only those ships based in Japan. But to conduct it out of U.S. ports would require building and operating four more carrier battle groups, which would increase costs to the United States about $10 billion a year. Benefits of comparable scale accrue from the air force and marine fixed-wing air capabilities in Japan. Budgetary benefits from marine ground forces on Okinawa are a factor of ten less.

In all, fixed-wing planes in Japan provide more than half the combat aircraft that the United States has immediately available for a possible war in Korea. And the Kadena Air Base on Okinawa could be particularly useful for other contingencies in the region. Aircraft operating from there can bring most of Southeast Asia within fighter range (using refueling aircraft when necessary). The base is also well suited to serve as a regional hub for military air transport operations.

U.S. military aircraft and ships have the added advantage of not taking up much space in a country that is one of the most densely populated in the world. Marine ground combat forces, with their associated requirements for training ranges, are far more onerous to support in Japan.

The clinching argument is perhaps the availability of alternatives. Marine capabilities on Okinawa do remain important for the defense of Korea. It would also be desirable to keep sailing marine patrols from Okinawa. That might be done by retaining the Thirty-first Marine Expeditionary Unit on Okinawa. Although it would be more complicated logistically, it could also be accomplished by flying MEU-sized units from the United States to Okinawa for brief periods, during which they would conduct exercises with the amphibious ships from Sasebo and then go on deployment (doing additional exercises in other areas). Finally, it would be desirable to retain the capacity to stage larger operations from Okinawa even once Korea is reunified.

But these functions can be satisfied without large numbers of resident ground forces. No more than 5,000 marines would be adequate as a permanent presence. With this presence the United States could pre-position equipment stocks on Okinawa. Consistent with the thrust of the 1997 U.S.-Japan Defense Guidelines, it could also make arrangements for contingency access to commercial ports and airfields there in emergencies—assuming Japan is also willing to enter into such a new bargain, as I believe that it should.

The options presented here are not all or nothing. They could be put in place gradually. Given the reluctance of many policymakers to consider major changes in U.S. military forces in Japan so soon after publication of the so-called Nye report in 1995, which effectively promised to maintain the status quo for the foreseeable future, a gradual course may be the most realistic.[4] But it should also be borne in mind that this chapter's options would not begin to affect the numbers of deployed marines until 2000 and would not be fully in place until 2003 in any event.

These arguments are developed in more detail in the rest of the chapter, after a summary of the present arrangements by which U.S. Forces/Japan maintain what is the Pentagon's second-largest military presence in a foreign country.

Current U.S. Forces in Japan

The United States stations an average of 45,000 uniformed military personnel in Japan. About three-fifths, or roughly 28,000, are on Okinawa. The 45,000 troops are about 10 percent less than the number based in Japan during the late 1980s, and 6 percent less than the 1980s average of 48,000. Of the 45,000 in Japan, 21,000 are marines, 18,000 of them on Okinawa; the remainder of the marines, among other things, fly about fifty fixed-wing planes featuring thirty-six F/A-18 aircraft at Iwakuni on the main island of Honshu.[5]

The total numbers of marines on Okinawa (and in Japan overall) are slated to decrease by about 2,000 when the Futenma Marine Air Station in Ginowan is closed. At that time the fifteen or so KC-130 marine transport and refueling aircraft will relocate to Iwakuni, and the fifty or so rotary-wing aircraft (of which fourteen are Cobra attack helicopters and most of the rest transport helicopters) will under current plans operate out of an offshore facility on the northeast Okinawan coastline. (For more discussion about the nature of the U.S. military presence in Okinawa and the recent changes in the U.S.-Japan security relationship, see chapter 2.)

U.S. Forces in the East Asia–Pacific Region

Together with 37,000 forces in South Korea, nearly 15,000 afloat in the Western Pacific and Southeast Asia regions, and 7,000 on Guam, the United States has a total East Asia–Pacific troop strength of about 104,000 (table 6-1). The 1995 Pentagon white paper known as the Nye report promised to retain that level for the "foreseeable future." Even though the report included Alaska, Hawaii, and Diego Garcia in its definition of the East Asia–Pacific region, it chose not to count the additional 60,000 U.S. military personnel stationed in those places as part of its regional presence. Nor did it count the 25,000 or so troops based in the United States that could quickly man additional ground-combat equipment stored in Guam, South Korea, and Diego Garcia. Adding in the forces from Alaska and Hawaii would make for a regional total of about 165,000; adding in those for whom equipment is predeployed in the region would push the number to 190,000.

Neither the Nye report nor the April 1996 Clinton-Hashimoto summit statements committed the United States to keep a specific number of U.S. troops in Japan. But the Nye report promised to keep in place the basic U.S. force structure now there. That includes one marine expeditionary force with its helicopters and fixed-wing aircraft, one amphibious ready group of ships, one aircraft carrier battle group, and more than one air force tactical combat wing. It also encompasses support capabilities such as the marines' KC-130 aircraft, fifteen KC-135 aerial refuel-

Table 6-1. *U.S. Active-Duty Uniformed Forces in the East Asia—Pacific Region, 1995[a]*

Country of basing	U.S. military service	Average number of troops	Additional troops with equipment stored in region	Subtotal (and with additional)
Japan	Air force	15,200	0	45,500
	Army	2,000	0	. . .
	Marine Corps	21,000	0	. . .
	Navy	7,300	0	. . .
South Korea	Air force	8,950	0	36,450
	Army	27,500	5,000	(41,450)
Diego Garcia	Marine Corps	0	10,000	900
	Navy	900	0	(10,900)
Other foreign		1,000	. . .	1,000
Guam	Air force	2,200	0	6,800
	Navy	4,600	10,000	(16,800)
Afloat	Navy/Marine Corps	13,000	0	13,000
Subtotal		. . .	. . .	103,650
				(128,650)
Alaska	Air force	10,000	. . .	19,600
	Army	9,600	. . .	
Hawaii	Air force	4,400	. . .	46,400
	Army	24,600	. . .	
	Marine Corps	2,900	. . .	
	Navy	14,500	. . .	
Grand Total		. . .	. . .	169,650
				(194,650)

Sources: International Institute for Strategic Studies, *The Military Balance 1995/1996* (Oxford University Press, 1995), pp. 30–31; Secretary of Defense William J. Perry, *Annual Report to the President and the Congress* (March 1996), p. C-2; and Office of International Security Affairs, *United States Security Strategy for the East Asia–Pacific Region* (Department of Defense, 1995), p. iv.

a. Totals for Marine Corps and navy forces based in Hawaii are reduced by 1,000 and 5,000, respectively, because some are already counted in the "afloat" category. Diego Garcia is not in the Pacific Ocean, but U.S. troops there are counted by the Department of Defense as contributing to the 100,000 in the region.

ing aircraft, and depot repair facilities on Okinawa and elsewhere. And President Clinton has also promised to keep "about the current number" of U.S. forces in Japan for the foreseeable future.[6]

Costs of the U.S. Presence

Japan pays the yen equivalent of $5 billion a year to accommodate and support the U.S. forces based on its territory. Those payments are for the local costs of housing, base construction, maintenance, utilities, fuel, many other supplies, and salaries of Japanese support personnel. They do not cover U.S. military and civilian salaries or the purchase costs of most U.S. equipment.

Japan forgoes another $1 billion in annual revenue that could be realized by renting the ninety-six bases that U.S. forces now employ (forty on Okinawa and fifty-six on the main islands). The acreage of that land is only one-quarter as great, countrywide, as when the United States occupied Japan. But much of what is left is in choice urban areas and thus valuable. In addition, 85 percent of the original Okinawan acreage remains in American hands; U.S. bases there now account for 75 percent of the total American military acreage in Japan as well as about one-fifth of the island's total land area. The number of U.S. bases on Okinawa will be reduced by seven and their combined acreage there by about 20 percent as a result of the 1996 Clinton-Hashimoto summit.[7]

Japan's support is by far the most generous of any country hosting U.S. military forces. (It also has the largest defense budget of any country with which the United States has a security relationship. But that budget is small as a percentage of Japanese GDP, funds forces that do not accept as many security responsibilities as do those of U.S. allies in Europe, and is based on a strategy that avoids power projection.) Japan hosts about 25 percent of U.S. forces based abroad but provides, in dollar-equivalent value, more than half of all contributions that the United States receives in military support from foreign countries. And its support stands to increase by $1.5 billion a year for the next five to seven years under the proposed relocation of the functions performed by the existing Futenma base.[8]

The cost of the Futenma relocation plan has not been publicly explained piece by piece as of this writing. But it is worth highlighting that the one piece of it that cannot be avoided, cleanup of the existing site, is probably not a major component. The U.S. base closure effort involves shutting down about one hundred major facilities at a total cleanup cost of $5 billion, or $50 million per site. Even allowing for the possibility that the Futenma site may be larger than the average facility closed in the United States, more in need of careful restoration due to its urban location, and more expensive to clean on an item-by-item and man hour–by–man hour basis, it is hard to believe that the operation could cost more than $500 million, or ¥50 billion.[9]

The United States pays about $1.5 billion in operations and maintenance costs for forces in Japan. The amount is considerably less than the $3 billion or more one would expect for a representative 45,000 troops in the U.S. military.[10] Thus the United States, although not saving the full $6 billion a year that Japan in effect pays to support U.S. forces, is probably getting a value of nearly one-third that amount. As estimated below, it is also probably realizing $25 billion a year in indirect savings from its bases in Japan, given the efficiencies of maintaining an East Asia–Pacific presence from nearby rather than from the continental United States.

Specific Military Purposes of U.S. Forces in Japan

Leaving aside the broad geopolitical purposes of the bilateral security relationship (see chapters 2 and 3 for more discussion of the subject), what are the main military functions of the U.S. forces and bases in Japan?

To begin, those forces and bases tie the United States to the defense of Japan. This was the original rationale for the security relationship, one that was particularly important during the cold war. Second, the base infrastructure provides a forward logistics capability for U.S. forces in any war in Korea. For example, the U.S. military has enough fuel stored on Okinawa—50 million gallons—to support a 100,000-strong marine force for nearly two weeks in combat; the marines also have 5,000 pieces of equipment there.[11] Equally important, bases in Japan would provide a regional hub for sending supplies for all military services from the United States to Korea and for servicing and repairing equipment. They could also provide staging for a large-scale amphibious operation in the region.

Third, Japan would almost certainly provide bases for U.S. combat operations in Korea. Those could involve U.S. fighter and attack aircraft operating over Korea and ports for U.S. ships and submarines patrolling in the region. Although they would probably prefer to operate primarily from South Korea, U.S. forces could in theory fly about 500 combat aircraft out of Japan from their own bases and possibly those of the Japan Defense

Agency's as well, if Tokyo agreed. Likewise, at least 75 principal surface combatants and 20 submarines, perhaps some American and others from the self-defense forces, could operate out of Japanese ports.[12]

Fourth, facilities in Japan provide forward operating bases for U.S. forces conducting other missions in the region. In addition to providing general reassurance, the units conducting those patrols could respond to a number of crises. Potential crises involving China, for example, might be handled by aircraft from the carrier *Independence*, the Kadena airfield in Okinawa, or the Iwakuni airfield on the mainland.[13] Routine marine patrols could handle certain limited crises on their own. They might, for example, help ensure access to the Malacca and Singapore Straits during a local disturbance by deploying forces ashore on either side of the narrow channels to prevent harassment of shipping. (However, they would probably require reinforcement and aerial support from carriers or nearby land bases if the disturbance was significant or protracted and if the United States elected to quell it rather than simply reroute commercial shipping out of harm's way.)[14]

Finally, forces and facilities in Japan provide a convenient and money-saving hub for U.S. operations in the Persian Gulf and other distant theaters. The value of this hub is especially great for aerial transport missions but also is considerable for the marines. It is not the only hub U.S. forces have in the area; facilities on Guam also being important. But bases in Japan increase total throughput capacity, constituting part of an air bridge using the northern continental states and Alaska (whereas Guam is better positioned to be a stopover for flights going through Hawaii).

Which of these bases and capabilities could the United States really count on in a crisis, though? For the immediate defense of Japan, all bases would be fully available and supported logistically. Of the ninety-six U.S. bases in Japan, seven of the most important—Futenma, Kadena, and White Beach on Okinawa, Sasebo in Kyushu, and Yokosuka, Yokota, and Zama on Honshu—are UN command bases that could be used (at least for logistical purposes) in the event of another Korean conflict without prior approval from Tokyo.

Use of all other bases in a conflict in Korea or elsewhere in the Far East region (corresponding to the zone within a 1,000-mile radius from Tokyo) would require official Japanese permission. Those other bases include a number of critical ones: notably Misawa Air Force Base on northern Honshu Island and Iwakuni Marine Air Station as well as Atsugi Naval Air Station. Even if permission to use the bases was granted, Japan could under the 1997

Defense Guidlines support U.S. troops with operations such as transportation and provision of nonlethal supplies, although it could probably only service weapons and work with amunition if it were itself under attack or at dire risk.[15]

A Brief Survey of Japan's Self-Defense Forces

As for Japan, its active-duty uniformed forces today number 235,500, with 148,000 in the army, 43,000 in the navy, and 44,500 in the air force. The army is organized principally into twelve relatively small infantry divisions, averaging fewer than 100 tanks and about 50 armored personnel carriers apiece. It has about 80 attack helicopters and 350 transport helicopters. The navy has 18 submarines, 8 destroyers (with several modern Aegis-class destroyers on the way), and 55 frigates specializing principally in antisubmarine warfare. It also operates about 100 P-3 maritime patrol aircraft and 100 antisubmarine helicopters. The air force includes 450 combat aircraft, of which 50 F-1's specialize in ground-attack missions. Most of the rest of the aircraft, F-15s and F-4s, are fighters specializing in air defense, but the air force also operates about 30 transport planes.[16]

Options for U.S. Forces and Bases in Japan

Chapters 2 and 3 address the ways Japan might expand its military roles and responsibilities to give the security relationship a more equitable and robust character. The focus of this chapter is on alleviating the pressures currently facing the alliance, notably Okinawans' preference that the U.S. military presence on their island be reduced and other Japanese citizens' typical views that although Okinawans deserve a reprieve, they do not wish to see the U.S. bases relocated on the main Japanese islands near their own communities. The chapter also explores ways in which U.S. military capabilities in Japan could be improved even as marine forces and bases on Okinawa are cut back.

Criteria for Devising the Options

The following options seek to protect what are the most critical U.S. military assets in Japan: ships, fixed-wing aircraft, and storage and staging facilities.

Apart from geostrategic arguments about the types of interests that Japan and the United States have in East Asia and plausible risks to those interests, a good way to compare the importance of the various U.S. bases in Japan is to estimate their respective dollar values. Which bases save the United States the most money in operational efficiencies? To put it another way, how much more would the United States need to spend if it did not have access to those bases but wished to retain comparable military capabilities in the region? The calculations show that what Tokyo pays in host-nation support, although generous, is actually only a small part of what the United States saves by virtue of its current force configuration in Japan. Moreover, the savings are greatest for air force and navy operations.

Consider first the navy. Its aircraft carrier battle group based in Yokosuka is principally charged with maintaining American presence in the western Pacific and is considered by virtue of its location to do so nearly continuously (even when in port). Were it necessary to maintain permanent carrier presence in the region out of U.S. ports, four more carrier battle groups would need to be added to the fleet. That is because any U.S. Navy ship operates on a twenty-four-month cycle, only one six-month segment of which is spent at sea. (The other three are spent on crew training, exercises in home waters, and major ship maintenance, respectively.) Moreover, during the six-month deployment, more than a month is usually lost in transit to and from U.S. ports.

The cost implications are enormous. A carrier battle group and associated aircraft cost nearly $15 billion to purchase; annual personnel, operating, and support costs are $2 billion. Averaging out the procurement costs over a typical thirty-year equipment lifetime, the cost per carrier group is $2.5 billion a year. Being able to maintain a permanent presence out of Japan rather than San Diego or San Francisco thus saves the United States more than $11 billion a year (adding in host-nation support). Additional savings accrue from basing amphibious ships and attack submarines in Japan.

If the navy lost its bases in Japan, it might well elect to tolerate times when the western Pacific was left uncovered by a carrier or compensate in some other way. But the effective fiscal value of navy bases in Japan can still be thought of as more than $10 billion a year.

For the air force and marine airpower, the economic benefits are less easily estimated. But one rough way to gauge the importance of the bases for U.S. tactical combat aircraft in Japan is to assume that, were they not available, the navy might have to maintain additional deployments in the region. If it deployed one additional carrier in the region continuously—only half compensation for the loss of the air force and marine fixed-wing airbases, since they can host 150 U.S. combat aircraft whereas a carrier only has capacity for about 75—the added costs for the five necessary carrier battle groups would again be more than $10 billion a year (table 6-2). If a second carrier were deployed part time instead, and perhaps supplemented with additional U.S. combat aircraft based in Korea, added costs might be half as much—still a large amount.

The air force also benefits, as do the marines, from having a regional hub for transport and logistics operations in Japan. It is difficult to calculate these benefits, but they are considerable in terms of the supply ships, refueling aircraft, and many other additional support capabilities that would be needed to compensate for a loss of bases in Japan.

But the savings are small for marine ground combat forces per se. Although there are some intangible benefits to the Okinawa bases, such as jungle training facilities, the main military benefit is that Japan pays for many host-nation support costs the United States would otherwise need to assume. Associated savings to the United States, while not insignificant, are in the hundreds of millions of dollars a year rather than the billions.

Options that Preserve or Enhance Key U.S. Bases in Japan

The first option developed in this chapter would end the permanent stationing of Marine Corps ground combat troops in Okinawa. It might start to be put in place in 2000 and be fully implemented by 2003. All major training bases would be closed and returned to Japanese control. Those few Futenma Air Station functions still deemed important would be relocated to existing military and civilian facilities. Most marine barracks would be returned to local control as well. But enough would be kept for personnel maintaining Marine Corps equipment and facilities on the island, as well as for 2,000 marines forming an MEU for deployment on navy amphibious vessels from Sasebo.

The major innovation of this option, shared by all variants of option two, would be to permanently store more marine equipment on Okinawa. Warehouses would be built to store enough equipment for a brigade equivalent, roughly 10,000 troops. This approach would be modeled on the POMCUS (prepositioned material configured to unit sets) program used by the army during the cold war in Europe. Additional equipment

Table 6-2. *Implicit U.S. Savings from Selected Bases in Japan*[a]

Billions of dollars

U.S. military service	Chief assets in Japan	Alternative approach without bases in Japan	Total savings to U.S. (annualized)
Navy	Carrier battle group, naval air wing	Possess five times as many ships and planes, operate from United States	11.5
Air force and marines	150 fixed-wing combat aircraft	Add base in Korea, keep another carrier group with air wing in western Pacific by adding five of each to navy	14
Navy	Amphibious group, submarines	Possess five times as many as are in Japan, operate from United States	2.5
Marines	Training ranges, barracks for ground combat units	Base and train troops in U.S., keep staging capabilities and extra equipment in Okinawa	0.5

Source: See text.

a. Added costs to the United States for any of these options would of course be less if Japan helped pay the costs. Costs would be more if the Pentagon had to pay for appreciable new facilities in the United States, but I assume that in a period of general defense downsizing, existing facilities would become available and be used with limited refurbishment.

There would be many ways, some better than others, to compensate for any loss of U.S. military bases in Japan. But the approaches presented here are representative of the cost associated with keeping aircraft in the western Pacific in the absence of bases.

would have to be purchased or refurbished, since the marines returning to stateside basing would take their first set of equipment with them.

Under option one, marine fixed-wing aircraft in Iwakuni and marine helicopters on Okinawa would return to the United States with their units. To compensate, the army might modestly augment its helicopter fleet in Korea to ensure no net degradation in forward-deployed U.S. airpower; alternatively or additionally, the air force could place about two squadrons of fighter-attack aircraft at the Iwakuni facility.

The United States would keep 100,000 troops deployed abroad or at sea in East Asia through 2000, and 90,000 even after 2003. This approach would also allow time for the POMCUS-like arrangements to be completed before the marines departed, so that the ability to deploy marines and their equipment to Korea would never be compromised should the peninsula remain divided for an extended period.

Option two is really a set of possible approaches. It would, albeit at somewhat greater cost and difficulty, have several advantages over the first option. It would combine the force cuts and POMCUS initiative of option one with improvements to other U.S. capabilities in the region, generally ships of one type or another—and if not in Japan then somewhere else in the Pacific. Doing so would result in a U.S. regional force structure that would be even more capable than today's. That might satisfy those who could support a Marine Corps withdrawal from Okinawa except for their worries that it be misread as signaling lessened U.S. commitment to the region. Total U.S. troop levels west of Alaska and Hawaii would remain close to the 100,000 goal for the East Asia–Pacific region.

The Sea-Based Heliport Concept

Before proceeding to a detailed analysis of these two options, a word is in order about current official U.S.-Japanese policy to build a facility just off Okinawa as a substitute site for Futenma's helicopter operations— most likely, it appears, a fixed asset rather than a mobile offshore base.

This facility would be a less militarily effective use of scarce resources than option two, which would add either U.S. amphibious ships, an aircraft carrier, or sea-based equipment storage ships to what is already based in Japan. The heliport seems likely to be an inefficient and expensive way of generating a modest military capability. Nor will it likely represent a meaningful technological innovation.

Options One and Two and the U.S. Defense Debate

Neither option one nor option two would necessarily have significant implications for the U.S. defense debate. Both could ease the process of further cutbacks that might eventually become necessary on fiscal grounds in the United States. In particular, the marines now based in Okinawa could be deactivated rather than relocated to the United States, if that was deemed a sensible way to make further reductions in forces and budgets. Also, by forward-basing additional ships in Japan, the United States could modestly reduce the size of its navy at little or no detriment to its global peacetime presence.

But almost surely major Defense Department reductions will not be made in the next few years. The real defense budget is about one-third less than it was at the end of the cold war in 1990. Neither the Republican Congress, nor Secretary of Defense William Cohen (former Republican senator from Maine), nor President Clinton for that matter, appears interested in cutting it further at this time, as evidenced by the recent completion of the quadrennial review.

Option One: Reduce Marine Presence on Okinawa to 3,000 to 5,000 Troops

Option one would reduce the marine presence on Okinawa by about 15,000 troops. Combat troops would return to the United States; all training ranges and most barracks would be returned to Japan; most infrastructure for staging marine operations from the island would be retained; and special POMCUS-like storage capabilities for enough equipment to outfit a brigade would be constructed there, as would facilities for helicopter maintenance and storage.

The option would leave up to 12,000 total U.S. troops from all services on Okinawa, of which air force personnel would constitute the majority. The overall number of uniformed U.S. personnel in Japan would decline to about 30,000 in 2003. The transition could be made entirely in that year, although it might better be spread out over the 2000–2003 time frame to soften whatever symbolic and perceptual effects could accompany it.

Option one may seem extreme, given the ongoing problems on the Korean peninsula and the difficulty of backing off the 100,000-troop level of the Nye report. But it is not extreme when one considers that the requirement of 100,000 troops is arbitrarily established and also a significant understatement of the actual number of U.S. military personnel focused primarily on the East Asia–Pacific region. More to the point, it should not degrade U.S. military capabilities in the region.

Resulting Marine Corps Force Structure on Okinawa

About 2,000 to 3,000 marines based on Okinawa for two-to-three-year periods (with their families, if married) would maintain installations for staging, supply, and equipment storage. The Thirty-first Marine Expeditionary Unit might or might not remain as well. The Third MEF headquarters would probably be relocated to Hawaii or the mainland United States.

By keeping its equipment and depot capabilities as well as access to wharves and a major airfield, the Marine Corps could continue to perform important functions from Okinawa. On a routine basis the most important would probably be to use Okinawa as a hub for MEUs in the region. MEUs, 2,000 troop units made up of an infantry battalion and some artillery and air power as well as logistics support, conduct Marine Corps ship-based presence operations around the world.[17] In the future, marine crews might fly from their U.S. bases to Okinawa, where they would join up with their equipment and board ships from Sasebo. After several days or at most weeks of exercises, they would set sail for the region's waters and some other countries, where they would conduct additional exercises. Alternatively, the Thirty-first MEU might remain permanently on Okinawa and retain responsibility for the deployments itself. The equipment for a single MEU, together with the brigade equivalent of material in POMCUS storage, would keep the total amount of Marine Corps equipment on Okinawa unchanged from what it is today.

Even from the corps's perspective, this option could come to have advantages. Keeping several thousand troops on deployment in Okinawa is difficult for a shrinking service that must also maintain deployments, conduct exercises, and respond to crises or other special requirements in many other parts of the world. Marines who make a six-month deployment to Okinawa are then supposed to be given a rest and returned to their home bases for a comparable length of time, meaning that all told they are unavailable for other assignments for a full calendar year.

This problem is not acute for the Marine Corps at its present size. But further reductions to the service's active-duty troop strength could well occur. After all, the Bush administration's base force, although more than 10 percent larger and more expensive than the overall force recommended by the Clinton administration's quadrennial defense review, actually envisioned a Marine Corps of only 159,000 active-duty uniformed troops in contrast to the bottom-up review's 172,000.[18] Should additional reductions take place while other marine activities around the world remained constant, the corps would not be large enough to comfortably handle today's presence on Okinawa.

Korea

In the event of war in Korea, option one would provide virtually the same capability as today's force posture because it would leave unchanged the total amount of Marine Corps equipment on Okinawa. Actually, U.S. capabilities for a war in Korea would suffer only modestly even if all Marine Corps equipment now in Okinawa were returned to the United States. The most important U.S. military capabilities in the critical early stages of a war would be the ground forces already there and tactical combat aircraft already in the region or quickly deployable from the United States. Marines from Okinawa would be part of a second echelon of capability that would also include ground-force reinforcements to join up with army and marine equipment pre-positioned in Korea and Guam, and the army's Twenty-fifth Light Infantry Division from Hawaii.

Why would the contribution of the Okinawa-based marines to a war in Korea be so limited in the first week of war? In addition to being relatively few in number, the marine ground units on Okinawa are not particularly mobile. At any time, there are perhaps 10,000 marine combat troops stationed there. But there are only enough amphibious ships in Japan to transport one MEU, about 2,000 troops, at a time. Other troops would have to get to Korea in other ways. They could be moved by Japanese commercial shipping, if that proved legally feasible in a Korean crisis, but then they would have no amphibious assault capability and would probably need more than a week to arrive in Korea because of the slowness of loading and unloading equipment on commercial vessels. They could, of course, await more amphibious ships from U.S. ports, but that would negate the principal military benefit of forward deployment. Or they could deploy with rifles and other light equipment by airlift, getting to Korea slightly more quickly than if they had been based in Hawaii or the United States, but they would not be particularly well suited for most types of combat once they had arrived.

For the sake of military conservatism, however, this option assumes that the POMCUS capability would be developed. The only slight degradation to U.S. capabilities that would result is that the marines now on Okinawa would have to be flown further to get to Korea, meaning that some other U.S. troops who would have flown over in the first stage of a massive airlift operation would have to postpone their arrival in Korea by a few days. But this problem is modest. U.S. airlift, especially when augmented by the civil reserve air fleet, can carry at least 50,000 soldiers overseas at a time if need be, or at least 100,000 to Korea per week.[19] That is far faster than heavy equipment can be transported to the region for them to operate. The real difficulty in preparing for regional war is not moving people but equipment.

Futenma

What would be the importance of the Futenma Marine Air Station, or its successor, under this option? It would no longer be needed for training. But its staging capabilities would remain useful for an amphibious armada that might still congregate at Okinawa in the event of war in Korea or elsewhere in the region.

In an amphibious staging operation, a Marine Corps airfield on or near Okinawa would need to host perhaps 100 to 200 aircraft. They would be mostly helicopters but could include some Harrier jets. These aircraft would not need to do a lot of flying during the preparation for the assault; they would simply be congregating there after deploying by air from the United States and undergoing last minute maintenance. What would be needed would be depots and hangar space.

Given the one-time nature of such an operation, if it ever occurred at all, Naha International Airport should be able to fulfill these functions. There would be significant disruption to its commercial air traffic, but only in the event of war, and even then only for a few weeks. Intense disruptions to commercial flights might last only a few days. Some improvement of facilities at Naha might be required to provide hangars, maintenance depots, and increased fuel storage capacity. But additional runways and air traffic control capabilities would not be required.

Budgetary and Economic Issues

Option one would preserve what are the chief economic benefits of the U.S.-Japan security relationship. The United States would retain access to bases that have a dollar equivalent value of at least $25 billion a year and would continue to receive several billion dollars a year in host-nation support. Japan would continue to benefit from U.S. security guarantees and the immediate presence and protection of the U.S. forces most able to defend its territory and other critical interests in the region. But relative to what is now planned, this option would modestly increase costs for the United States, reduce them for Japan, and create an economic drag on Okinawa's economy.

Consider first the U.S. balance sheet. Tokyo now pays $5 billion a year in costs associated with the U.S. military presence in Japan. About $1.8 billion of that amount is spent on Okinawa and $1 billion on the Marine Corps, half in rent for land and half in other costs.[20] If the marines relocated to somewhere on the U.S. West Coast, the U.S. government would presumably pick up these costs. But such costs are generally less in the United States by a factor of two to three, so marine costs might increase by only $400 million a year. Such expenditures are not insignificant, but they are modest and they would help mitigate some of the economic pain associated with base closures in the United States.

There would be some one-time costs associated with relocation that Japan and the United States might share. First, taking the Desert Storm experience as a rough guide for many of the costs of moving troops and equipment, it might cost $300 million to move 15,000 marines to the West Coast. Comparable costs would be associated with remodeling barracks and classroom facilities and various other capabilities at a base in the United States otherwise slated for elimination by the base-closure process.

Costs associated with the POMCUS site would add a bit to these sums, probably $50 million a year for several years for construction and lesser sums thereafter for operations and maintenance. In addition, Japan might help the United States purchase the equipment to be stored on Okinawa (marines returning home would also need equipment in the United States for training and other purposes). Fully outfitting a brigade of marines with new equipment such as M1 tanks and Bradley fighting vehicles would cost $1 billion according to Bill Myers of the Congressional Budget Office.[21] But that quality of equipment is probably not needed; it would be more modern than standard Marine Corps weaponry. Costs might reach half that amount, however, for a grand total in POMCUS-related costs of $750 million (and modest recurring costs for upkeep).

The costs for upgrading Naha International Airport to make it capable of serving as part of a marine staging operation from Okinawa would be modest. Because additional runways and most other airport infrastructure would not be needed, costs would be much less than for a replacement facility. Based on what can be gleaned from NATO debates over replacing an air base in southern Europe several years ago and from improvements made by the United States to various facilities in Southwest Asia over the years, the costs would probably total in the high tens of millions of dollars or, at most, the low hundreds of millions.[22] In all, the one-time costs associated with relocation would be less than $2 billion. Because most of it would be spent on facilities in Japan, most would presumably be paid by Tokyo.

Japan would still need to pay some additional costs, notably those for environmental cleanup and conversion of the Futenma site. But those costs should be no more than $1 billion. In sum, then, if Japan paid all relocation and cleanup costs, it would spend less than half of what is now anticipated to be spent for the Futenma replacement facility. And Tokyo would start to save $1 billion a year in host-nation support beginning in 2003.

What of the economic effects on Okinawa? Tokyo now puts $1.8 billion a year into the island's economy in support of the U.S. bases; related indirect spending adds another $1.3 billion. The total represents about 10 percent of the island's economic activity.[23] Okinawa's reliance on defense spending is thus comparable to that of the most defense-dependent U.S. states at the end of the cold war—8 to 10 percent of the economic output of California, Alaska, Hawaii, Mississippi, Washington, Maryland, and Virginia was due to defense spending. From 1990 to 1995 U.S. defense spending declined by a third; California in particular suffered recession for several years as a result. Okinawa would lose half of its defense dollars (even after considering the modest economic stimulus of environmental cleanup and restoration efforts on the island), and in a shorter time. Left to its own devices, therefore, it would probably suffer a recession as a result.[24]

Results could improve if Tokyo and Okinawa designed a plausible economic conversion strategy. But conditions could just as easily get worse if Tokyo decided to reduce its payments to the prefectural government on the grounds that having been relieved of its overbearing defense responsibilities, Okinawa no longer was entitled to unusually generous financial support. (Tokyo provides nearly 80 percent of the prefecture government's total fiscal resources, corresponding to about one-sixth of the prefecture's annual economic product, although on average it provides only 50 percent of other prefectural governments' funds.)

Option Two: Implement Option One and Improve Other Capabilities

The military implications of withdrawing 15,000 marines from Okinawa would be minor if staging and storage facilities on Okinawa were retained and POMCUS-like storage capabilities with a brigade's equivalent of marine combat equipment were constructed and maintained there. Option one further assumes that if a replacement facility for Futenma Air Station is not built, as I believe it should not be, the Naha International Airport will be available as a marine aircraft staging base in the event of war (and that Kadena will handle whatever limited helicopter operations are needed for the Marine Expeditionary Unit and related peacetime purposes).

But implementing option one could give the impression of a lessening of the U.S. commitment to Asia or a weakening of the Japanese commitment to its security partnership with the United States. To avoid these potential drawbacks, U.S.-Japan military capabilities could be strengthened, in particular U.S. forces in Japan.

Four plans could work. All would build on the changes in option one, which they take as a starting point. Any could be adopted, as could some combination. They are

—homeport at least three more U.S. Navy amphibious ships in Japan;

—build four more maritime pre-positioning ships for Marine Corps equipment and base them in Japan;

—homeport an additional U.S. aircraft carrier and associated escort vessels in Japan (although without necessarily basing the crews for those ships permanently in Japan); and

—pursue any of these approaches or the permanent basing of Marine Corps combat forces in some other country in the western Pacific, perhaps Australia.

All of these approaches would increase the U.S. military presence in Asia relative to option one, although only the last would keep total troop levels at their current number. Using the Nye counting scheme, the first three approaches would produce a U.S. military presence of 90,000 to 95,000 uniformed personnel.

Homeport Three More Amphibious Ships in Japan

Homeporting three more ships would double the number of troop-carrying U.S. amphibious ships based in Japan from three to six, meaning that about 15 percent of the total U.S. amphibious fleet would be based in Japan (and the rest still in the continental United States). The vessels would be based on the main islands of Japan, perhaps at Sasebo where the other amphibious ships are now. The ships could pick up equipment and marines on Okinawa (the equipment stored there and the troops flown in from stateside bases) and be quickly available for regional contingencies in Korea or elsewhere. There would probably be little difficulty of finding berths as well as accommodations for 1,000 additional sailors in Sasebo.

The additional ships might be accommodated in port by making reductions in the size of the Japanese navy. Additional reductions, beyond the cuts from sixty-eight principal surface combatants to sixty-three that have occurred since 1990, may make sense anyway. Or if necessary, Japan could construct new berths, probably at a cost of less than $100 million.[25]

Even with six ships in Japan, the United States would not have enough forward-based capability to make most types of amphibious assaults without reinforcements. An amphibious assault would generally be conducted by, at a minimum, a brigade-size force (formerly designated a marine expeditionary brigade and now known as an MEF-forward). It is the size of five MEUs and requires fifteen to twenty amphibious ships for its assault echelons and initial supplies.[26] But the added amphibious capability could come in handy for a limited operation such as an evacuation of noncombatants or a humanitarian assistance mission.

Station Four New Maritime Pre-positioning Vessels in Japan

The Marine Corps now uses three squadrons of so-called maritime pre-positioning vessels to warehouse equipment at sea. Each squadron is made up of four ships and holds enough equipment for a full marine brigade. The squadron focused on the East Asia–Pacific region is normally found in Guam.

Building four new vessels and stationing them in Japan would complement the POMCUS element of option one.[27] It would cost somewhat more than the POMCUS option because of the need to procure ships and the added, if modest, difficulty of maintaining equipment stored at sea. The cost of the ships might reach half a billion dollars, making for a total price tag of about $1 billion. Afterward, operating the ships would cost about $50 million a year.[28]

This option would improve the marines' ability to deploy quickly to Korea. Equipment could be unloaded on the peninsula in the first few days of a crisis, up to a week faster than much of the Okinawa-based equipment could arrive now. Marines could be flown in from the United States by the civil reserve air fleet. This would add at least 25 percent to the number of relatively heavy U.S. ground forces (those with substantial numbers of tanks and other armored vehicles) that could be there in the period from day five until day ten of a Korean contingency.

As with the amphibious ship option, the need for extra sailors in Japan would be modest. These ships would offer the further attraction of being relocatable should another part of the world become more troublesome than Northeast Asia.

Homeport Additional Aircraft Carrier, Escort Ships, and Naval Air Wing in Japan

Homeporting an additional aircraft carrier, escort ships, and a naval air wing in Japan would be the most forward looking of the ideas considered here. First, it would augment capabilities that seem most likely to be relevant to longer-term strategic challenges for the United States and Japan. The carrier would also be available to help maintain presence in the Persian Gulf—only 14,000 kilometers from Japan, although more than 20,000 from mainland U.S. ports. In fact, the carrier might conduct many routine patrols in the Persian Gulf. But it would clearly be available for patrols, exercises, and crisis response in the East Asia–Pacific region as well and would signal an increased U.S. emphasis on the area.[29]

Second, this configuration would provide an opportunity for the navy to experiment with a novel yet commonsense idea for its forward operations in the post–cold war world. It could homeport an additional carrier battle group in Japan but base sailors for the vessels in the United States, shuttling them to their ships by air just before a deployment. Doing so would not be essential, but given the expense of building substantial apartments for another 7,500 U.S. military personnel and their families, it might be appealing just to build dormitories for the sailors who would occasionally be in port in Japan but would continue to live in the United States. Japan's major expenses would consist of building additional berths for a carrier battle group and dormitories for 7,500 sailors. Because they could be small and modest, the dormitories would not be particularly expensive.

The U.S. Navy would need to make some adjustments. Today a crew generally stays with its ship permanently, but under this option crews would rotate out to the ships in Japan and train at home on different vessels. If the navy could make this plan work, however, it could save a great deal of money. Today, with the exception of its carrier presence near Japan, it needs four to six ships in the fleet for every one on forward station. This is because to maintain morale, the navy sends ships out for six-month deployments only once every two years, and during the six-month tours one or two months are wasted in transit.[30] During the cold war, no one minded this arrangement because a large carrier force was thought necessary for a possible conflict with the Soviet Union. But now it is the peacetime presence mission that determines the size of the carrier fleet and most other parts of the navy.[31] If defense budgets get tighter, more efficient approaches to presence could gain considerable appeal.

This option would rotate crews but would leave the ships on forward station for an extended period. Eventually, if applied more generally, this could help the navy maintain its global commitments with a smaller fleet in the event that budget cuts force such a choice.[32] At first, making the idea work would be challenging: crews would have to get accustomed to operating on different ships, and the logistics of transporting and transferring them would need to be worked out. But there are already precedents in the mine countermeasures fleet for how to solve both problems.

Indeed, the costs for this option could be kept even lower if the carrier *Independence,* now homeported in Japan, were kept there but its crews also rotated. In that event, apartments now used by the crews of ships already based in Japan could also be used for the crews of the additional ships, assuming of course that both battle groups were homeported at or near Yokosuka. The apartments would essentially become spacious dormitory chambers, each of which would be shared by two sailors (at different times in almost all cases) rather than a single family. This option would necessitate more housing for sailors in the United States, unless future force cuts coincided with its adoption. Such cuts seem moderately likely over the next decade. If they do not occur, however, some added costs would be incurred. But potential savings would be much greater than costs.

U.S. Navy air facilities in Japan would also need to be shared by rotating air crews. Routine training missions might be cramped during periods when both carriers were in port, and some additional depot and hangar space at Atsigi Naval Air Station might need to be constructed. But the associated costs would not include construction of major new facilities, and would therefore probably remain in the low hundreds of millions of dollars at most. These costs would presumably be paid by Tokyo. Alternatively, the space freed up at Iwakuni could be used by the additional navy air wing rather than supplemental air force squadrons.

Another complication could accompany this option. The *Independence* is one of the navy's only remaining non-nuclear carriers. If a two-carrier option were adopted, the second carrier would probably have to be nuclear powered. There might be modest political resistance to accepting the permanent stationing of such a ship in Japanese ports. In the end, however, it seems unlikely that a country already accustomed to servicing nuclear-powered U.S. Navy ships and to generating much of its own electricity from nuclear reactors would find this problem insurmountable.

This option could be expected to meet resistance from the U.S. Navy. It would require substantial logistical and operational adaptations. Although it appears feasible, as a practical matter the navy would probably need to gain experience rotating more crews on smaller ships such as destroyers before seriously considering the idea for aircraft carriers. The idea should not be dismissed, but in the context of 1997 it is admittedly ambitious.

Base Marine or Navy Forces in Australia

For an amphibious ship, Australia is a week's sail from Korea and two from the Persian Gulf. Sailing times are a third less for a destroyer or carrier.[33] For quick response to a crisis in Korea, forces would thus be less ideally positioned than forces in Japan, but if adequate ships were immediately available, the troops could arrive as fast as most units from Okinawa today. Putting the roughly 10,000 marines now in Okinawa in Darwin, Australia, and also basing perhaps six to eight amphibious ships there would be helpful in a Korean emergency. It would be helpful for a Persian Gulf action, and most of all for areas around the Indonesian straits. All this would be contingent on basing both ships and troops in Australia.

For the United States there would be many advantages to basing troops and ships in Australia. Even without the generous host-nation support provided by Japan, overseas access provides a visible demonstration of U.S. commitment and allied cohesiveness, keeps forces closer to where they might be used, and reduces excessive dependence on other bases in the region. The main potential drawbacks are the costs of relocation and the risks of further relocation should the new bases not prove dependable.

Conclusion: Augmentations in Japan's Defense Capability

Given the changes to U.S. defense posture in the Asia Pacific that I have considered, how could Japan improve its own forces in ways that would help strengthen the security relationship? The two types of ideas presented here are perhaps not within the bounds of normal discourse in

Japan. But neither type is extreme. That is, they are consistent with the assumption that Japan will continue to place major constraints on its independent military capabilities, and particularly those types that would cause its neighbors greatest concern.

The first choice might be for Japan to join the U.S. Navy in conducting peacetime patrols, particularly in the East and South China Seas and Indonesian straits. The second would be to buttress Japan's ability to provide significant help in peace operations and perhaps also in military transport in support of U.S. wartime operations. U.S.-Japan naval patrols would show important solidarity between the two principal maritime powers of the region. Japan might provide several destroyers for such purposes, reducing the demands on the U.S. destroyer fleet in the region. The patrols would serve not only to deter large-scale aggression by a large power, but also to check piracy and otherwise maintain confidence in the critical waterways of the southwest Pacific. Such goals are important to Japan as much as to the United States and should be appreciated by China and other regional powers as well.[34]

Conducting these patrols, and even using force in self-defense if necessary, might not represent a fundamental change in Japanese military practices (although it would represent a significant departure). It would require a modification to the 1,000-nautical-mile limit on Japanese maritime operations, but that limit is an interpretation of the existing constitution rather than an inherent element of it. The ships would not have to include any long-range strike capabilities against land targets.[35] They could be considered largely as backup for U.S. ships that would take the lead in any policing action, for example. Japanese ships would only come to their aid when needed. Doing so might be justifiable under Japan's self-defense rights because if one ship in a squadron is threatened, all are arguably in danger.

In some situations Japan could, if necessary, choose to withdraw from the joint patrols. It would be inappropriate to do so during the heat of battle, because U.S. ships would be counting on the Japanese destroyers for help. But if a military strike was anticipated, Japan could elect not to participate if it found the circumstances inappropriate. This might delay a U.S. response and inconvenience an operation, but it would not negate the value of Japan's peacetime contribution to the patrols.

The second major option would have Japan reorient some of its military procurement toward strategic lift as well as trucks, water purification systems, mobile hospitals, and other mundane types of logistics support needed in peace operations. These assets are not very expensive per unit but are needed in significant quantities for distant operations (most of the world's militaries have not made the investments because they prefer to spend limited procurement dollars on weapons). Japan, with its orientation to multilateral security policy and reluctance to use offensive military power itself, might therefore do the world a great service by providing the kinds of support needed in distant and difficult peace operations.

In a more ambitious form, this option could also transform certain Japanese ground forces into units better suited for peace operations, including combat-intensive enforcement operations. If only a few thousand troops were involved in the change, Japan's ground-force capabilities could hardly be thought of as a threat to the powers of the Pacific Rim. Yet they could be useful as part of a multilateral coalition for operations in places such as Bosnia, Liberia, or Burundi.

More realistic, perhaps, is for Japan to focus just on transport and logistics. For a large peace operation involving 10,000 combat troops, 20,000 to 30,000 support troops might be needed. Japan could restructure that many of its own ground forces for such support purposes, also buying them the equipment needed to get where they are going and function there for many months. The associated procurement costs would be less than $1 billion for trucks and ancillary ground gear, but could reach $5 billion for a fleet of twenty-five wide-body transport aircraft (enough to transport 10,000 troops by themselves, or perhaps 3,000 to 5,000 troops with light equipment, at a time).[36] This type of mission would not be risk free. Flying forces into a combat zone, even if local factions are limited in their capabilities, is dangerous. Japan might even need to participate in combat operations to drive resistance out of airport areas and ensure the safety of incoming flights. But the risks would be limited in scope and probable duration.

These options need not be acted upon immediately, nor must a major restructuring of the U.S. military presence in Japan await their adoption. But they might be sensible actions for Japan to take as the new bargain discussed in this book is put into effect.

Notes

1. See John Lewis Gaddis, *Strategies of Containment* (Oxford University Press, 1982), pp. 25–53.

2. Ibid.

3. See, for example, International Institute for Strategic Studies, *The Military Balance 1996/97* (Oxford University Press, 1996), p. 308.

4. Office of International Security Affairs, *United States Security Strategy for the East Asia–Pacific Region* (Department of Defense, February 1995), pp. 24–25.

5. See Secretary of Defense William J. Perry, *Annual Report to the President and the Congress* (Government Printing Office, March 1996), p. 176. About 15,000 of the other U.S. troops in Japan are air force personnel, 7,000 are navy, and 2,000 are army. The respective numbers from each service on Okinawa are 7,000, 2,000, and 1,000. About 45,000 family members of U.S. troops live in Japan; 5,000 Defense Department civilians also work there, and 22,000 Japanese are in the employ of the Defense Department.

6. International Institute for Strategic Studies, *The Military Balance 1995/96* (Oxford University Press, 1995), pp. 30-31; Caspar W. Weinberger, Secretary of Defense, *Annual Report to the Congress, 1986* (GPO, 1985), p. 300; Perry, *Annual Report* (1996), p. C-2; Office of International Security Affairs, *United States Security Strategy for the East Asia–Pacific Region* (Department of Defense, February 1995), pp. 1, 24–27; U.S. Armed Forces, Japan, "Briefing," January 28, 1994, slides 5 and 6; Michael H. Armacost, *Friends or Rivals?: The Insider's Account of U.S.-Japan Relations* (Columbia University Press, 1996), p. 86; and Stewart M. Powell and Holly Yeager, "U.S. to Reduce GIs on Okinawa by 10 Percent," *Pacific Stars & Stripes*, April 11, 1996, p. 1.

7. U.S. Armed Forces, Japan, "Briefing," January 28, 1994, slides 9, 39; Department of Defense, "Report on the Security Relationship between the United States and Japan," March 1, 1995, p. 17; Powell and Yeager, "U.S. to Reduce GIs on Okinawa," p. 1; Bill Nichols, "Okinawa Move Is Not a Retreat," *USA Today*, April 15, 1996, p. 1; Kevin Sullivan and Mary Jordan, "U.S. to Trim 11 Bases on Okinawa," *Washington Post*, April 16, 1996, p. 1; and Steve Glain, "Closing U.S. Air Base Won't Stop Outcry," *Wall Street Journal*, April 15, 1996, p. 1.

8. Institute for National Strategic Studies, *Strategic Assessment 1996* (Washington: National Defense University, 1996), p. 118; and "U.S. Base Plan Costly," *Aviation Week and Space Technology*, April 29, 1996, p. 66.

9. Perry, *Annual Report* (1996), p. 128.

10. Institute for National Strategic Studies, *Strategic Assessment 1996* (National Defense University, 1996), p. 118; U.S. Armed Forces, Japan, "Briefing," January 28, 1994, charts 37–40; and Office of the Under Secretary of Defense, Comptroller, *National Defense Budget Estimates for FY 1997* (Department of Defense, April 1996), pp. 60–61, 70–71, 92–93.

11. See, for example, Thomas C. Lin, "In Defense of East Asia's Quick-Reaction Force," *International Herald Tribune*, May 30, 1996, p. 9.

12. International Institute for Strategic Studies, *Military Balance 1995/1996*, pp. 182–83.

13. Indeed, concern over the tense East Asian theater has reportedly led the U.S. military to cancel training exercises for the *Independence* in the Middle East and keep the carrier in the western Pacific continuously. See Brian Williams, "U.S. Carrier to Remain in Waters of East Asia," *Washington Times*, June 17, 1996, p. 13.

14. Lin, "In Defense of East Asia's Quick-Reaction Force," p. 9.

15. U.S. Armed Forces, Japan, "Briefing," January 28, 1994, slides 7 and 8.

16. International Institute for Strategic Studies, *Military Balance 1995/96*, pp. 181–83.

17. See Congressional Budget Office, *Moving the Marine Corps by Sea in the 1990s* (October 1989), p. 15.

18. See Les Aspin, "An Approach to Sizing American Conventional Forces for the Post-Soviet Era," House Armed Services Committee, January 24, 1992.

19. Perry, *Annual Report to the President and the Congress* (1996), pp. 192–93; and Department of Defense, *Conduct of the Persian Gulf War: Final Report to Congress* (April 1992), pp. E-7–E-10.

20. U.S. Pacific Command, "Okinawa Economic Factbook," Camp H. M. Smith, March 1996.

21. Congressional Budget Office, *Moving U.S. Forces: Options for Strategic Mobility* (1997), p. 41.

22. Congressional Budget Office, *Rapid Deployment Forces: Policy and Budgetary Implications* (May 1983), pp. 38–39, 60.

23. United States Pacific Command, "Okinawa Economic Factbook," March 1996, pp. 9–10.

24. Defense Conversion Commission, *Adjusting to the Drawdown* (Department of Defense, 1992), pp. 11–12; and Congressional Budget Office, *Economic Effects of Reduced Defense Spending* (1992), pp. 11–12, 27–28.

25. International Institute for Strategic Studies, *The Military Balance 1990/1991* (Oxford, England: Brassey's, 1990), p. 165; and IISS, *Military Balance 1995/96*, pp. 26, 30–31, 182.

26. Congressional Budget Office, *Moving the Marine Corps by Sea* (1997), pp. 14–17; and U.S. Marine Corps, *Concepts and Issues 95* (1995), pp. 2-11, a-5.

27. Alternatively, this pre-positioning could replace that of option one, although it would obviously produce less added capability for the region and might not fit the more assertive spirit of the option two variants discussed here.

28. See Congressional Budget Office, *Rapid Deployment Forces*, p. 38.

29. Defense Mapping Agency, *Distances between Ports* (Department of Defense, 1976), pp. 107, 178–79.

30. Ronald O'Rourke, *Naval Forward Deployments and the Size of the Navy* (Congressional Research Service, 1992), pp. 13–23.

31. Les Aspin, *Report on the Bottom-Up Review* (Department of Defense, 1993), p. 50.

32. William F. Morgan, "Rotate Crews, Not Ships," annotated briefing CAB-94-40, Center for Naval Analyses, Alexandria, Va., June 1994.

33. See Defense Mapping Agency, *Distances between Ports*; and Navy League of the United States, *Almanac of Seapower*, vol. 37 (January 1994), pp. 124–50.

34. For a similar idea, see Asian Forum Japan, "A Call for a Multilateral Strategy for Japan," Tokyo, May 1995, p. 116.

35. For an argument that Japan should especially avoid deploying ships such as aircraft carriers and threatening long-range missiles, see Hashimoto Motohide, "Security in Asia," Policy Paper 149E, Institute for International Policy Studies, Tokyo, March 1996, p. 15.

36. The requirement of UN authorization might ease many concerns among Japanese and their neighbors about any possible resurgence of Japanese unilateralism or militarism. See William J. Durch, "Japan-U.S. Cooperation in U.N. Peace Efforts," in Selig S. Harrison and Nishihara Masashi, eds., *U.N. Peacekeeping: Japanese and American Perspectives* (Washington: Carnegie Endowment, 1995), pp. 158–59.

CHAPTER SEVEN

Theater Missile Defense and the U.S.-Japan Alliance

Michael O'Hanlon

IN ADDITION TO the subjects of U.S. forces on Okinawa, Japanese support for U.S. military operations in East Asia, and future roles for Japan's own defense forces, a crucial issue in contemporary transpacific relations is that of missile defenses. This chapter lays out some general considerations about missile defense that could lend perspective to a debate that may soon become dominated by more tactical diplomatic issues.

The promise of theater missile defense (TMD) is unclear because of technical uncertainties over the systems being developed and an uncertain future security environment in Northeast Asia. TMD systems would help defend Japan against some possible missile threats much better than against others. But their potential utility is considerable, both to the United States and Japan.

U.S. TMD programs would benefit from technical and especially financial support from Japan in both the development and procurement stages. Still, Tokyo is already spending a good deal of money on host-nation support for U.S. forces in Japan and relocation of the Futenma Marine Corps Air Station in Ginowan, Okinawa. So the Japanese government should not feel excessive pressure to please Washington on this matter. It should be doing more to contribute to a meaningful and balanced alliance, but not through more checkbook diplomacy unless its own interests are directly served by such financial assistance. Instead, it

179

should be working to become a more equal ally in matters such as response to possible military crises in East Asia.

Nevertheless, TMD programs, particularly Patriot PAC-3 and THAAD (theater high-altitude area defense) missiles and navy lower-tier systems, do merit Japanese support. And the investment would represent a much better use of Tokyo's money than would construction of an offshore airbase for the marines on Okinawa.

Japan should not be deterred from pursuing TMD by any North Korean or Chinese claims that such steps are provocative. Neither Pyongyang nor Beijing nor Moscow has an inherent right to hold the Japanese islands at risk of missile attack with conventional or unconventional weapons. China's concerns about its nuclear capabilities vis-à-vis those of the United States are understandable, and advanced TMD systems could indeed enter into that broader nuclear balance (at least in theory). But Beijing's pressure on non-nuclear Japan not to collaborate with the United States on TMD development and acquisition appears ill founded and unseemly, especially in regard to the PAC-3, THAAD, and navy lower-tier programs (given their very limited potential utility against longer-range missiles).

Japanese TMD would make the most sense against a small North Korean missile threat. It could be effective whether those missiles carried conventional, chemical, biological, or (although it is very unlikely on technical grounds) even nuclear warheads. Japanese TMD could also be useful against an accidental or unauthorized Chinese or Russian attack or an attack by a nonstate entity that gained access to several missiles and was prepared to launch them from a ship or a neighboring country's territory. Depending on the quality of the TMD system, that utility might be limited to defense against just short-range missiles or might have greater capabilities. Also, should Japan someday decide to assume an active role in dangerous peace operations, TMD could be helpful if a regional power attacked Japanese forces deployed as part of such a contingent.

The rest of this chapter is divided into three parts. The first reviews the basic logic of missile defenses and limits on them. The second summarizes the general state of play of missile defense research, development, testing, and procurement in the United States. And the third directly addresses the near-term situation in East Asia and choices for Japan.

What Are Missile Defenses For (If Anything)?

A historical perspective is useful for seeing how missile defenses gained a poor reputation among arms control advocates during the cold war. It can help identify which rationales if any may now be valid.

The nuclear arms competition between the United States and the Soviet Union began in 1949 with the first Soviet explosion of an atom bomb. It accelerated in the early 1950s with the development of thermonuclear technology as well as the intensification of the cold war in the Far East and Europe. The United States built huge numbers of nuclear weapons to compensate for Soviet conventional military superiority. America pursued the capability of launching a disarming nuclear first strike at a time when that seemed technologically feasible and when Moscow's global ambitions seemed without bounds and not easily deterred.

By the 1960s the plausibility of a disarming nuclear first strike launched by either superpower was gone for good. But war planners continued to develop weaponry requirements as if it remained, constructing elaborate theories of "damage limitation" and "escalation dominance" to justify the continued pursuit of nuclear superiority even as a nuclear war had become unthinkable for both sides (although not impossible).[1]

It was at this time that missile defense technologies made their first serious appearance. Both countries developed ground-based interceptors that would be guided to targets by large and vulnerable radar systems. The prospects for successful interceptions by these early missiles, known as Sentinel and Safeguard on the U.S. side, were not considered particularly good.[2] The offense had too many simple recourses, even if defenses wound up being capable of successfully maneuvering near a tiny object coming at speeds of three or four miles a second. The recourses included using chaff and decoys to confuse defenses trying to intercept missiles outside the atmosphere, attacking radars, saturating defenses with large attacks, detonating nuclear warheads high above radars, or developing maneuvering reentry vehicles to defeat defenses designed to destroy warheads that reentered the atmosphere. For those reasons, the U.S. system was deployed for only a short time in the mid-1970s and then disbanded.[3]

Spending a lot on defense systems thus did not seem promising, especially as the advent of multiple independently targetable reentry vehicle (MIRV) technology gave the offense a further way to overcome most defenses through saturation attacks. Yet in light of the excessively large nuclear target sets and warhead inventories, and the mindsets that justified them, any conservative nuclear war planner would have been sure to attribute greater capabilities to a defensive system than it deserved. The outcome would probably have been an unstable arms race.[4] These are the conditions that produced the 1972 Anti-ballistic Missile (ABM) Treaty.

Developing defenses became even more anathema to arms controllers when doing so threatened to upset a fragile U.S.-Soviet detente. Whether it was Soviet proliferation of air defense systems with possible missile-defense capabilities or President Reagan's Star Wars program, defenses jeopardized a continued easing of tension in the bilateral relationship.[5] In addition, technological improvements did not appear sufficient to justify the expense; the threat of countermeasures to newer missile defense technologies appeared every bit as great as to the older ones.[6]

Some of these same concerns and dynamics remain in the current U.S.-Russian relationship. But things have also changed. The Gulf War and the acquisition of ballistic missiles by various developing countries have greatly influenced the U.S. debate. To counter missile proliferation, a strong consensus in U.S. politics has endorsed developing and deploying improved theater missile defenses.[7]

Also, few observers take the details of the nuclear arms balance seriously anymore at a political level. Retaining a survival deterrent to a nuclear strike is still considered important, of course, but one hears little talk of maintaining strategic superiority or a "prevailing" or "countervailing" capability.[8] Moreover, theoretical analysis shows that if the nuclear superpowers deployed modest-sized strategic defenses with capabilities that were large relative to other countries' arsenals but small relative to each other's, nuclear stability might even be improved.[9] In this situation, defenses are not necessarily destabilizing in the way they were during the cold war.

On the other hand, no new consensus has formed in the United States (or Russia) on the proper role for national missile defense.[10] The Republican Congress has attempted to force legislatively a deployment by 2003.[11] But most Democrats and Secretary of Defense William Cohen are opposed to a schedule that leaves no flexibility for reassessing the threat, the state of defense technology, budget pressures in the United States, or the possible effects on U.S.-Russian relations, including strategic offensive arms control. Moreover, policymakers do still worry about the relative overall size of U.S. and Russian arsenals, condone ambitious war plans, and allow forces to remain on high alert.[12] In this setting they will not be entirely indifferent to the implications of defenses for the nuclear balance.

Given all these circumstances, old answers about defenses are no longer adequate, and the Chinese objection to Japanese TMD on the grounds of stability is suspect. But at the same time, enough technological and arms control issues remain similar to their cold war nature that the old questions will not go away. Missile defenses, especially those with potential strategic implications, will have to be subject to careful technical, budgetary, and strategic review at every stage of the policy process.

The State of Missile Defense Technology

In the Gulf War, the Patriot missile in its PAC-2 form performed poorly. There are no absolutely certain confirmations of successful interceptions of incoming SCUD missiles, and clear evidence of many failures (although the army and the manufacturer continue to maintain that about 50 percent of all SCUDs were successfully intercepted).[13]

Technology has improved since then. For example, as a result of initial post–Gulf War modifications as well as the so-called PAC-3 configurations 1 and 2, Patriot radars can now track more objects at once, see them at greater range, pick up fewer false targets from extraneous radar reflections, and exchange information with each other's computers. Interceptors can be based further away from radars, allowing a greater area of coverage. Starting in 1999 a new missile and more radar upgrades will allow a PAC-3 configuration 3 capability, which should for the first time allow the radar to discriminate automatically between a heavy warhead and light decoys or debris and also permit greater maneuverability of the interceptor itself. The system might be able to defend out to several tens of kilometers from the missile's launch point. Such a system should have a good chance of reliably handling the type of threat that Iraq possessed in 1991, particularly if the attacker employs single warheads rather than numerous smaller ones.[14]

The next generation of TMD includes the THAAD and the navy's lower-tier system. Likely to be more effective than Patriot, they will still be considerably limited in coverage. But if upgraded, these systems and the navy upper-tier program could raise issues about the potential for providing wide coverage. If they were coupled with space-based infrared sensors like the surveilliance and missile tracking system (SMTS) now under development, their coverage could even extend to wide-area defense against attack by strategic missiles.

This concern should not be overblown. These defenses generally function with infrared sensors that cannot work in the atmosphere because friction with the air heats them up and blinds them. Thus the missiles must intercept objects high in the sky. And the higher up objects are, the easier it is for an attacker to camouflage them because air resistance will not yet have slowed down lighter decoys that could accompany the warhead.

These systems are also having difficulties in tests. Pentagon acquisition chief Paul Kaminski recently put the army's THAAD program officials on notice that their program would have to start completing intercept tests successfully or risk a loss or even termination of funding.[15] Since then, another test failure has occurred.[16] The navy's lower-tier program with the Standard Missile 2 Block 4A interceptor, guided by the Aegis radars already deployed on cruisers and destroyers (as well as the interceptors' own terminal homing devices), recently had a successful test. But it was against a nonmaneuvering object with a predictable and known flight path, giving little reason for confidence yet about the more rigorous tests that are not expected to take place until the turn of the century.[17]

Indeed, because of budget constraints, missile defense research in general in the United States relies heavily on specific tests of individual systems as well as computer simulation of system performance. Integrated tests of entire systems are rare and expensive. This adds particular uncertainty to a type of military technology that is still in its infancy.[18]

Theater Missile Defense in East Asia: Choices for Japan

In making decisions about developing and buying TMD capabilities, how can Tokyo juxtapose these technological and arms control realities with the specifics of the East Asian–Pacific security environment? The United States appears committed to deploying theater missile defenses with its troops wherever they may be, but Japan may have different priorities and preferences.

There are at least three major issues involved: a possible North Korean threat, presumably in the near-to-medium term; concern over a possible threat from China but also a possible Chinese counterreaction to any deployment; and possible defensive requirements for Japanese forces that might someday be deployed to other regions on peacekeeping missions.

Policymakers have to wrestle with how long they believe the threat from North Korea may endure in its present form. Satoshi Morimoto (chapter 3) is probably right that the threat will not remain indefinitely, but because accurate prediction is impossible, the threat may endure longer than we now hope. Therefore, in my judgment, Japan would benefit from deploying theater missile defenses against a possible North Korean challenge. Relying on U.S. TMD deployed around U.S. military assets in Japan could leave important cities unprotected, since the extent of coverage of any next-generation defense system could be only tens of kilometers. So Japan will have to provide defense itself or risk being left vulnerable.

Would the systems work? Probably, at least against a simple threat. But North Korea has been reported to be developing warheads that break up into large numbers of smaller grenadelike explosives. That would render interception impractical (unless boost-phase interception technologies are someday developed by the air force, an ambitious hope that is beyond the scope of this chapter). Fortunately, although still dangerous, such explosives would be unlikely to destroy an entire building in a Japanese city even if they made a direct hit. So the potential for casualties would be reduced.[19] And North Korea is probably not in a position to develop much more sophisticated countermeasures than those it already has.

If the North Korean regime decays and collapses violently, any ensuing missile launches by renegade commanders or factions would probably be small, meaning that a good TMD capability might be able to intercept all incoming reentry vehicles of substantial size. This would provide some defense against chemical attack and a good defense against large conventional warheads or nuclear warheads (although it is extremely doubtful that North Korea could deliver a nuclear warhead by missile even if it had one, given the primitiveness and bulkiness of most nuclear weapons developed without testing).[20]

North Korea might well be upset by a TMD deployment, but it would be hard pressed to construe it as aggressive. Moreover, Seoul would remain at risk of artillery attack in any case, so Pyongyang would still have a ready terror card against one member of the Japan-U.S.-South Korea triangle and also against U.S. troops. Japan itself would be safer with a TMD deployment, however, and U.S. military forces could benefit by being able to deploy all their own defenses closer to the battlefield.

The argument may also someday be strong for buying theater missile defense capability for Japanese forces on peacekeeping or collective security missions. Granted, most traditional peacekeeping missions do not involve missile threats. And most hypothetical combat missions under a collective defense approach of the type advocated in this book would presumably involve U.S. forces, which could provide defenses for all coalition troops. But other scenarios could develop in which the United States might not participate.

Of greater immediate interest is China. Here, the calculus for Japan is more complicated, particularly as concerns higher-performance systems capable of intercepting fast reentry vehicles at higher altitudes. But the overall case for deploying theater missile defenses seems strong. At the broadest level, it is hardly clear that Japan should concede to China any right to hold it permanently at nuclear risk. Japan has no intention of developing nuclear weapons. Nor does its alliance with the United States link it to any U.S.-Chinese nuclear issues. The alliance does not provide the United States with nuclear capabilities vis-à-vis China that it would not have anyway. Japan has no power to make Washington launch a nuclear attack on China against U.S. leaders' own will, and there is no treaty language that would require it.

To revisit the earlier discussion, the history of superpower arms control during the cold war never recognized any inherent right of one country to hold another nuclear hostage. The limits on defenses grew out of an arms competition that would in all likelihood have been worse without those limits. Such was the origin of the ABM Treaty. Some of that logic may still apply to the U.S.-Chinese nuclear situation, but not to Beijing and Tokyo.

These theoretical aguments aside, Japanese deployment of next-generation theater missile defenses would not make it safe from Chinese attack in any case. China has roughly 10 longer-range nuclear-tipped ICBM missiles, 20 medium-to-long-range ICBMs, 12 shorter-range SLBMs on a submarine, about 85 shorter-range land-based missiles, and some 150 bombers. Its total nuclear warhead inventory approaches 300.[21]

Systems such as Patriot PAC-3 would almost certainly never be tested against high-speed reentry vehicles like those on China's longer-range and medium-to-long range ICBMs. So those thirty missiles would assuredly provide an unmitigated threat in any case (similar conclusions would, of course, apply to Russian ICBMs and SLBMs that could be targeted against Japan). The shorter-range ICBMs and SLBMs could also saturate defenses in one or two parts of the Japanese islands, exhausting the local supply of interceptors and rendering that part of Japan completely vulnerable. Even if THAAD and the navy's lower-tier defense achieved some theoretical capability against longer-range missile reentry vehicles—a dubious but possible proposition—they could be defeated by a saturation attack in one region or, in all likelihood, by only relatively sophisticated countermeasures. Navy upper-tier defense would share this latter vulnerability. Yet Tokyo might still find defenses useful against an unauthorized or accidental Chinese attack or that of a nonstate group that acquired several missiles.

Conclusion

I have little reason to believe that there should be serious problems with Japanese deployment of next-generation missile defenses, especially for Patriot PAC-3, but also for THAAD and the navy lower-tier and upper-tier systems. TMD technologies that approach strategic defense capabilities, as later generations might, would be a more sensitive matter, although even there the inherent right of any other country to hold Japan at permanent risk of attack seems difficult to reconcile with Japan's presumably permanent non-nuclear status.

Thus I believe that Japan should adopt the option developed elsewhere in this volume and instead of spending large sums replacing Futenma Air Base use some of the funds to cooperate fully in TMD acquisition. But it is clearly a matter for the Japanese people and government to decide, based on their own interests and assessments of the regional security picture.

Notes

1. See, for example, Janne E. Nolan, *Guardians of the Arsenal* (Basic Books, 1989); Lawrence Freedman, *The Evolution of Nuclear Strategy* (St. Martin's Press, 1983); and David Alan Rosenberg, "U.S. Nuclear War Planning, 1945–1960," and Desmond Ball, "The Development of the SIOP, 1960–1983," in Desmond Ball and Jeffrey Richelson, eds., *Strategic Nuclear Targeting* (Cornell University Press, 1986), pp. 35–83.

2. David N. Schwartz, "Past and Present: The Historical Legacy," in Ashton B. Carter and David N. Schwartz, *Ballistic Missile Defense* (Brookings, 1984), pp. 330–49.

3. Arms Control Association, "Strategic Defensive Arms Control," in *Arms Control and National Security* (Washington, 1989), pp. 66–85.

4. Charles L. Glaser, "Do We Want the Missile Defenses We Can Build?" in Steven E. Miller and Stephen Van Evera, eds., *The Star Wars Controversy* (Princeton University Press, 1984), pp. 98–130; Stephen Weiner, "Systems and Technology," in Carter and and Schwartz, *Ballistic Missile Defense*, pp. 49–97.

5. See, for example, Strobe Talbott, *Deadly Gambits* (Knopf, 1984); McGeorge Bundy, *Danger and Survival* (Vintage Books, 1988), pp. 549–615; and Sidney D. Drell, Philip J. Farley, and David Holloway, "Preserving the ABM Treaty: A Critique of the Reagan Strategic Defense Initiative," in Steven E. Miller and Stephen Van Evera, eds., *The Star Wars Controversy* (Princeton University Press, 1986), pp. 57–97.

6. Union of Concerned Scientists, *The Fallacy of Star Wars* (Random House, 1984).

7. For one early expression of the consensus that has prevailed since the Gulf War, see Representatives Les Aspin and William Dickinson (then chairman and ranking Republican, respectively, of the House Armed Services Committee), *Defense for a New Era* (Riverside, N.J.: Brassey's, 1992), pp. xxvi–xxvii.

8. William J. Perry, *Annual Report to the President and the Congress* (Department of Defense, 1996), pp. 213–18; and Institute for National Strategic Studies, *1997 Strategic Assessment* (Washington: National Defense University, 1996), p. 245.

9. Jerome Bracken, "Multipolar Nuclear Stability: Incentives to Strike and Incentives to Preempt," Yale University, December 1996, p. 22. Given the low alert levels of Russian forces today, however, their survivability may not be adequate for this model to apply unless the forces are kept on hair-trigger alert, as now appears the case. In this situation, defenses may worsen things if they make it more difficult to take superpower forces off alert. See Bruce G. Blair, "Where Would All the Missiles Go?" *Washington Post*, October 15, 1996.

10. Paul Mann, "ABM Treaty at 25: Relic or Rebirth?" *Aviation Week and Space Technology*, February 24, 1997, pp. 50–53.

11. See Lisbeth Gronlund and others, "The Weakest Line of Defense: Intercepting Ballistic Missiles," in Joseph Cirincione and Frank von Hippel, eds., *The Last 15 Minutes* (Washington: Coalition to Reduce Nuclear Dangers, 1996), p. 46.

12. Bruce G. Blair, *Global Zero Alert for Nuclear Forces* (Brookings, 1995), pp. 58–78.

13. Robert M. Stein and Theodore A. Postol, "Patriot Experience in the Gulf War," *International Security*, vol. 17 (Summer 1992), pp. 199–240.

14. David Hughes, "Patriot PAC-3 Upgrade Aimed at Multiple Threats," *Aviation Week and Space Technology*, February 24, 1997, pp. 59–61; and Gronlund and others, "Weakest Line of Defense," pp. 57–58.

15. "Do or Die?" *Aviation Week and Space Technology*, February 24, 1997, p. 19; and Gronlund and others, "Weakest Line of Defense," pp. 45–60.

16. John Mintz, "Missile Defense System Fails Fourth Test," *Washington Post*, March 7, 1997, p. G1.

17. David Hughes, "Navy Readies Fleet for Anti-Scud Warfare," *Aviation Week and Space Technology*, February 24, 1997, pp. 61– 63.

18. William B. Scott, "Mix of Simulation, Flight Testing Troubles BMDO Leaders," *Aviation Week and Space Technology*, February 24, 1997, pp. 64–67.

19. Gronlund and others, "Weakest Line of Defense," p. 51.

20. Congressional Budget Office, *The Bomb's Custodians* (July 1994), p. 3.

21. Stockholm International Peace Research Institute, *SIPRI Yearbook 1996* (Oxford University Press, 1996), p. 619.

Part Three

POLICY
RECOMMENDATIONS

CHAPTER EIGHT

Policy Recommendations

THE FOUR contributors to this volume reached agreement on the following six policy recommendations.

1. Establish a bilateral task force on East Asia–Pacific security policy.
   The working-level dialogue between U.S. and Japanese officials on security, the so-called Nye Initiative, was a constructive beginning for revitalizing the U.S.-Japan alliance. It laid the groundwork for the successful April 1996 summit between President Clinton and Prime Minister Hashimoto in Tokyo and the historic Japan-U.S. Joint Declaration on Security. We applaud this effort to redefine the alliance in terms of common values and interests rather than primarily of meeting a common threat. For both the United States and Japan, economic development in the East Asia–Pacific region based on greater openness and equity also serves their security interests. As the nations in the region become more prosperous, respect for democratic principles and human rights is likely to grow. Consequently, we reject the arguments made by some that a clash of civilizations or values is inevitable across the region and that the United States and Japan will find themselves on opposite sides in such a conflict. Instead, there is now a historic opportunity for the two most powerful democracies in the region to use their influence to shape a security environment in which societies can continue to become more prosperous and political systems more democratic and respectful of human rights.

The collapse of the Soviet Union removed one of the most acute threats to East Asia–Pacific security, but destabilizing factors remain, including tensions on the Korean peninsula, territorial disputes, the China-Taiwan confrontation, military modernization by many states in the region, and the proliferation of weapons of mass destruction. These and other security challenges require at a minimum a robust U.S. military presence in the region and a strong U.S.-Japan alliance for deterrence, reassurance, and crisis response. But simply having U.S. forces deployed and maintaining the bilateral alliance are not enough to promote regional peace and stability. The United States and Japan should work more closely together to reduce tensions and prevent crises and military conflicts as well as respond to crises and deter aggression.

Unfortunately, bilateral consultations and coordination on the many aspects of regional security policy are woefully inadequate. The U.S.-Japan Security Consultative Committee, composed of the U.S. secretaries of state and defense and the Japanese ministers of foreign affairs and defense, has not sufficiently increased public understanding about the importance of the bilateral alliance for regional and global security. This so-called 2-Plus-2 mechanism has failed to tackle in an integrated way the complex diplomatic, military, and economic dimensions of security challenges and opportunities in the region and develop a coordinated strategy between the United States and Japan. Nor will the bureaucratic review now under way to strengthen U.S.-Japan defense cooperation mobilize the public support necessary in both countries to sustain this alliance well into the twenty-first century.

To help correct this situation, the Japanese prime minister and the U.S. president should establish a high-level bilateral task force to assess the regional security challenges and opportunities, evaluate policy options, and recommend coordinated policies to strengthen security. This task force should include members of the Japanese Diet and the U.S. Congress as well as prominent private citizens and experts. Its agenda should encompass such pressing matters as reducing tension on the Korean peninsula, firmly integrating China into the East Asia–Pacific region, managing the China-Taiwan issue, achieving the appropriate U.S. force structure and levels in Japan and rest of the region, and encouraging nuclear nonproliferation. Such a commission would contribute greatly to deepening public understanding of and support for the U.S.-Japan security relationship and the responsibilities it does and can fill both in the region and the world at large.

2. Restructure U.S. military forces in Japan by removing marine combat forces from Okinawa by 2003.

U.S. forces in Japan are essential not only for Japan's defense, but also for security in the East Asia–Pacific region and beyond. But the changing strategic environment and developments in defense technologies make it possible to streamline these forces to increase military efficiency while preserving their ability to perform critical military missions. Restructuring would also respond to a growing Japanese desire to reduce the American military presence, especially to lighten the burden on the people of Okinawa. In April 1997 the Japanese Diet passed with an overwhelming majority a law that permits U.S. forces to continue the use of military bases in Okinawa. Although this legislation was both necessary and inevitable, it does not provide a solid political basis for the U.S.-Japan alliance in the future.

America's most important military assets in Japan are its air force and navy units, as well as its logistics and staging bases for all the military services. To sustain Japan's willingness to host them, the United States should withdraw forces that are not as essential. Although the Third Marine Expeditonary Force (III MEF), stationed in Okinawa, performs important functions in U.S. global and regional defense strategies, maintaining this presence at current levels jeopardizes the long-term political support in Japan for both the U.S. military presence and the U.S.-Japan alliance. Moreover, many of the military missions assigned to the III MEF can be executed adequately by redeploying the marines elsewhere (to Guam, Hawaii, or even the continental United States) if U.S.-Japanese defense cooperation can be strengthened at the operational level. Moreover, potential security challenges, as well as burden-sharing concerns, suggest that it may be more appropriate to position marines in Australia, Southeast Asia, and other parts of the region. Such a change in marine deployments would have the added benefit of strengthening security ties among U.S. allies and friends in the region.

Therefore, the U.S. government should adopt a more flexible approach to its military presence and policy, an approach similar to the one recommended by the East Asia Strategic Initiative (EASI), adopted by the Bush administration. This process involved a periodic evaluation of the East Asia–Pacific security environment and modifications in military deployments in response to regional developments (see chapter 1). And Washington should stop defining America's security commitment in terms of the number of forces; instead it should define it in terms of military roles and missions.

Our view is that the United States can and should remove the marine *combat* forces from Okinawa when the Futenma Marine Air Station is returned to Okinawa sometime between 2001 and 2003. The necessary logistical facilities of the U.S. Marine Corps, however, should be maintained on Okinawa, and marine combat equipment should be pre-positioned there for ready use in a crisis and for routine Marine Expeditionary Unit patrols in the western Pacific Ocean. As part of this restructuring, Japan should take the appropriate steps to support U.S. military operations in regional contingencies and facilitate rapid deployments into and out of Japan during a military emergency. These steps would include allowing U.S. use of civilian as well as military facilities in Japan, passing legislation to deal with military emergencies, and providing comprehensive logistical support for U.S. forces in the rear. The review of the bilateral guidelines for defense cooperation that is now under way provides a good opportunity for Japan to move forward on these matters.

Depending on the evolution of the security environment, Japan and the United States might consider ways to bolster the U.S. military presence in Japan, including augmenting the U.S. naval and air capabilities at Sasebo and Iwakuni.

3. Reinterpret the Japanese constitution to enable Japan to participate in collective self-defense and collective security operations.

Japan makes a valuable contribution to regional security by providing bases for U.S. forces to deal with contingencies beyond the defense of Japan. But in the post–cold war context, as Americans tend to turn inward to concentrate on domestic renewal, the current arrangement may no longer be politically viable in the United States. A passive role, not to mention an obstructive one, by Japan during a regional crisis in which vital interests are involved will severely test the alliance, if not rupture it. Conversely, an implicit American policy of containing Japan strategically offends Japanese national honor and perpetuates insecurity about their own democratic institutions and their ability to control the military.

Japan is now in the throes of a debate about its constitution and the country's responsibilities for international security. This debate will increase public awareness about security issues and eventually make decisionmaking on defense policy more transparent and more reassuring to Japan's neighbors. Rather than adhering to defense minimalism to

avoid political controversy, Japanese leaders should address the fundamental constitutional questions head on and work to harmonize the constitution, the UN Charter, and the Japan-U.S. Security Treaty, the three
pillars of Japanese security policy. Reinterpreting or revising the constitution to permit Japan to exercise the right of collective self-defense, a
right recognized in both the UN Charter and the bilateral security pact,
would go far in strengthening the U.S.-Japan alliance and enabling Japan
to contribute more to UN-sponsored security operations.

Considering the Japan-U.S. Joint Declaration on Security, Tokyo and
Washington have been reviewing the 1978 guidelines on bilateral
defense cooperation and will announce new guidelines in fall 1997. To
strengthen the alliance, the Japanese Diet should pass the necessary legislation to fully implement these new guidelines. This may require that
Japan engage the issue of exercising the right of collective self-defense.

Meanwhile, the U.S. government should refrain from inadvertently
intervening in the Japanese constitutional debate. Statements by American high officials that the United States expects the improvement of
bilateral defense cooperation to "be conducted within the framework of
the constitution of Japan" can be misinterpreted by the Japanese to mean
that the United States does not want either a reinterpretation or a revision
of the constitution. Such a misinterpretation could stifle a healthy debate
in Japan. Although the United States need not take sides in this debate, it
should also not unintentionally weaken those in Japan who seek to transform the bilateral security relationship into a true alliance by allowing
Japan to exercise its right to collective self-defense.

A Japan that can exercise its right to collective self-defense would be
able to cooperate with the United States in the defense of common interests during a crisis, even without a military attack on Japanese territory.
But exercise of this right does not mean that Japan must act in concert
with the United States in every circumstance. The Japanese people,
through their own political process, would still retain the right to determine whether to support U.S. military operations. This judgment,
however, would be made on policy grounds rather than on the basis of
constitutional interpretation. By embracing the collective self-defense
right, Japan would evolve into a more equal strategic partner of the
United States. It would not only share more of the burden of maintaining
security, but would also acquire more of the power in determining how
the alliance should function to promote security. Such a change should
bring to life the prior consultations process mandated by the U.S.-Japan

security treaty. By having the ability to say yes to collective defense and security missions, Japan would also gain the right to say no to the United States when it disagrees with U.S. policy. Washington would thus have a greater incentive to consult more vigorously with Tokyo as policies are being formulated, rather than merely informing Tokyo of decisions that have already been made.

4. Revitalize relations among the United States, Japan, and the Republic of Korea as the first step to reducing tensions on the Korean peninsula.

Good relations among the United States, Japan, and the Republic of Korea are essential for increasing the prospects of peaceful Korean reunification and for constructing a stable Northeast Asian security order after Korea is reunified. The three countries are cooperating effectively to implement the agreed framework between the United States and North Korea regarding the latter's nuclear programs. Nevertheless, Japanese food aid to North Korea and U.S. negotiations with Pyongyang have provoked suspicions and misinterpretations in South Korea. To revitalize the political-security relationship between the United States and South Korea, Washington should initiate a working-level dialogue on security issues with Seoul similar to the Nye Initiative between Washington and Tokyo. One of the objectives would be to reaffirm and redefine the U.S.-ROK security alliance not only for the post–cold war era, but also the period after Korean reunification. This process should culminate in a joint security declaration similar to the one signed by President Clinton and Prime Minister Hashimoto. At the same time, Tokyo should renew its efforts to improve relations with Seoul. After Japan revises its guidelines for U.S.-Japan defense cooperation, Washington and Tokyo should expand their dialogue on defense cooperation into a trilateral process that includes Seoul.

These initiatives would lay the foundation for a constructive dialogue between Washington and Pyongyang and Tokyo and Pyongyang while encouraging progress in relations between Pyongyang and Seoul. Strong trilateral relations among South Korea, the United States, and Japan will help constrain North Korea from engaging in aggressive behavior and from driving wedges between the three partner countries. This constraint would in turn encourage North Korea to resume its dialogue with the South as well as to be more cooperative about reducing tensions on the peninsula. A workable formula for holding four-party talks among the two Koreas, China, and the United States as proposed by Washington seems to have emerged. As the discussions move forward, Japan and Russia should be formally included, not only to support a peaceful reunification of the peninsula, but also to participate in constructing a stable Northeast Asian security order.

5. Integrate China into the regional and international community.

Peace and stability in the East Asia–Pacific region will not be possible without the comprehensive integration of China into the regional and international community. Only then will China fully embrace the peaceful resolution of international disputes, nonproliferation of weapons of mass destruction, military transparency, freedom of navigation, and other international norms shared by the United States and Japan. But Japan and the United States must actively encourage China to support these norms and behave accordingly as part of its responsibilities as a great power, and they should persuade Beijing that the institutionalization of these norms will ultimately serve China's long-term interests. Multilateral settings such as the Asia-Pacific Economic Cooperation process and the ASEAN Regional Forum provide excellent venues to get this message across and should be used to the greatest extent possible.

The two countries should also continue to support China's economic development and facilitate its accession to the World Trade Organization as soon as possible. Chinese membership in the WTO would enable the advanced industrial states to apply international rules in a multilateral context to deal with economic disputes with China and stimulate Chinese institutional reforms. It would also boost Washington's policy of engaging Beijing by helping alleviate the suspicion that engagement is merely a means to contain China. As for the terms of China's accession to the WTO, Japan and the United States should insist that Beijing grant broader import rights for foreign firms in China and make its regulations and plans on foreign trade more transparent. While allowing China some time to dismantle trade barriers that protect politically and socially sensitive state-owned enterprises, Tokyo and Washington should press Beijing to reduce quickly protectionist barriers in other industries.

In addition, the United States and Japan should develop their respective bilateral diplomatic exchanges (including summits) and security dialogues with China to nurture a mutual strategic understanding, identify common interests, and build on these common interests to deal constructively with regional and global security challenges.

Because an improvement of relations between China and Taiwan

serves the security interests of both Japan and the United States, Tokyo
and Washington should vigorously urge Beijing and Taipei to commence
a dialogue designed to defuse tensions while deepening economic links.
As they applaud Taiwan's democratization as well as its economic suc-
cesses, the United States and Japan should work out a modus vivendi
with China about Taiwan within the framework of a one-China policy. To
facilitate such an arrangement, the United States should abide by the
August 1982 communiqué on arms sales to Taiwan.[1] Both the United
States and Japan should publicly and unequivocally oppose not only a
formal declaration of independence by Taiwan but also efforts by Taiwan
to move toward independence.

This would go beyond current official statements made by both Washington and Tokyo. At the same time, however, both countries should urge
China to respect Taiwan's quest for greater international recognition by
accepting its membership in various international economic organizations. The United States and Japan should also emphasize that they have
a major stake in a peaceful solution to the issue of Taiwan's future status
and would interpret aggressive military behavior against it as a threat to
their security interests. The U.S.-Japan alliance is indeed critical for
encouraging a peaceful handling of the Taiwan issue.

Efforts should be made to convince China that the reinvigoration of
the U.S.-Japan security alliance is not directed at a third country and is
definitely not meant to contain China. The purpose of the redefined
alliance between Japan and the United States is more to promote their
common interest in regional peace and stability and ensure that the
alliance can survive domestic political challenges within their respective
countries than it is to contain a common threat. But Washington and
Tokyo should also remind Beijing that this alliance will have both the
will and capacity to counter clear military threats to regional security if
they do emerge. To mitigate misunderstanding, the United States and
Japan should initiate trilateral security discussions with China at the min-
isterial level.

Finally, the United States and Japan can support China's integration
into the international community by inviting China to participate in the
enlarged Group of Seven (G-7) summit process (now called the Summit
of Eight with the recent inclusion of Russia), first as an observer and
later as a full member. The mode of participation should be contingent
upon China's progress in economic and political liberalization as well as
its contribution to regional stability and global order. In this regard,

Tokyo and Washington should carefully watch how China respects free speech and other human and political rights in post-unification Hong Kong and how the Fifteenth Congress of the Chinese Communist party charts the future course of Chinese society and politics.

6. *Fund cooperative research on theater missle defense systems with the United States, but in full recognition of the technical risks.*

The promise of theater missile defense (TMD) technology is unclear both because of technical questions about the systems being developed and an uncertain future security environment in Northeast Asia. But TMD's potential utility is considerable to the United States as well as Japan. U.S. TMD programs would benefit from technical and financial support from Japan in development and perhaps someday also in procurement and operation.

However, Tokyo is already spending a great deal of money on host-nation support for U.S. forces in Japan and relocation of the Futenma Marine Air Base on Okinawa. It also faces budget constraints. It should be doing more to contribute to a meaningful and balanced alliance, but not necessarily through more checkbook diplomacy. That said, TMD programs would probably represent a better use of Tokyo's money than would construction of an offshore heliport for the marines on Okinawa.

TMD systems owned and operated by Japan would make most sense against a small North Korean missile threat. They might prove effective whether the missiles carried conventional, chemical, biological, or even nuclear warheads. They could also be of some use against an accidental or unauthorized Chinese or Russian attack, or an attack by a nonstate entity that gained access to several missiles and was prepared to launch them from a ship or a neighboring country. And should Japan someday decide to become an active participant in dangerous peace operations, TMD could be helpful if a regional power attacked forces deployed as part of such a contingent. Depending on the quality of the TMD system, its use might be limited to defense against rudimentary short-range missiles or it might have somewhat greater capabilities.

Japan should not be deterred from pursuing TMD by North Korean or Chinese claims that such a step would be provocative. Neither Pyongyang nor Beijing nor Moscow has an inherent right to hold the Japanese islands at risk of missile attack by conventional or unconventional weapons. China's concerns about its nuclear capabilities vis-à-vis those of the United States are perhaps understandable, and advanced

TMD systems could indeed enter into that broader nuclear balance, at least in theory. But Beijing's direct pressure on nonnuclear Japan not to collaborate with the United States on TMD development and acquisition seems unreasonable. In any case, Beijing will almost certainly retain some ability to hold the Japanese islands at risk of missile attack. The magnitude of that risk might be reduced somewhat by advanced TMD such as the navy's upper-tier system, but even that conclusion hinges on the dubious assmption that such systems will prove technically feasible and perform well against countermeasures.

Expectations about TMD should therefore be kept in check. But the programs appear worthwhile to pursue jointly, at least in the research and development phase.

Note

1. In this document the U.S. government stated that "it does not seek to carry out a long-term policy of arms sales to Taiwan, that its arms sales to Taiwan will not exceed, either in qualitative or in quantitative terms the level of those supplied in recent years since the establishment of diplomatic relations between the United States and China, and that it intends to reduce gradually its sales of arms to Taiwan, leading over a period of time to a final resolution." For the full text of this communiqué see Harry Harding, *A Fragile Relationship: The United States and China since 1972* (Brookings, 1992), pp. 383–85.

Japan-U.S. Joint Declaration on Security—Alliance for the 21st Century

1. Today, the Prime Minister and the President celebrated one of the most successful bilateral relationships in history. The leaders took pride in the profound and positive contribution this relationship has made to world peace and regional stability and prosperity. The strong Alliance between Japan and the United States helped ensure peace and security in the Asia-Pacific region during the Cold War. Our Alliance continues to underlie the dynamic economic growth in this region. The two leaders agreed that the future security and prosperity of both Japan and the United States are tied inextricably to the future of the Asia-Pacific region.

The benefits of peace and prosperity that spring from the Alliance are due not only to the commitments of the two governments, but also to the contributions of the Japanese and American people who have shared the burden of securing freedom and democracy. The Prime Minister and the President expressed their profound gratitude to those who sustain the Alliance, especially those Japanese communities that host U.S. forces, and those Americans who, far from home, devote themselves to the defense of peace and freedom.

2. For more than a year, the two governments conducted an intensive review of the evolving political and security environment of the Asia-Pacific region and of various aspects of the Japan-U.S. security relationship. On the basis of this review, the Prime Minister and the President

reaffirmed their commitment to the profound common values that guide our national policies: the maintenance of freedom, the pursuit of democracy, and respect for human rights. They agreed that the foundations for our cooperation remain firm, and that this partnership will remain vital in the twenty-first century.

The Regional Outlook

3. Since the end of the Cold War, the possibility of global armed conflict has receded. The last few years have seen expanded political and security dialogue among countries of the region. Respect for democratic principles is growing. Prosperity is more widespread than at any other time in history, and we are witnessing the emergence of an Asia-Pacific community. The Asia-Pacific region has become the most dynamic area of the globe.

At the same time, instability and uncertainty persist in the region. Tensions continue on the Korean Peninsula. There are still heavy concentrations of military force, including nuclear arsenals. Unresolved territorial disputes, potential regional conflicts, and the proliferation of weapons of mass destruction and their means of delivery all constitute sources of instability.

The Japan-U.S. Alliance and the Treaty of Mutual Cooperation and Security

4. The Prime Minister and the President underscored the importance of promoting stability in this region and dealing with the security challenges facing both countries.

In this regard, the Prime Minister and the President reiterated the significant value of the Alliance between Japan and the United States. They reaffirmed that the Japan-U.S. security relationship, based on the Treaty of Mutual Cooperation and Security between Japan and the United States of America, remains the cornerstone for achieving common security objectives, and for maintaining a stable and prosperous environment for the Asia-Pacific region as we enter the twenty-first century.

(a) The Prime Minister confirmed Japan's fundamental defense policy as articulated in its new "National Defense Program Outline" adopted in November, 1995, which underscored that the Japanese defense capabilities should play appropriate roles in the security environment after the Cold War. The Prime Minister and the President agreed that the most effective framework for the defense of Japan is close defense cooperation between the two countries. This cooperation is based on a combination of appropriate defense capabilities for the Self-Defense Forces of Japan and the Japan-U.S. security arrangements. The leaders again confirmed that U.S. deterrence under the Treaty of Mutual Cooperation and Security remains the guarantee for Japan's security.

(b) The Prime Minister and the President agreed that continued U.S. military presence is also essential for preserving peace and stability in the Asia-Pacific region. The leaders shared the common recognition that the Japan-U.S. security relationship forms an essential pillar which supports the positive regional engagement of the U.S.

The President emphasized the U.S. commitment to the defense of Japan as well as to peace and stability in the Asia-Pacific region. He noted that there has been some adjustment of U.S. forces in the Asia-Pacific region since the end of the Cold War. On the basis of a thorough assessment, the United States reaffirmed that meeting its commitments in the prevailing security environment requires the maintenance of its current force structure of about 100,000 forward deployed military personnel in the region, including about the current level in Japan.

(c) The Prime Minister welcomed the U.S. determination to remain a stable and steadfast presence in the region. He reconfirmed that Japan would continue appropriate contributions for the maintenance of U.S. forces in Japan, such as through the provision of facilities and areas in accordance with the Treaty of Mutual Cooperation and Security and Host Nation Support. The President expressed U.S. appreciation for Japan's contributions, and welcomed the conclusion of the new Special Measures Agreement which provides financial support for U.S. forces stationed in Japan.

Bilateral Cooperation under the Japan-U.S. Security Relationship

5. The Prime Minister and the President, with the objective of enhancing the credibility of this vital security relationship, agreed to undertake efforts to advance cooperation in the following areas.

(a) Recognizing that close bilateral defense cooperation is a central element of the Japan-U.S. Alliance, both governments agreed that continued close consultation is essential. Both governments will further enhance the exchange of information and views on the international situation, in particular the Asia-Pacific region. At the same time, in response to the changes which may arise in the international security environment, both governments will continue to consult closely on defense policies and military postures, including the U.S. force structure in Japan, which will best meet their requirements.

(b) The Prime Minister and the President agreed to initiate a review of the 1978 Guidelines for Japan-U.S. Defense Cooperation to build upon the close working relationship already established between Japan and the United States.

The two leaders agreed on the necessity to promote bilateral policy coordination, including studies on bilateral cooperation in dealing with situations that may emerge in the areas surrounding Japan and which will have an important influence on the peace and security of Japan.

(c) The Prime Minister and the President welcomed the April 15, 1996 signature of the Agreement Between the Government of Japan and the Government of the United States of America Concerning Reciprocal Provision of Logistic Support, Supplies and Services Between the Self-Defense Forces of Japan and the Armed Forces of the United States of America, and expressed their hope that this Agreement will further promote the bilateral cooperative relationship.

(d) Noting the importance of interoperability in all facets of cooperation between the Self-Defense Forces of Japan and the U.S. forces, the two governments will enhance mutual exchange in the areas of technology and equipment, including bilateral cooperative research and development of equipment such as the support fighter (F-2).

(e) The two governments recognized that the proliferation of weapons of mass destruction and their means of delivery has important implications for their common security. They will work together to prevent proliferation and will continue to cooperate in the ongoing study on ballistic missile defense.

6. The Prime Minister and the President recognized that the broad support and understanding of the Japanese people are indispensable for the smooth stationing of U.S. forces in Japan, which is the core element of the Japan-U.S. security arrangements. The two leaders agreed that

both governments will make every effort to deal with various issues related to the presence and status of U.S. forces. They also agreed to make further efforts to enhance mutual understanding between U.S. forces and local Japanese communities.

In particular, with respect to Okinawa, where U.S. facilities and areas are highly concentrated, the Prime Minister and the President reconfirmed their determination to carry out steps to consolidate, realign, and reduce U.S. facilities and areas consistent with the objectives of the Treaty of Mutual Cooperation and Security. In this respect, the two leaders took satisfaction in the significant progress which has been made so far through the "Special Action Committee on Okinawa" (SACO), and welcomed the far reaching measures outlined in the SACO Interim Report of April 15, 1996. They expressed their firm commitment to achieve a successful conclusion of the SACO process by November 1996.

Regional Cooperation

7. The Prime Minister and the President agreed that the two governments will jointly and individually strive to achieve a more peaceful and stable security environment in the Asia-Pacific region. In this regard, the two leaders recognized that the engagement of the United States in the region, supported by the Japan-U.S. security relationship, constitutes the foundation for such efforts.

The two leaders stressed the importance of peaceful resolution of problems in the region. They emphasized that it is extremely important for the stability and prosperity of the region that China play a positive and constructive role, and, in this context, stressed the interest of both countries in furthering cooperation with China. Russia's ongoing process of reform contributes to regional and global stability, and merits continued encouragement and cooperation. The leaders also stated that full normalization of Japan-Russia relations based on the Tokyo Declaration is important to peace and stability in the Asia-Pacific region. They noted also that stability on the Korean Peninsula is vitally important to Japan and the United States and reaffirmed that both countries will continue to make every effort in this regard, in close cooperation with the Republic of Korea.

The Prime Minister and the President reaffirmed that the two governments will continue working jointly and with other countries in the region to further develop multilateral regional security dialogues and cooperation mechanisms such as the ASEAN Regional Forum and, eventually, security dialogues regarding Northeast Asia.

Global Cooperation

8. The Prime Minister and the President recognized that the Treaty of Mutual Cooperation and Security is the core of the Japan-U.S. Alliance, and underlies the mutual confidence that constitutes the foundation for bilateral cooperation on global issues.

The Prime Minister and the President agreed that the two governments will strengthen their cooperation in support of the United Nations and other international organizations through activities such as peacekeeping and humanitarian relief operations.

Both governments will coordinate their policies and cooperate on issues such as arms control and disarmament, including acceleration of the Comprehensive Test Ban Treaty (CTBT) negotiations and the prevention of the proliferation of weapons of mass destruction and their means of delivery. The two leaders agreed that cooperation in the United Nations and APEC, and on issues such as the North Korean nuclear problem, the Middle East peace process, and the peace implementation process in the former Yugoslavia, helps to build the kind of world that promotes our shared interests and values.

Conclusion

9. In concluding, the Prime Minister and the President agreed that the three legs of the Japan-U.S. relationship—security, political, and economic—are based on shared values and interests and rest on the mutual confidence embodied in the Treaty of Mutual Cooperation and Security. The Prime Minister and the President reaffirmed their strong determination, on the eve of the twenty-first century, to build on the successful history of security cooperation and to work hand-in-hand to secure peace and prosperity for future generations.

April 17, 1996 Tokyo

Prime Minister of Japan   President of the United States

Index

209